Walks of a Lifetime

FALCON®

An imprint of Globe Pequot
Falcon and FalconGuides are registered trademarks and Make Adventure Your Story is a trademark of Rowman & Littlefield.

Distributed by NATIONAL BOOK NETWORK

Copyright © 2017 Rowman & Littlefield
Maps by Melissa Baker and Alena Joy Pearce © Rowman & Littlefield

All photos by Robert Manning unless otherwise noted

Title page photo: Amalfi Coast
Front cover: Maroon Bells–Snowmass Wilderness
Back cover: Amalfi Coast

British Library Cataloguing-in-Publication Information available

Library of Congress Cataloging-in-Publication Data available

ISBN 978-1-4930-2641-8 (paperback)
ISBN 978-1-4930-2642-5 (e-book)

♾™ The paper used in this publication meets the minimum requirements of American National Standard for Information Sciences—Permanence of Paper for Printed Library Materials, ANSI/NISO Z39.48-1992.

Printed in the United States of America

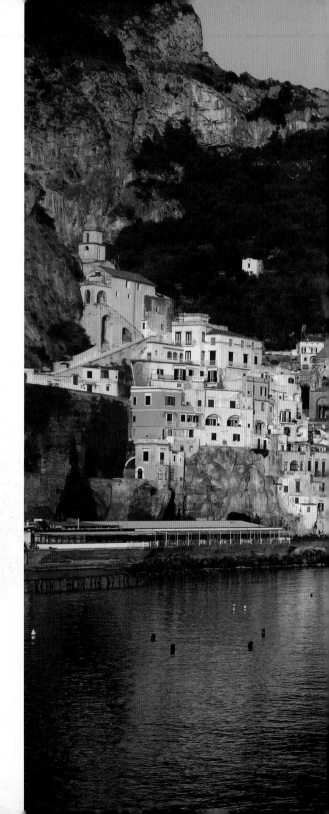

Walks
of a
Lifetime

EXTRAORDINARY HIKES FROM AROUND THE WORLD

Robert and Martha Manning

FALCON®

GUILFORD, CONNECTICUT

Great Wall of China

Ala Kahakai National Historic Trail

Contents

High Sierra Camps Loop   Aravaipa Canyon   Sydney

The Opera House is an icon of Sydney and recognized around the world.

Introduction

We had an amusing but meaningful experience a few years ago. We were enjoying walking the Pennine Way in England and Scotland and were staying the night at a traditional English B&B in the beautiful village of Keld. Keld is the point at which the Pennine Way crosses England's Coast-to-Coast Trail (which we walked several years ago and described in our earlier book, *Walking Distance: Extraordinary Hikes for Ordinary People*). At breakfast the next morning we were talking with another US couple that was walking the Coast-to-Coast Trail. When they found out we lived in the small state of Vermont, they asked us if by any chance we knew the Vermont couple who wrote the book *Walking Distance*, as it had inspired them to start long-distance walking. We don't know who was more excited—we or they—when we told them we were that couple. *This* is why we write books about walking: to encourage people to walk as a celebration of life and to enjoy the diverse, beautiful, and curious world in which we live. It's especially satisfying when we see such obvious evidence that we've succeeded.

We're fond of saying that walking is simple, but that it can also be profound. Yes, walking is easy for most of us; indeed, it's the most universal and accessible form of transportation, exercise, and recreation. But walking can also stimulate our thinking, slow our frantic lives, allow us to more deeply experience and appreciate the world, express our commitment to the environment, explore spirituality, and make us healthier and happier in the process. Now *that's* profound! We explore these and related ideas in this book.

We've prepared this book to encourage you to walk more in your everyday life and, in particular, to try some longer walks—long-distance trails and multi-day walks through the world's great cultural landscapes. Walk through some of America's "crown jewel" national parks—Grand Canyon, Yosemite, Denali, Zion, Acadia, and Canyonlands. Follow in the footsteps of pilgrims who have been walking to Santiago de Compostela in Spain and to the shrines of Japan's Kumano Kodo for a thousand years. Follow England's Thames River from its source in the Cotswolds through London and then on to the sea. Walk the Abel Tasman Coast Track, one of New Zealand's "Great Walks." Walk across Italy's Tuscany and along its Amalfi Coast. Walk through the great mountain ranges of North America—the Appalachians, the Rockies, and the Sierra Nevada. Walk among the world's great cities—New York, San Francisco, Los Angeles, Paris, and Sydney. Walk the Great Wall of China. And much more.

(ABOVE) The Virgin River Narrows is one of the most iconic walks in the national parks; it asks a lot of hikers, but it returns even more.

(BELOW) The Thames Path ends at the unusual Thames Barrier, designed to protect London from tidal surges.

Our book includes two major components. First, we include descriptions of thirty of the world's great long-distance and multi-day walks. The thirty walks we describe here should be added to the thirty walks we include in our previous book, *Walking Distance*. Together, these walks span much of the geography of the world, including six continents (sorry, there are no reasonable walks in Antarctica), offer an array of natural and cultural attractions, and range from easy to more challenging. A few walks are backpacking trips, but most offer a variety of options for accommodations. Most of these walks can be done in their entirety or in sections, even as a series of day hikes. We've chosen these walks very deliberately; these are *extraordinary* hikes for *ordinary* people. All these trails are highly accessible—they're well marked and maintained and can be walked by most people (though we offer some advice on how to prepare for these walks). We've chosen not to include any "super" long-distance trails, such as the Appalachian Trail, as this would not be in keeping with our objective of writing for ordinary people. It's simply not feasible for most people to hike these trails in their entirety. However, we suggest some exceptional sections of these trails. For example, we include the Presidential Traverse, one of the most dramatic and iconic sections of the Appalachian Trail, and the High Sierra Camps Loop, which includes a short but delightful section of the Pacific Crest Trail.

We've been deliberate about using the word "walk" in much of our writing, as the word "hike" may sound needlessly intimidating in many cases. We use both words as they are appropriate to the context. Most of the walks we describe are long-distance trails, such as the Pembrokeshire Coast Path in Wales and the Backbone Trail in California, while others are multi-day walks that can be done as a series of day hikes, such as on the carriage roads of Acadia National Park, Maine, and in the distinctive neighborhoods of Paris. All of the walks can be done in a few days to a few weeks. We've compiled a table at the end the book that summarizes the essential features of all these walks to help you find the trails that best meet your needs.

We've had the privilege of walking all the trails we include in the book, nearly all in their entirety, thus our descriptions are firsthand. We begin each description with a short anecdote about our walk, then describe the walk, including its major attractions and natural and cultural history. We conclude with a short discussion of logistical considerations. Our color photographs offer a first-person sense of the walks; these are some of the places, events, and people that captured our attention and imagination. Maps accompany each trail description.

The second component is comprised of short essays interspersed with the trail descriptions. We're fortunate to be in a period of history when many people are rediscovering the benefits and joy of walking, and a rich literature has been evolving. We sense a growing yearning among many people for more "authentic" experiences, and walking promotes more intimate and genuine contact with local people and places. Walking can also be adventurous; though guidebooks can offer a day-by-day description of a trail, one can never be quite sure what's around the next bend, and every day brings new and

sometimes unexpected experiences. Walking vacations can also help protect the places we walk, as walking has little environmental impact if done in a knowledgeable and careful manner (as we describe later in the book). When walkers use local services such as B&Bs, small inns and refuges, and eat local foods, the resulting economic impact can be reinvested in stewarding and sustaining these local areas.

As our essays suggest, our evolutionary heritage—particularly the unusual bipedal character of the human body—is especially well adapted for walking. Moreover, the great network of trails throughout much of the world (a very different type of "World Wide Web") offers many lifetimes of walking opportunities. Our essays address these and an array of related topics, as well as offer some personal advice about preparing for long walks and walking in a responsible manner.

If you haven't tried long-distance or multi-day walking, we hope this book will encourage you to consider it. If you're already a confirmed walker, the book is designed to stimulate your thinking about where to walk. We hope we'll cross paths with you soon; in the meantime, you can always reach us through our website, www.extraordinaryhikes.com.

Bob Manning   Martha Manning

—Robert and Martha Manning
Vermont, 2017

The Abel Tasman Coast Track is a good example of the biologically rich interface of the sea and the land.

Abel Tasman Coast Track

We had decided to "slackpack" the Abel Tasman Coast Track, staying in local B&Bs and small inns instead of camping or staying in huts, and we contacted a local company to make reservations for us. One of the places along the trail had few options, so the company recommended innovative lodging—a boat anchored offshore with several sleeping cabins. We looked it up online and the home page featured an image of several bikini-clad young women jumping off the upper deck of the boat into the water. We concluded that this wasn't what we were looking for and chose another option. This was a "bach"—the word New Zealanders use for a cabin—to rent onshore, near the vessel, and this turned out great. That night we took a dinghy ride to have dinner on the boat and were pleased to find that all the people onboard were much like us—there for the hike, not a party. We decided either option would have worked, and this way we got to experience both the boat and the bach.

LOCATION
New Zealand

LENGTH
32 miles

ACCOMMODATIONS
Commercial: Yes
Huts/refuges: Yes
Backpacking/camping: Yes

BAGGAGE TRANSFER AVAILABLE
Yes

OPTION TO WALK SECTIONS
Yes

DEGREE OF CHALLENGE
Low-Moderate

ABEL TASMAN NATIONAL PARK lies at the northern tip of New Zealand's South Island. It's a large area where the sea meets the land in a series of rocky bluffs and steep slopes thickly covered in lush rain forest. Scattered throughout the park are iconic sand beaches that glow a rich golden color. Add in the blues and turquoises of the sea, and the park is a strikingly beautiful place and a vital ecological reserve. The Abel Tasman Coast Track runs directly along the coastline of the park for 32 miles, between Wainui and Marahau, and is the most popular of New Zealand's system of Great Walks.

The interface of the sea and land is nearly always biologically rich, and the Abel Tasman Coast Track is a good example. The headlands feature forests of black beech on the ridgelines and the drier upper slopes, and rain forest with abundant tree ferns in the wetter lower elevations. Kanuka and manuka are present where the forest has been disturbed. This diverse forest offers habitat for many species of birds. Tuis and bellbirds are the glamour species, with their distinctive and showy calls. The flightless and entertaining weka will be seen by all walkers as wekas have lost their fear of humans and are perpetually curious and hungry. The sea, its estuaries, and the lagoons behind many of the beaches

(ABOVE) The sea, its estuaries, and the lagoons behind many of the beaches feature shorebirds and wading birds, such as these oystercatchers.

(RIGHT) Hikers on the Abel Tasman Coast Track must cross tidal estuaries at low tide.

feature shorebirds and wading birds such as cormorants, gannets, and oystercatchers. Little blue penguins (sometimes called fairy penguins) swim in the sea during the day and live in burrows onshore at night. Marine mammals include dolphins and fur seals. Park staff conducts an aggressive program of capturing invasive predators such as rats, possums, and stoats through traps set in the forest; these traps have poisonous bait and should not be touched or tampered with. The Tonga Island Marine Reserve is located just off the coast and contributes to conservation of marine mammals.

Abel Tasman was a Dutch explorer who is credited with being the first European to "discover" New Zealand in 1642. He and his party were met by hostile native Māori people who quickly drove the explorers away. Starting in the early nineteenth century, the area was subject to logging, mining, and agriculture. The national park was established in 1942 thanks to the persistence of Pérrine Moncrieff (from the nearby town of Nelson) who was determined to save the beautiful coastline from the ravages of economic development.

We were struck by the especially large tidal fluctuations along the track, and were amused to see boats in some of the small harbors sitting high and dry on the mud at low tide. But more importantly, the track includes several inlets (at Awaroa, Torrent Bay, and Bark Bay) that can only be

crossed during the roughly two hours before and after low tide. Walkers should carry a tide table and know how interpret it (which is not difficult). All but Awaroa have an alternative inland route, but these can be lengthy. The crossing at Awaroa has no alternative and is long—nearly a mile. We got to this crossing early (as did most other walkers) and enjoyed hanging out for an hour with this small group of people representing a number of countries, swapping stories about our adventures. You walk on the muddy bottom of the inlets, portions of which are carpeted in clam shells; it's important to wear shoes of some kind. Most folks bring a pair of shoes that can get wet, useful because a few knee-deep channels have to be waded.

Of course, swimming is a favorite activity of many walkers on the track. The famous golden sand beaches are magnetic, as is the warm, transparent aquamarine water. The main track descends to many of these beaches, but other smaller and remoter beaches can be reached by side trails. Some of the beaches are served by a system of water taxis and other boats based primarily in Kaiteriteri (just south of the track) and the large town of Nelson (still farther south). These taxis are used primarily by day-trippers—folks who want to spend the day at the beach or who wish to kayak along the coast when the weather allows—but the taxies can be useful to walkers who wish to hike the track in sections. Walkers seem to especially enjoy the suspension bridges that cross some of the larger streams that drain off the headlands and into the sea; we found the one at Falls River to be especially exciting. A nice hour-long side trip is the trail to Separation Point, which is the dividing point between the two major bodies of water along the track, Golden Bay and Tasman Bay. The beaches and rocks off Separation Point are a breeding ground for fur seals. There is a very nice park visitor center in the small village of Marahau at the southern end of the track.

This walk is not difficult and is family friendly—we saw people of all ages enjoying the track and especially the beaches. Most walkers take three to five days to walk the length of the Abel Tasman Coast Track. Be advised that the track along the headlands can be steep as it climbs among many small river valleys, but the

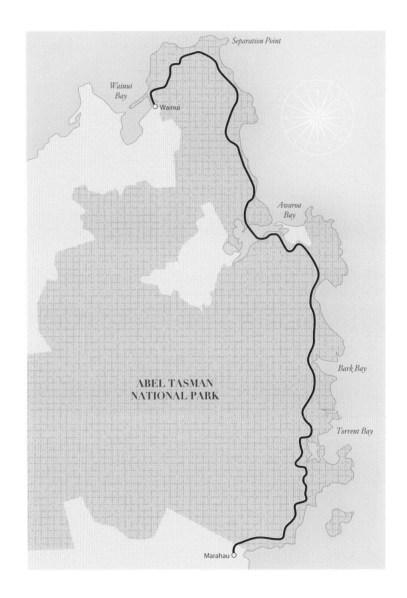

(LEFT) The portions of the trail on the headlands offer rich rain forests with many species of tree ferns.

(RIGHT) The waters of the Tasman Sea are a striking turquoise color.

trail is well marked and maintained, and the climbs are not long. (The maximum single elevation change along the track is 700 feet.) The track is served by a system of four huts and eighteen camping sites, and these must be reserved from the New Zealand Department of Conservation. The huts are basic—bunk beds and communal kitchen and bathroom services, but they are well designed and maintained, and are a bargain. There are a few small commercial lodgings on private property within the boundaries of the park.

Of course, you can walk the track in either direction—we chose to walk from north to south, using local buses to position ourselves. Because the northern section is farther removed from surrounding towns, it offers more solitude (solitude is considerably more difficult to find on the southern sections, especially on weekends). Access to the northern end of the trail takes two-and-a-half hours by bus, but it is a pleasant ride, mostly through agricultural areas featuring hops, apples, kiwifruit, and vineyards. We were amused by our friendly bus driver, who seemed to know just about everyone in the small towns we traveled through. The track can be walked year-round, but the main swimming season is December through March.

Coastal trails are among our favorite kinds of walks—nearly always varied and interesting. The Abel Tasman Coast Track is a quintessential example. The track is highly accessible, well-used, and richly rewarding, and we encourage you to put this walk high on your to-do list.

WALKING THROUGH THE DICTIONARY

The standard English dictionary definition of walk, at least in the context of this book, is "travel by foot." (Walk has other meanings in different contexts—for example, to be awarded first base in baseball because the pitcher throws four balls; to be set free in a criminal court; to leave or resign one's professional position; to take too many steps in basketball.) As it applies to this book, the word "walk" can be both a verb and noun. It was probably derived from the Middle English *walken* and the Old English *wealcan*. The richness of walking is evident in the scores of sometimes colorful synonyms that parse its many nuances: stroll, march, trek, saunter, strut, flounce, promenade, amble, trudge, meander, wander, slog, stagger, limp, career, cruise, tiptoe, lope, ramble, stride, etc., etc. It can be entertaining to brainstorm as many synonyms as you can—a good activity on a long walk, especially on a rainy day.

Some words for walk are a function of nationality. In Britain, the word "walk" is used even for long journeys along the region's national trails. The Brits also use "ramble," "hillwalk," and "fellwalk," the latter two associated with walking in the mountains. In the United States and Canada, "walk" is normally reserved for covering only a short distance—around the block, to the market, etc., while the word "hike" is used to describe covering relatively long distances—several miles or more, especially in a park or other natural area. Moreover, "day hike" is used to differentiate a hike of a day or less from a "thru-hike," a multi-day hike on a long-distance trail. Australians "bushwalk," New Zealanders "tramp," and people "trek" in the Himalayas.

Rebecca Solnit, in her book, *Wanderlust*, offers many examples of the ways in which the word "walk" and its companion "travel" are embedded in our language. For example, we can steer straight, go the distance, and get ahead. We hit our stride, but sometimes lose our direction, go in circles, or even go nowhere. We can be lost souls and go downhill. We can be on the primrose path, the road to ruin, on the high or low road, or on easy street. We can set the pace, make great strides, take a big step forward, keep pace, toe the line, and follow in another's footsteps.

We primarily use the word "walk" in this book because it sounds less intimidating than hike (and certainly less demanding than bushwalk!). We want to encourage people to walk more in their everyday lives and to try long-distance and multi-day walks. To do this, we outline many of the reasons people might want to walk more, offer advice on how to prepare for long-distance walks, and include only descriptions of trails that can be walked by most people. We've walked all of these trails, and they're all extraordinary and fully accessible to ordinary people.

Australians "bushwalk" along the trails in and around Sydney Harbour.

The carriage roads are wide and gently graded as they were originally developed to accommodate horse-drawn carriages.

Acadia's Carriage Roads

We were spending the week at Acadia National Park walking the park's famous carriage roads. The weather report for the next day was especially fine, so we planned our route very carefully, making sure we'd be walking by Jordan Pond House at the opportune moment—just in time for afternoon tea. Tea and popovers are a longstanding tradition at Jordan Pond House, going back to the days when John D. Rockefeller Jr. and other rich and famous summer residents of Mount Desert Island rode in horse-drawn carriages around the island, stopping at Jordan Pond House for refreshments. Our timing was impeccable, and we sat at a table on the lawn overlooking glacially carved Jordan Pond with the distinctive twin mountains called "The Bubbles" in the background. It was idyllic. And the popovers were delicious!

ACADIA NATIONAL PARK offers dramatic evidence that the significance of national parks is not measured by their size. Less than 50,000 acres, Acadia is among the smallest national parks, but its combination of natural, cultural, and recreational resources places it among the "crown jewels" of the US national park system. And visitors clearly agree, flocking to the park by the millions each year, making Acadia one of the most intensively visited national parks.

Acadia is located in northern coastal Maine and protects the finest remaining examples of New England's rocky, rugged, undeveloped shoreline. It's part of the vast Gulf of Maine and its associated archipelago, which includes nearly a thousand islands. Although the park is spread among fifteen islands and the mainland, the heart of the park is Mount Desert Island. Iconic features include the 27-mile Park Loop Road, which connects many of the park's scenic and recreational attractions, a network of hiking trails, Cadillac Mountain (the highest point on the East Coast and the first place the sun strikes in the continental United States from late fall through most of winter), and the highly unusual and richly rewarding 50-mile network of carriage roads.

LOCATION
Maine, United States

LENGTH
50 miles

ACCOMMODATIONS
Commercial: Yes (Nearby)
Huts/refuges: No
Backpacking/camping: Yes
(Nearby)

BAGGAGE TRANSFER AVAILABLE
No

OPTION TO WALK SECTIONS
Yes

DEGREE OF CHALLENGE
Low

(LEFT) Tea and popovers at Jordan Pond House are a tradition among walkers on the carriage roads.

(RIGHT) Two grand gatehouses were built to control access to the carriage roads.

The carriage roads were constructed at the direction of John D. Rockefeller Jr. over a period of three decades beginning in the early twentieth century. Mr. Rockefeller and his friends were summer residents of Mount Desert Island and were disturbed when cars were allowed on the island. The cars detracted from their horse-and-carriage rides along the local roads, so Mr. Rockefeller, as few other Americans could do, decided to build his own system of nonmotorized roads. Design of the carriage roads was under the guidance of prominent landscape architects such as Frederick Law Olmsted Jr., and construction crews included a group of Italian stonemasons. Mr. Rockefeller generously gave the carriage roads and much of the land on the island to the nation as the first national park in the eastern United States.

The carriage roads gracefully weave through the cultural landscape on the eastern side of Mount Desert Island; they follow the contours of the land and are designed to take maximum advantage of the views. The road network includes seventeen strikingly beautiful bridges—each unique in design

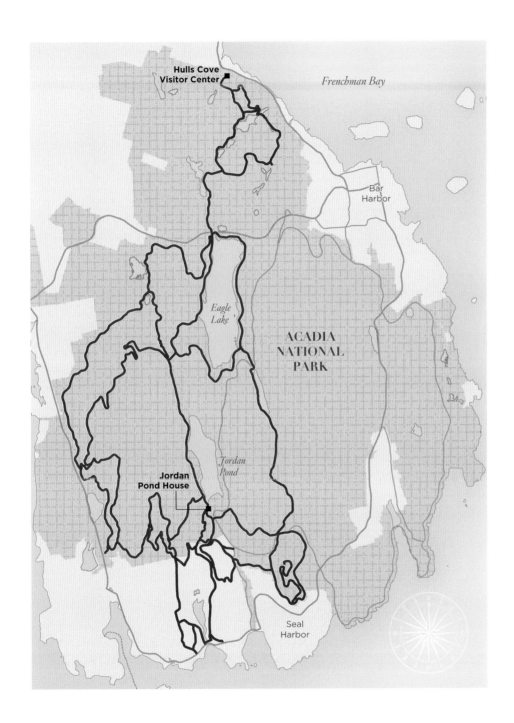

Wayfinding along the carriage roads is relatively easy as all intersections are marked with distinctive and historic signposts; the signposts are numbered and keyed to locally available maps and guides.

Lichens, mosses, blueberries, and other low-growing plants thrive along the margins of the carriage roads.

and crafted of local granite—and two large stone gatehouses. The roads are 16 feet wide, surfaced with well-groomed gravel, and lined with granite copingstones that locals fondly call "Rockefeller's teeth." The roads have gentle grades and wide curves to accommodate horses and carriages, and take walkers through spruce and hemlock forests lined with blueberries and ferns to open-ocean views, follow the shorelines of glacially carved lakes, and cross numerous streams on the graceful historic bridges. The carriage roads are one the most distinctive assets of the US national park system and a joy to recreationists, especially walkers and bikers.

The carriage roads form a dense network of routes that include a number of entrances/exits, and this presents many appealing options for walkers. You can do walks of many lengths featuring a variety of terrain and attractions. Part of the fun will be planning your walks, and we ensured that we ultimately walked the full network by the end of our week in the park. Our favorite route is called "Round Mountain," one of the longer but classic walks offering so many of the features that make the carriage roads distinctive and attractive. Round Mountain, at just over 11 miles, makes a loop around three mountains—Sargent, Parkman, and Penobscot—and the walk can easily be shortened or lengthened. The route takes walkers to the highest point on the carriage roads (780 feet) and offers outstanding views of Somes Sound, Jordan Pond, and Eagle Lake. But be sure to look closely at the features in the foreground—huge slabs of the park's distinctive pink granite sporting numerous species of lichen, artful wind-gathered groupings of pine needles, dense forests of evergreens, and an understory of blueberries and other shrubs. This section of the carriage roads features seven bridges, all different in character and style. About halfway around this section, there's a short spur trail to Jordan Pond House. We recommend starting this walk at the Parkman Mountain parking lot a half-mile north of Upper Hadlock Pond (off ME 198).

The story of the carriage roads and Acadia National Park can be told through both natural and cultural history. Geology has had the most dominant and obvious effect on the landscape, sculpting the massive granite-domed mountains and the distinctive U-shaped valleys with plentiful lakes and wetlands. Evidence of glaciers is everywhere: Look for glacial erratics (large rocks carried by glaciers and deposited far from their origin) and glacial polish, striations, and chatter marks on the park's bare granite summits. Plant and animal life is rich and varied as the park is a transition zone where land meets the sea and the southern deciduous and northern coniferous forests meet. Iconic wildlife includes harbor seals, bald eagles, peregrine falcons, and occasional visits from moose and black bears. Whale-watching excursions are available in the tourist-friendly gateway town of Bar Harbor.

The park's human history is just as significant. The small visitor center at Sieur de Monts and the larger Abbe Museum in Bar Harbor feature the vital Native American presence. Mount Desert Island takes its name from its treeless granite mountains; in 1604 early explorer Samuel de Champlain called it "Isle des Monts Desert" or "Island of the Barren Mountains." The name "Acadia" reflects the history of the French maritime provinces and settlements in this part of the New World. In the early 1800s, Hudson River School painters Thomas Cole and Frederick Church came to Mount Desert Island and the surrounding area to celebrate the region's wild, "sublime" landscape. They were followed in the mid to late-nineteenth century by wealthy families from Boston, New York, and Philadelphia in search of cooler summers and beautiful scenery. The park was established in 1916 thanks to conservation-minded residents, including George Dorr (often referred to as the father of the park), Charles Eliot (president of Harvard University), and oil magnate John D. Rockefeller Jr. (who donated millions of dollars and thousands of acres to the park). The park is highly unusual in that it is comprised almost entirely of donated land.

Wayfinding along the carriage roads is relatively easy as all intersections are marked with distinctive and historic cedar signposts; the signposts are numbered and keyed to locally available maps and guides. No motorized use is allowed, but the carriage roads are used by bikers and horseback riders (there are very few of the latter today) as well as walkers. This requires all users to respect the others. Horses always have the right-of-way, and bikers must yield to walkers. Bikers are asked to watch their speed and not startle walkers, and walkers are asked to not walk abreast in large groups, thereby blocking the trail to bikers. In addition to the carriage roads, the park includes 120 miles of hiking trails, some of which intercept the carriage roads, expanding the walking possibilities.

Acadia is often crowded in the summer, and parking lots at entrances to the carriage roads can fill up early. This can be avoided by using the free Island Explorer shuttle bus system; using the bus also allows for one-way walks along the carriage roads.

Both the carriage roads and trails are in excellent condition thanks to endowments that have been established by the nonprofit group Friends of Acadia. A full range of accommodations can be used as "base camp" while you walk the carriage roads; there are two campgrounds in Acadia National Park and many choices of motels and B&Bs in Bar Harbor and the other small towns and villages in and around the park.

We've had the pleasure of walking on the carriage roads for many years and have noticed that nearly everyone—couples, extended families, groups of youngsters—seems to be having fun. Including us! Maybe it's the popovers.

The carriage road network includes seventeen strikingly beautiful bridges, each unique in design and crafted of local granite.

Walking is one of the things that makes us human.
(Maroon Bells–Snowmass Wilderness)

HUMAN BEING, BEING HUMAN

Walking is one of the things that make us human. While scientists debate the origins of walking, it's generally agreed that walking on two feet, or "bipedalism," emerged several million years ago as an evolutionary adaptation. There is more consensus on its implications. Rebecca Solnit writes that "[t]he only given is that upright walking is the first hallmark of what became humanity" and "[w]hatever its causes, it caused much more." It freed what are now our arms and hands, allowing humans to evolve into the ultimate toolmaker, and our brains responded to this opportunity. Science writer John Noble Wilford writes, "Anthropologists and evolutionary biologists are now agreed that upright posture and two-legged walking—bipedality—was the crucial and probably the first major adaptation associated with the divergence of human lineage from a common ancestor with the African apes." And renowned paleoanthropologist Mary Leakey wrote:

One cannot overemphasize the role of bipedalism in hominid development. It stands as perhaps the salient point that differentiates the forbears of man from other primates. This unique ability freed the hands for myriad possibilities—carrying, toolmaking, intricate manipulation. From this single development, in fact, stems all modern technology. Somewhat oversimplified, the formula holds that this new freedom of forelimbs posed a challenge. The brain expanded to meet it. And mankind was formed.

In his book *On Foot: A History of Walking*, Joseph Amato writes that "With a rotating periscope head, strong legs, and unbounded dreams, the walking species became the ruler of the world." To reject walking is to turn our backs on our evolutionary history.

But just as importantly, walking is a miracle—a biological and mechanical marvel. Of course, most of us take walking for granted; it's simple, even "pedestrian." But in reality it's a symphony of our highly developed nervous, skeletal, and muscular systems; the balance and strength to hold ourselves upright on our two relatively small feet while moving one foot in front of the other for miles on end, over all sorts of terrain, without falling, and doing all this with little conscious thought. Buddhist monk and peace activist Thich Nhat Hanh observed that "People usually consider walking on water or in thin air a miracle. But I think the real miracle is not to walk either on water or in thin air but to walk on the earth."

The biomechanics of human walking have been described as a "double pendulum" or "inverted pendulum" process. In this motion, the back foot leaves the ground and swings forward from the hip, using the other, rigid leg as a fulcrum. This foot then reaches the ground, rolls forward from heel to toe, and the process is repeated. In this way, one foot is always in contact with the ground, and this is what distinguishes walking from running.

Fortunately, walking is instinctual and this complex biomechanical process is hardwired in our brains. The aesthetics of walking were widely appreciated for the first time with publication in the 1880s of Eadweard Muybridge's photographic "motion studies," which used a battery of linked cameras to record the act of walking. In *The Lost Art of Walking*, Geoff Nicholson writes that "for me the walking pictures reveal the magical nature of something we take so much for granted." We should appreciate and celebrate this gift by taking a daily walk.

The Ala Kahakai National Historic Trail offers a great way to appreciate the tropical beauty of Hawaii.

Ala Kahakai National Historic Trail

The Hawaiian language is beautiful—even musical—when spoken, but we were challenged to pronounce many of the place-names (even the name of the trail we were walking!). Fortunately, National Park Service bookstores offer a handy language guide and we found it very useful. Hawaiian is not an especially difficult language; just get in there and sound those vowels—all of them! Diphthongs (adjacent vowels) add a layer of complication and are pronounced as a unit. Thus, Ala Kahakai is "ah lah KAH hah KY ee." Don't worry, we found local people happy to help. It's wonderful how deeply the Hawaiian language is embedded in the islands, an indication of deep respect for the history and culture of the area.

THIS IS A RARE OPPORTUNITY to be among the first to walk one of the newest national historic trails in the United States. In fact, it's so new that much of it wasn't yet accessible when we walked this evolving trail. But some of the finest sections of the trail are available, and our experience walking these sections prompted us to include it in this book. The trail is a bit of a paradox—it's one of the most recently designated national trails, but the route itself is ancient.

The trail is on the island of Hawaii ("the Big Island") and was designated a national historic trail by Congress in 2000. It's managed by the National Park Service, though like many components of the national trails system, much of the on-the-ground work of planning, managing, and maintaining the trail is done by a local nonprofit group, in this case the Ala Kahakai Trail Association. The association states that the trail is "a path that joins the past to the present and the future," and they've adopted the old Hawaiian philosophy that "no task is too big when done together by all."

Following existing routes laid down hundreds of years ago, the trail will ultimately run 175 miles around much of the perimeter of the island, from Upolu Point in the north, down the west side of the island, around the southern end of the island, and north along the east side to Waha'ula Heiau in Hawai'i Volcanoes National Park. Most of the trail is either directly on the beach, on cliff tops, or

LOCATION
Hawaii, United States

LENGTH
Up to 175 miles

ACCOMMODATIONS
Commercial: Nearby
Huts/refuges: No
Backpacking/camping: Yes

BAGGAGE TRANSFER AVAILABLE
No

OPTION TO WALK SECTIONS
Yes

DEGREE OF CHALLENGE
Low-Moderate

(ABOVE) Some of the Ala Kahakai National Historic Trail on the western, or Kona Coast, passes through vast fields of *a'a*, composed of a layer of brittle fragments or cinders called "clinkers."

(BELOW) *Pahoehoe* is formed by extremely hot liquid lava flows and is characterized by ropey, corrugated surfaces and cracks caused by contraction when cooling.

across long stretches of large lava flows. Ala Kahakai means "shoreline trail" in Hawaiian. The trail is stunningly beautiful in many places, but was established primarily to celebrate the rich ancient Hawaiian culture.

The route used by Native Hawaiians to link the many settlements along the coast forms the foundation of the trail. Of course, the people often traveled by sea (what is sometimes referred to as the "blue" trail), but also traveled around the island extensively by land (the "brown" trail). The trail traverses more than 200 *ahupua'a*, the traditional sea-to-mountain land divisions used by Native Hawaiians. An *ahupua'a* included all the necessities of life—access to the sea to catch fish and gather other marine life, opportunities to farm in the fertile and well-watered uplands, and timber and wildlife in the mountains. Extended family groups lived in each *ahupua'a* and cooperated closely by sharing resources.

By hiking the trail, you'll learn much about the life and culture of Native Hawaiians, as well as experience the Big Island's natural history. Like all the Hawaiian Islands, Hawaii is volcanic, a process that is both evident and ongoing. Release of magma from the ocean floor several miles beneath the present-day islands slowly accumulated to form the islands and their volcanoes. Two nearly 14,000-foot volcanoes, Mauna Loa and Kilauea, dominate the landscape of the island, and the Ala Kahakai Trail crosses many of the massive lava flows from these volcanoes. The lava forming these flows is of two basic types. *A'a* lava flows are composed of a layer of brittle fragments or cinders called "clinkers"; it's very rough and challenging to walk on even where it's been fashioned into the Ala Kahakai and other trails—and it's tough on shoes. This type of lava is characteristic of the portion of the trail on the west side or Kona Coast portion of the island. *Pahoehoe* lava flows are formed by extremely hot liquid lava and characterized by ropey, corrugated surfaces and cracks caused by contraction during cooling. It can also be rough, but is generally easier to walk on than *a'a*. This type of lava is characteristic of Hawai'i Volcanoes National Park in the south.

The four major sections of the trail that are easily accessible are associated with the four units of the national park system on the island. Pu'ukoholā Heiau National Historic Site is located on the northern part of the island. The trail runs through the park and then continues south for about 15 miles to the Waikoloa Beach area. The park offers a fascinating glimpse into the prehistory of Native Hawaiians and features three *heiau*, or temples, built of native volcanic stone. Pu'ukoholā Heiau is one of the last major sacred structures built in Hawaii before outside influences dramatically changed traditional life. Constructed in 1790-91 by Kamehameha I, this temple played a major role in his ascendancy. It's believed that the stones used to construct the temple came from the distant Pololū Valley, and that workers formed a human chain at least 20 miles long, passing the stones from one worker to another. On the hillside between Pu'ukoholā Heiau and the sea are the ruins of Mailekini Heiau. This is an older temple that is not as finely crafted as Pu'ukoholā and thought to

The Ala Kahakai National Historic Trail offers stunning views of the Hawaiian coastline.

have either war or agricultural significance. Hale o Kapuni Heiau was constructed underwater just offshore, and was dedicated to sharks believed to be *'aumakuas* or ancestral deities.

Leaving the park to the south, the trail is marked in places and leads along cliff tops and isolated beaches to Waikoloa Beach, an area that is highly developed for tourism. The walk can be rough in places and is accessible (or at least approached) by road at several points. The trail in the Waikoloa Beach area is interesting as it includes a number of anchialine ponds, small ponds that rise and fall

(ABOVE) Along the trail in Kaloko-Honokōhau National Historical Park, you are likely to see some of the more than 100 *honu*, or large green sea turtles, that live in waters of the park. This is an ancient species, a survivor of the age of dinosaurs.

(BELOW) The Pu'u Loa Petroglyphs Trail is a gem, offering close-up views of the largest concentration of petroglyphs in Hawaii.

with the tides but have no surface connection to the sea. The water is brackish but often fresh and clear enough for the ponds to serve as highly valued sources of drinking water for Native Hawaiians. This area also includes a major petroglyph field that features nearly 30,000 ancient rock carvings thought to have religious or celebratory meanings.

Kaloko-Honokōhau National Historical Park lies south, near the town of Kona. Much of the area is covered in seemingly uninhabitable *a'a*, but the area was attractive to Native Hawaiians due to its freshwater springs and small natural harbor. The area includes two large fishponds—Kaloko and 'Aimakapa—that were vital sources of food; these ponds demonstrate the ingenuity and engineering skill of their builders. Young fish entered the ponds though a grate constructed of poles and fed on algae, plankton, and small shrimp. As they grew, they became too large to escape the ponds and were netted for food. The walls are perfectly sited and their angles just right to dissipate the power of the incoming waves. Although they were built with no mortar, they have mostly withstood the weather for hundreds of years. (Portions repaired by the National Park Service have proven inferior and are being re-repaired in the traditional manner.) The equally ingenious 'Ai'opio fishtrap was built out into the sea and sited so that fish were trapped at low tide. Near the harbor and 'Ai'opio fishtrap you are likely to see some of the more than 100 *honu*, or large green sea turtles, that live in the waters of the park. This is an ancient species, a survivor of the age of dinosaurs. The park is also a refuge for wetland birds, drawn by the ponds and marshes.

Pu'uhonua o Hōnaunau National Historical Park lies still farther south along the Kona Coast. This park teaches visitors about the Hawaiian ideas of sanctuary and offering a second chance for someone who had broken a *kapu* (sacred law) or had been defeated in war. Features include the stone ruins of the ancient village (including an impressive dry-stacked lava stone wall), two more fishponds, a collapsed lava tube (through which molten lava flowed), and the Keokea Hōlua, a paved hillside that royalty (*ali'i*) used as a toboggan run. Some of the trail in this park was modified in the nineteenth century in response to Western influences; the trail was straightened and widened to allow for pack animals.

Hawai'i Volcanoes National Park occupies much of the southern portion of the island, including Kilauea Volcano, which is active. Much of the backcountry portion of the park is laced with trails, and those along the coast will be important components of the Ala Kahakai Trail. This includes the Puna Coast Trail, the short trail to Pu'u Loa Petroglyphs, and parts of the Hilina Pali Trail and Ka'aha Trail. The three-quarters-of-a-mile trail to the petroglyphs is a gem, giving walkers a good feeling for the area's characteristic *pahoehoe* and offering close-up views of the largest concentration of petroglyphs in Hawaii. This is a revered and sacred site: Many families with genealogical ties to these lands continue their ceremonial practice of placing the *pikos*, or umbilical cords, of their children in the rocks in hopes of blessing them with a long life. Much of the Puna Coast Trail can

be walked as an out-and-back excursion, but the Hilina and Ka'aha trails require a short but demanding backpacking trip.

The Hawaiian Islands are natural treasures, where plant and animal life have been left (until recently) to evolve in relative isolation. For example, the birds of the island changed remarkably over time in response to the variety of specialized habitats. Ornithologists hypothesize that as few as fifteen original colonist species account for what are now more than fifty species or sub-species. *Nēnē*, the Hawaiian goose, is the state bird and endangered, but you will see nēnē along roads and trails. Drive slowly so as not to strike them and don't be tempted to feed them—it habituates them to humans and ultimately threatens them. The shallow, warm water surrounding the island is a sanctuary for humpback whales—watch for them from the trail from December through May.

Much of the Ala Kahakai National Historic Trail runs directly on the gorgeous coastline.

As with most trails, walking the Ala Kahakai Trail takes some planning and attention to logistical details. We advise consulting closely with the National Park Service as we found this very helpful. Most of the trail is fully exposed to the elements, so you must be prepared with proper sunshade, rain gear (especially in Hawai'i Volcanoes National Park), and lots of water. The portions of trail in the national parks are well marked and maintained, but the portions outside the parks require more caution—carry a map and be especially careful on cliff tops and on beaches that may flood at high tide. Swimming in the open ocean can be especially dangerous due to rough seas and unpredictable currents. Because this is an active geologic area, earthquakes can cause tsunamis; scan the landscape occasionally to get a sense of how you can get to higher ground. Volcanic activity at Hawai'i Volcanoes National Park can cause the National Park Service to close trails periodically; check on the status of trails at the park's visitor center.

Walking the Ala Kahakai Trail can be an adventure, and we found it well worth the effort. It's historic, beautiful, and enlightening. We enjoyed our several days of walking, and hope to return as the trail continues to be developed. *Mahalo* to all those who are making this trail a reality.

RITES OF WAY

So, where can one go to practice the kind of walking described in this book? That's a seemingly simple and fair question. But the answer is more complicated, steeped in history, culture, and controversy. Let's start in Europe, where the history is long.

Many countries in Europe have been aggressive in ensuring the public's "right to roam," also referred to as "everyman's right." England is a good example. More than a century ago, a well-to-do elite enacted policies in the form of "enclosures" that retracted public access to the nation's private but open lands. However, reforms were ultimately enacted, and the process of reopening lands continues to play out. For example, the Property Law Act of 1925 spurred a campaign to make the great open spaces of Britain more accessible to the public. This led to what has been described as "the most successful direct action campaign in British history," the most famous of which was a mass trespass at Kinder Scout in 1932 (see the description of the Pennine Way). Organized by the British Workers' Sports Federation, 400 walkers from the nearby towns of Manchester and Sheffield met on the Kinder edge path to assert their "right to roam." Arrests were made, but ultimately the public's right to roam on private lands—on historic rights-of-way and through open moors and related areas—was widely recognized. This right continues to expand. The result is a rich stock of walking opportunities, including a well-developed national trails system.

Similar rights are recognized in many other European countries. Scotland and the Scandinavian countries have especially broad policies that are codified through historical practice, constitutional provision, and national legislation, or some combination of the three.

The concept of the "right to roam" is advancing as a basic human right that should be available to all without regard to class. (Backbone Trail)

Of course, there's wide recognition that there are reasonable limitations to these rights, and that rights come with responsibilities. For example, the public is often restricted from entering active agricultural lands where people might damage crops, and they may not walk through gardens or in very close proximity to private homes. Certain activities are also prohibited, such as use of motorized vehicles and camping without explicit permission of the landowner. Moreover, there is the expectation that walkers will not leave trash or otherwise diminish the value and economic use of the land.

The United States presents quite a different situation. Private property and associated rights of ownership are pillars of American values and law. In fact, many immigrants settled in America to escape prohibitions on private property. The public may not cross or otherwise use private lands without explicit permission of landowners, and this has tended to limit opportunities for walking.

But this is greatly offset by an especially large system of public lands—national parks and forests and related reserves—that comprise nearly a third of the country. Of course, there are rules that mandate responsible use of these lands, but the lands are generally open for walking/hiking-related recreation activities

Moreover, there is a national trails system that totals more than 60,000 miles, including such iconic trails as the roughly 2,200-mile Appalachian National Scenic Trail. Many private lands are also available for walking thanks to the goodwill of many landowners, legal easements that have been negotiated

In 1932, 400 walkers from the nearby towns of Manchester and Sheffield met on the Kinder Scout edge path to assert their "right to roam." (Pennine Way)

by hiking and related organizations, and state legislation that limits landowner liability for injuries or other damages that might occur to hikers.

The concept of the "right to roam" is advancing as a basic human right that should be available to all without regard to class. Celebrate this right with a long walk! But be careful to exercise this right in a responsible manner, and be sure to express your thanks to private landowners and public land managers.

Amalfi's small medieval towns cling to the hillsides and spill down to the sea.

Amalfi Coast

Everyone's heard of the Mediterranean diet—eating primarily plant-based foods such as fruits, vegetables, and whole grains; drinking red wines; using healthy fats such as olive oil; and using herbs and spices instead of salt. The benefits are good health and prolonged life. But we think we've discovered another important ingredient—walking up and down long flights of steps! We were introduced to this at the apartment we rented in the charming town of Amalfi: up seventeen steps to get to the door of the building, up eighty-five steps to our apartment, and then a final eighteen steps to the rooftop terrace. Of course, this is nothing compared to the long flights of steps that take residents and visitors from town to town and connect the vast network of trails and paths throughout the Amalfi Coast. We worked up a vigorous appetite for the Mediterranean dinners we ate each night, confident that we were not just having fun and enjoying ourselves, but making ourselves healthier in the process.

LOCATION
Italy

LENGTH
Variable (a few days to a few weeks)

ACCOMMODATIONS
Commercial: Yes
Huts/refuges: No
Backpacking/camping: No

BAGGAGE TRANSFER AVAILABLE
Yes

OPTION TO WALK SECTIONS
Yes

DEGREE OF CHALLENGE
Moderate

THE AMALFI COAST lines the shores of the Gulf of Sorrento in southern Italy. The area's impossibly steep slopes plunge from the 4,500-foot ridgelines of the Lattari Mountains into the sea, supporting a series of small towns that line the coast and climb the hillsides. There is little flat land here, so generations of farmers have terraced the land using dry stone walls (called "*macerine*") to support a vibrant agriculture that includes olive groves, vineyards, and world-famous lemons. The lemons grow on trees that have been trained across wooden frames and pergolas. Seafood is another "crop" that has been harvested for centuries, with small colorful boats lining the harbors (along with the yachts of the rich and famous).

Before there were roads connecting the towns, there was an intricate network of trails that is still used by locals (it's not unusual to encounter farmers and shepherds along the trails, accompanied by mules loaded with firewood, vegetables, and fruit) and adventurous visitors. There are many

(ABOVE) The architecture of the impressive Amalfi *duomo* shows Moorish influences.

(ABOVE RIGHT) The medieval town of Amalfi is the heart of a former regional republic that rivaled the powerhouse of Venice to the north.

days of walking to be done here, but be sure you train before you come so you can take maximum advantage of these trails, many of which climb and descend with the landscape.

A string of beautiful towns lies along the coast, the most prominent of which are Salerno, Ravello, Amalfi, and Positano. Salerno is the gateway town on the eastern end of the region, and the area's transit hub offering train and bus stations. It has a long and eventful history, briefly serving as the capital of Italy after World War II. It's the largest town on the Amalfi Coast and docks cruise ships that frequent the area. Ravello has a deserved reputation as sophisticated—it sits high on the slopes above the sea and boasts the ruins of great estates and an assortment of contemporary five-star hotels. A bus system serves Ravello (and many other towns), and the town makes a great starting point for one-way (downhill!) walks to villages and other destinations along the sea. Amalfi is the heart of a former regional republic that once rivaled the powerhouse of Venice to the north. It's a small medieval town squeezed into a tight ravine that tumbles down from the mountains and spills into the sea. Its important place in history is manifested by its large *duomo*, or cathedral, which includes strong Moorish elements of design and decoration. Positano is often described as chic and elegant, and is highly popular with the "stars" and their accompanying paparazzi. It sits on the shore of the sea and climbs the hills behind it in a series of pastel buildings and stepped lanes. In addition, smaller towns lie on the coast or cling to the hills above, all of which make prized walking destinations.

The walking alternatives on the Amalfi Coast are nearly infinite, with so many routes between towns, agricultural areas, and other destinations, and so many ways to combine them into a series of day hikes. But everyone agrees that the *Sentiero degli Dei*—the Walk of the Gods—should be on the itinerary. This walk starts high in the hills in the town of Bomerano; Positano is the ultimate goal. The trail passes large and fragrant bushes of rosemary, works through forests of oak and strawberry trees, and makes its way along the tops of steep cliffs that offer stunning views of the dramatic coast. Picnic tables are generously scattered along the trail, which comes to its official end in the village of Nocelle, high above the sea. There are several alternatives from here: The local bus runs to Positano and is a good option. Or you can take the 1,700 steps down to the bus stop on the main road at Arienzo and then ride to Positano. Or you can walk along the road from Nocelle to the town of Montepertuso, at the foot of Monte Gambera and its iconic hole in the mountain, and then on to Positano. In any case, you'll be fully justified in rewarding yourself with a lemon gelato in town.

We enjoyed several walks from our home base in Amalfi. We walked up the steep hillsides at the back of the town to the village of Pontone, where we admired the vegetable gardens, and then worked our way west through a deep ravine that includes a large natural area featuring streams and waterfalls running off the surrounding mountains, and then through the Valley of the Mills ruins with their iron and paper works for which Amalfi was once famous. This is a circular route that ultimately

The town of Positano offers dramatic views of the sea, punctuated by distinctive umbrella pines.

brings you right back down to Amalfi. On another outing, we again walked to Pontone, but turned east and ultimately made our way to the ruins of La Torre dello Ziro, an outpost and watchtower constructed in the twelfth century to guard against attack by Saracen pirates.

On two other days, we took the bus from Amalfi to Ravello and made our way back to Amalfi via different routes. Before leaving Ravello, we suggest walking through the ruins of the town's magnificent Villa Rufolo (said to have once had more rooms than days in the year) and its extensive gardens. Our first exploration made a large loop around Ravello and several other villages, and then traveled down the hillsides to the town of Atrani, which shares the seashore with Amalfi. On the other outing, we descended to the seaside village of Minori, where we walked through the ruins of an impressive, two-thousand-year-old Roman villa and then traversed the slope to the neighboring town of Maiori, with its lovely and extensive public beach. The route between the two towns is called the Lane of the Lemons. When finished, we took the bus back to Amalfi. These are only a few of our favorite walks, and everywhere we went was authentic, historic, and gorgeous.

The Amalfi Coast occupies the southern side of the Sorrento Peninsula. The northern side includes the appealing town of Sorrento and, farther north on the Italian coast, Naples and Pompeii. Off the tip of the peninsula is the "perfect" island of Capri. All these areas warrant a visit, but if you're primarily interested in walking in this appealing part of the world, don't be tempted to spread yourself too thinly; be sure to spend adequate time on the Amalfi Coast.

But don't be tempted to drive! The road built to connect the towns of the Amalfi Coast in the nineteenth century is narrow, twisty, crowded, and carries lots of buses; it's hair-raising, and many of the towns don't allow parking anyway. There's lots of good public transportation, including

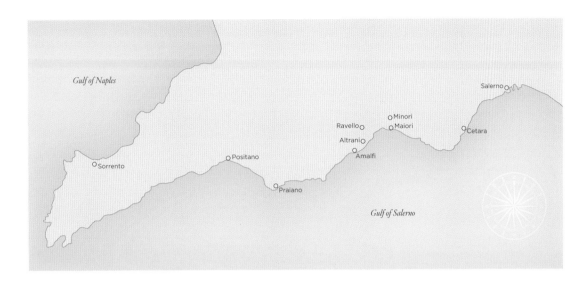

the very inexpensive local Sita bus system. A system of ferries also connects many towns from early spring through late fall. You can visit this area year-round, though summer is usually hot and very crowded. We were there in December and January, and the daytime temperatures were in the mid to high 50s (good walking temperatures) and mostly sunny. Many types of accommodations are available.

We took hiking poles and found them very useful, especially for descending steep steps. Many hiking companies offer walks on the Amalfi Coast, moving from town to town every couple of days, but we enjoyed basing ourselves in Amalfi and using local transportation to get to and from other towns. This allowed us to really get to know Amalfi, and we avoided having to frequently pack and repack clothes and other gear. We suggest taking a good hiking guidebook and maps with you to Italy, as they weren't readily available there. And there's not much English spoken in many of the rural villages, so prepare yourself as best you can.

We walked for ten days and didn't tire of the stunning, dramatic, and historic landscape of the Amalfi Coast. The views of the coast varied with every turn in the trail, and the scene included craggy mountains, rich forests, endless terracing and associated agriculture, iconic umbrella pines, fragrant wildflowers and herbs, groups of dramatic islands off the coast, and one historic town after another. At the end of each day of walking we were rewarded with local foods and wines, and still more of that lemon gelato. Our stay in Amalfi was over the Christmas and New Year's holidays, and we were treated to multiple fireworks displays and several parades that culminated in local folk song and dancing. We'd waited years to walk the Amalfi Coast and we weren't disappointed!

TRAIL ANGELS

Nearly all long-distance walkers have met at least one "trail angel" who generously dispensed a little "trail magic." Often these moments occur at the time and place they're most needed—at the end of an especially long day, when persistent cold, heat, or rain has taken a toll, or when food or water is running low. Trail magic is a tradition of charity on long-distance trails, unexpected acts of kindness offered by fellow hikers and people who live near the trail. Trail magic can take many forms—food and beverages left for hikers at strategic spots, rides to nearby towns to resupply, low-cost or even free meals and accommodations, helpful advice from local people familiar with the trail, an offer of much-needed laundry service.

Lloyd Gust was a quintessential trail angel on the Pacific Crest Trail. Lloyd and his wife had hiked most of the trail themselves and knew what hikers needed and when they needed it. He adopted a 300-mile section of the trail in Oregon near where he lived, refilling water caches, giving rides when needed, helping out with medical emergencies, and doing many munificent acts of kindness for up to 300 hikers a year. This was a heroic effort, and many of the hikers he helped feel he should be considered a charter member of the unofficial Trail Angel Hall of Fame.

We've benefited from trail magic. A kind family operating the B&B where we were staying on a long hike in the Rocky Mountains of Colorado insisted on giving us a ride to the trailhead, saving us some road walking, and asked us only to send them a postcard when we finished the hike. When we were walking along Italy's Amalfi Coast, we were concerned that we'd taken a wrong turn. We were standing on the trail studying and restudying our map when a young man from a local village approached. Though we didn't share a language, we all tried hard to understand each other, and he offered a reassuring affirmation that we were, indeed, on the intended trail. We've found that there's a certain romanticism associated with long-distance walking, and that many people just seem to want to help.

Of course, if you've benefited from trail magic, that means you should consider being a trail angel yourself when the opportunity arises. We often carry individually wrapped hard candies to dole out to walkers who look like they could use a little magic in their day; we share our maps and trail information with folks who are less informed; and we've used our first aid skills at strategic times, treating strangers' blisters, sore knees, etc. Our experience is that these wonderful moments are mutually beneficial and a meaningful way to connect with fellow walkers.

We've found that there's a certain romanticism associated with long-distance walking, and that many people just want to help. (Great Glen Way)

A trail angel left apples for pilgrims on the Camino Portugués.

Aravaipa Canyon is
a hidden oasis in the
Sonoran Desert.

Aravaipa Canyon Wilderness

We found a great place for lunch—in the shade of a giant cottonwood with a big boulder that served as a backrest. After eating, we were about to gather our gear and continue on down the canyon when we saw some movement downstream. It took a few minutes to figure out what we were seeing, but then we realized we were watching a herd of javelinas cross the creek and nose about. Javelinas, also known as collared peccaries, are medium-size animals (3 to 4 feet long, 2 feet tall, and up to 55 pounds) that resemble wild boar. They evolved in South America and have migrated north, only recently arriving in Arizona. They're herbivores and generally not dangerous, but have long, sharp canine teeth that protrude from the jaws about an inch. Javelinas live in large family groups, and have scent glands on their rumps used to mark their territories and to identify individuals in the herd. (Even people can smell them at some distance—ugh.) Javelinas were a new entry on our life list of wildlife, and we were fascinated to watch them. After about ten minutes, they moved on into the dense vegetation, and we decided to move on downstream as well.

LOCATION
Arizona, United States

LENGTH
22 miles

ACCOMMODATIONS
Commercial: No
Huts/refuges: No
Backpacking/camping: Yes

BAGGAGE TRANSFER AVAILABLE
No

OPTION TO WALK SECTIONS
No

DEGREE OF CHALLENGE
Moderate

ARAVAIPA CANYON is an 11-mile-long winding oasis in southeastern Arizona, about 120 miles south of Phoenix and 50 miles northeast of Tucson. A rare and valuable perennial stream, Aravaipa Creek flows through the canyon creating lush riparian habitat for many species of wildlife. This is a land of little precipitation, but the creek is fed by springs, seeps, and tributary streams. The canyon is narrow, varying from about 50 to 300 feet in width, and canyon walls rise to as much as 1,000 feet above the stream. Managed by the US Bureau of Land Management and the nonprofit Nature Conservancy, which owns some adjoining uplands, the lush canyon makes a stark and beautiful contrast to the surrounding Sonoran Desert. Most of the canyon—nearly 20,000 acres—is designated wilderness, which means the area is intended to be preserved, though some recreational use is allowed.

Surrounded by the Galiuro and Santa Teresa Mountains, Aravaipa Canyon is classic basin-and-range country, a vast geographic region of the western United States characterized by mountain chains

(ABOVE) Saguaro are in abundance on the dry canyon walls and arid uplands surrounding the canyon.

(ABOVE RIGHT) Steep sandstone walls rise above Aravaipa Creek.

(BELOW) In the canyon, the creek is lined with mature cottonwood, sycamore, and willow trees, offering shade and shelter.

divided by flat, arid valleys. American geographer Clarence Dutton likened the region to an "army of caterpillars marching toward Mexico." At the west entrance, the canyon is relatively wide, but it narrows very quickly. In the canyon, the creek is lined with mature cottonwood, sycamore, and willow trees, offering shade and shelter, and saguaro grow in abundance on the dry canyon walls and the arid uplands surrounding the canyon. The canyon is home to an estimated 300 animal species, most of them birds such at the canyon wren, peregrine falcon, zone-tailed hawk, and the yellow-billed cuckoo. Walkers might see black bears, bobcats, coyotes, mountain lions, rattlesnakes, gila monsters, and nine species of bats (though we weren't fortunate enough to see any of these animals). Two species of endangered fish are found in the creek. Several side canyons flow into Aravaipa Creek, but only Deer Creek is open enough for serious exploration (the other canyons require scrambling and bouldering). This dead-end canyon features a short but impressive narrows section where the canyon walls close to within 20 feet of each other, and a gushing spring in a fern-covered grotto. Deer Creek is worth the side trip.

People have coveted Aravaipa Canyon for hundreds—and probably thousands—of years. Native Americans used the canyon for agricultural purposes, but its small size was limiting. They also used many of the plants that grow in the canyon and hunted and fished here. The canyon was abandoned by AD 1450, but evidence of native culture can be seen at the Turkey Creek cliff dwelling, located about 1.5 miles from the east end of the canyon.

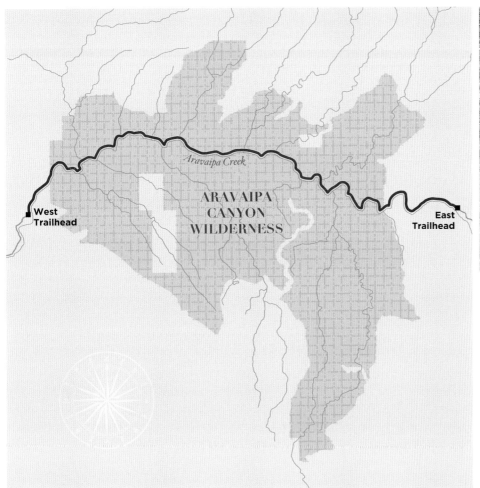

There isn't a maintained trail on the floor of the canyon—it's more of a route, and it's recommended that you use social trails that have already been created.

The area was used in the mid-1800s by the Aravaipa band of the Western Apache, who hunted, fished, grew corn, and collected acorns from the canyon's Emory's oaks. The Aravaipa band fought many battles with the US Cavalry, ultimately being moved out of the canyon area. Soon thereafter Hispanic and Anglo settlers started grazing stock here and developed copper mines in the watershed. Limited ranching in the area continues today, but the town of Aravaipa in now a ghost town. If you look closely as you walk through the canyon, you may see evidence of this complicated history in the form of cabin ruins and traces of Native American occupation.

You must cross the stream many times, sometimes wading through water that's typically no more than knee-deep.

Aravaipa Canyon can be sampled in a day hike, but is best experienced as a two- to three-day backpacking trip. There isn't a maintained trail on the floor of the canyon—it's more of a route that may require occasional bushwhacking (though it's recommended that you use the social trails that have already been created). Moreover, you must cross the stream many times, sometimes wading through water that is typically no more than knee-deep. All this adds to the adventure, but for most people, walking the length of the canyon (about 11 miles) makes for a very long day.

We found our hiking poles to be very helpful. Wayfinding is not difficult, as you simply walk up- or downstream, depending on whether you start from the east or west entrance. There are several short side canyons, but the only one we'd recommend exploring is Deer Creek (as noted above). There are lots of potential campsites scattered along the canyon floor, and water is readily available from the creek (though it must be treated). A permit is required, even for a day hike, and permits must be reserved weeks or even months ahead; spring and fall are the most popular seasons and weekend quotas fill the fastest. A maximum of 50 people per day are allowed in the canyon and permits are available online from the Bureau of Land Management. You can drive to parking areas that serve the east and west entrances of the canyon, but the west entrance is much more convenient and the road is serviceable for a conventional car. It's quite a long drive to reach the east entrance and requires a four-wheel-drive vehicle with high clearance as the creek must be forded several times. Like most canyons in the Southwest, Aravaipa is subject to occasional flash floods—look for driftwood in the trees lining the creek for dramatic evidence. Check weather reports carefully before you enter the canyon.

Southwestern canyons with perennial streams like Aravaipa are a treasure—lush oases in the midst of the desert that offer precious wildlife habitat and an inviting retreat for hikers. Aravaipa's wilderness designation adds to the sense of adventure. We enjoyed the canyon so much, we walked it a second time a few years later.

"ARE WE THERE YET?"

We've all heard this one before, especially those of us who've walked with children. But admit it, haven't you muttered these words under your breath a few times yourself? For various reasons, it can be comforting to know how long a walk might take, and it can be frustrating if the walk takes substantially longer than you expect. If fact, it's wise to know how long a walk might take, at least within reasonable bounds. How much food and water will you need? When might family and friends expect to see you again, or, more pointedly, when should they worry if they haven't seen you?

For all these reasons and more, walkers have given this issue serious thought for more than a hundred years. For example, in 1892, Scottish mountaineer William Naismith devised what has become known as "Naismith's rule," a rule of thumb that helps estimate how long it will take to walk a trail based on both length of the trail and the amount of ascent. The rule suggests allowing one hour for every 5 kilometers (3.1 miles) forward, plus one hour for every 600 meters (roughly 2,000 feet) of ascent. Naismith and other walkers field-tested his rule on the fells of Scotland and found it generally accurate. However, the rule assumes a lot (we'll get to that in a moment) and doesn't account for rest breaks or sightseeing.

One way to employ this rule is to calculate the "flat distance" of a trail (calculated by taking into account both distance and ascent) and then estimating the time needed to walk this flat distance. Here's an example we found in the literature. As noted above, Naismith's rule suggests a standard relationship between distance and climb: 3 miles (15,840 feet) of distance is the time equivalent of 2,000 feet of climb. Therefore, 7.92 (15,840/2,000) units of distance are equivalent to one unit of climb. Rounding off, this is an 8:1 relationship.

Therefore, if a trail is 20 kilometers long (12.4 miles) with 1,600 meters (5,249 feet or about a mile) of climb, the equivalent flat distance of the trail is 20 + 1.6 x 8 = 32.8 kilometers (20.4 miles). Assuming a walker can maintain a speed of 5 kilometers (3.1 miles) per hour, the walk will take 6 hours and 34 minutes.

Of course, the speed (and therefore time) can be adjusted for individuals. (Don't worry, there are easier ways to do all this that we'll get to in a moment.) We should add here that walking at 3 miles per hour or faster for an extended period is ambitious, at least in our experience, and this pace leaves little or no time to appreciate the walk.

But wait—there's more. Recently several observers, mostly mathematicians and geographers, have offered some refinements to Naismith's rule, including some elegant (but sometimes obtuse) equations and graphs. For example, the

Walking speed is affected by distance, ascent, and a variety of other factors. (Maroon Bells–Snowmass Wilderness)

It's wise to know how long a walk might take, at least within reasonable bounds. (Maroon Bells–Snowmass Wilderness)

roughness of the trail can affect walking time; generally, when walking on rough trails, allow 1 hour for every 4 kilometers (2.5 miles) forward, instead of the rate suggested by Naismith's rule. Of course, walking downhill can make a difference too. For slopes that aren't steep (less than 12 degrees), subtract 10 minutes of walking time for every 300 meters (about 1,000 feet) of descent, and for steep slopes (greater than 12 degrees), add ten minutes of walking time for every 300 meters (about 1,000 feet) of descent.

Naturally, the fitness of the walker can also make a big difference in walking time. A series of "corrections" (called "Tranter's Corrections") to Naismith's rule have been suggested based on six categories of fitness that range from "unfit" to "very fit" (of course, walkers rate their own level of fitness, and this may be fraught with peril). And there are corrections to the corrections: drop a fitness level if you are carrying a heavy pack, walking into a headwind, or hiking at night (?!).

But don't take our word for all this—be sure to read more about it in the papers published on this topic in the scientific and professional literature. Examples include "Three Presentations on Geographical Analysis and Modeling: Non-Isotropic Geographic Modeling Speculations on the Geometry of Geography Global Spatial Analysis" and "GPS-Aided Walking Experiments and Data-Driven Travel Cost Modeling on the Historical Road of Nakasendo-Kisoji (Central Highland Japan)." Or not.

So, let's return to the question posed at the beginning of this essay: Are we there yet? Or more appropriately, how long will it take to get "there"? This is a reasonable question with potentially important consequences. But like many things, it's more complicated than it might seem. Naismith's rule is a reasonable place to start. However, the calculation should be tweaked based on the factors likely to affect walking time (simple awareness of these factors and how they're likely to affect hiking times can be useful).

Learn about the trail you intend to walk (we include much of this information in the trail descriptions in this book) and factor in your general walking times. Then take all this information and adjust Naismith's rule as warranted. Using a "pacing card" can be helpful; they're available online. Find your walking speed on one axis of the matrix and the distance of the trail on the other, and find the estimated walking time (adjustments or "corrections" are often built into these handy cards). Some guidebooks include estimated walking times, though how these times were calculated is not always specified. At the very least, we suggest starting with Naismith's rule, but adding as much as 25 percent more time to be sure you allow enough time to enjoy the walk.

Fortunately, there are several online walking time calculators that allow you to enter the kinds of information noted above—many walkers find them useful. Another approach is to keep track of your walking distances and times as a way to make you more aware of how long different types of walks tend to take. There are an increasing variety of sophisticated pedometers on the market (these have the added advantage of encouraging you to walk the recommended daily minimum of 10,000 steps), and several smartphone apps that will map your walk, including both distance and ascent/descent.

Lovely rocks and pygmy forests cover much
of the higher elevations of the Backbone Trail.

Backbone Trail

We started our walk on the Backbone Trail where we should have—at the impressive, newly renovated visitor center at King Gillette Ranch. This building was constructed in 1928 as the stables for the King Gillette Ranch in the Santa Monica Mountains in Southern California. The stables have been converted into the first "net-zero" building in the US national park system, meaning the building produces all the energy needed to function. Design and reconstruction of the building were based on the principles of reducing energy usage and CO_2 emissions, enhancing water efficiency, improving indoor environmental quality, and contributing to stewardship of natural and cultural resources. The building earned LEED platinum designation, the highest rating possible, from the Leadership in Energy & Environmental Design program. Here we talked with rangers about the trail, how to access it, and the types of environments we would find as we hiked. We left the visitor center with a good sense of how to plan our hike and a stronger appreciation of the possibilities for enlightened environmental design.

LOCATION
California, United States

LENGTH
65 miles

ACCOMMODATIONS
Commercial: Yes (Nearby)
Huts/refuges: No
Backpacking/camping: Some

BAGGAGE TRANSFER AVAILABLE
No

OPTION TO WALK SECTIONS
Yes

DEGREE OF CHALLENGE
Moderate

THE BACKBONE TRAIL is a 65-mile route that follows the ridges of the Santa Monica Mountains and lies within Santa Monica Mountains National Recreation Area, which is managed by the National Park Service. This is a new model of national parks in America, but one that has proven very productive in other places around the world, particularly those that have high population densities. This new type of national park relies heavily on collaborative relationships among public, private, and nonprofit groups; in this case the major entities are the California State Parks, the Santa Monica Mountains Conservancy, and the Mountains Recreation and Conservation Authority. The National Park Service owns some of the land within the park and also plays an important role in helping to coordinate management of the park in a unified and coherent way. The Backbone Trail is a good example of the possibilities of this collaborative approach. The park is also an exemplar of one of the

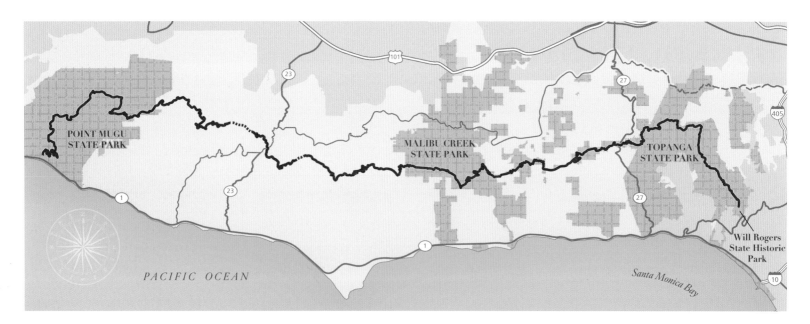

At the western end of the Backbone Trail, hikers can dip their toes in the Pacific Ocean at Point Mugu State Park.

ways in which the National Park Service has been trying to extend the reach of the national parks to urban areas and their diverse populations.

The Backbone Trail has been a vision of conservationists for decades, and creation of state parks in the area in the 1970s, along with establishment of Santa Monica Mountains National Recreation Area in 1978, led to substantial progress in the 1980s. By 1990, 43 miles of the trail had been completed. Two small sections of the trail are still not accessible to the public. The name "Backbone Trail" has a double meaning, signifying its path along the ridgetops of the park and its status as the backbone or unifying core of the area's extensive system of trails.

The trail stretches from Point Mugu State Park in the west to Will Rogers State Historic Park in the east. At Point Mugu State Park, walkers can dip their toes in the Pacific Ocean, while the trail in Will Rogers State Park leads right into the great city of Los Angeles. The trail follows ridges, traverses chaparral-covered hillsides, finds its way through shady oak woodlands, and crosses a number of creeks and valleys. The whole area has a coastal Mediterranean ecosystem that offers warm, dry summers and mild, wet winters. The route is comprised of singletrack trails that had their origins as game tracks, converted fire roads, and newly constructed trail sections. Construction of the trail has benefited from help by volunteers and the California Conservation Corps. It's expected the trail will be completed soon, but walkers can enjoy the vast majority of the trail now.

(ABOVE LEFT) The undeveloped lands of the Backbone Trail are in sharp contrast to downtown Los Angeles.

(ABOVE) Manzanita is easy to identify by its colorful bark.

Located near the geographic center of Los Angeles, the trail's proximity to this large urban population is, perhaps, its most defining characteristic. From the eastern end of the trail there are dramatic views of downtown Los Angeles, with the park's large, green canyons and ridgelines in the foreground. It's a stark and dramatic view that emphasizes the unusual opportunities the Santa Monica Mountains National Recreation Area creates for the city's residents and visitors. We saw many people as we walked the trail, particularly in the state parks, where they were playing ball, picnicking, and just generally enjoying the out of doors. Some were families with small children and others were in extended family groups. It was exciting to see so much racial and cultural diversity among visitors, a reflection of the diversity of the city and validation that the trail and the surrounding park are serving the needs of a cross section of the population.

We especially enjoyed Will Rogers State Historic Park, honoring one of America's best-loved and most-quoted humorists: Rogers is famous, in particular, for saying that he "never met a man [he] didn't like," a reflection of his outlook on life. The park was Rogers's 186-acre ranch in the first part of the twentieth century and was deeded to the state by his family in 1944. The park offers great views of Los Angeles and the Pacific Ocean. The Rogers ranch home is built in a sprawling western

Eagle Rock in Topanga State Park is a large area of exposed bedrock that's fun to climb on and provides panoramic views of the park and surrounding lands.

style and includes thirty-one rooms. It's listed on the National Register of Historic Places and is open to the public. The park also includes rolling lawns, stables, riding arenas, and a polo field that is still used today.

Other highlights included the Circle X Ranch, Point Mugu State Park, and Eagle Rock in Topanga State Park. Circle X Ranch rises above the town of Malibu and was once a camp for Boy Scouts; it's now a popular hiking destination. It includes Sandstone Peak, the highest point along the Backbone Trail, and offers great views of the Pacific Ocean, including (on clear days) the Channel Islands, a national park off the coast of California, and the inland valleys to the east. Point Mugu State Park has 5 miles of ocean shoreline with rocky bluffs, sand beaches, and rugged hills, and offers more potential views of the Channel Islands. This area encompasses the jagged peaks of the Boney Mountains, part of which is a state wilderness area. The word "mugu" has Native American origins; Native Americans inhabited this region of California for more than 10,000 years. A section of the park that includes the Backbone Trail has recently been burned by a wildfire, evidence of the historic

role fire has played in this ecosystem as well as the effects of the prolonged drought that has afflicted much of California. Eagle Rock in Topanga State Park is a large area of exposed bedrock that's fun to climb on and provides panoramic views of the park and surrounding lands.

The Backbone Trail is accessible via a network of roads that lace Santa Monica Mountains National Recreation Area and the surrounding lands; the roads cross the trail in many locations. This network allows the trail to be walked in a series of day hikes, the most common way to approach this trail. The state parks offer access to many portions of the trail, but require an entrance fee. The trail is only moderately challenging in most places, though there are a few steep sections. Trail running shoes are adequate, and hiking poles are recommended. It can be hot in the summer, so take plenty of water and wear sun protection. National Park Service rangers lead eight-day hikes that start on Saturdays twice a month from January through April, and this is an excellent way to walk the whole (existing) trail if you live in the Los Angeles area. A good map of the area is a requirement as wayfinding can be challenging, and there is not yet a comprehensive guidebook for the trail.

And, of course, visit with rangers at the King Gillette Visitor Center to get oriented to the park and trail and to ask about the latest trail conditions . . . and expect to be impressed with the qualities that make the visitor center "net zero."

(ABOVE LEFT) A recent fire has burned a section of the trail, evidence of the historic role of wildfires in this ecosystem.

(ABOVE) Early morning fog softens and quiets ranch views along the trail.

THE ETHICS OF WALKING

Walking can be one of the most sustainable forms of recreation and travel, having little impact on the environment. However, that doesn't mean walkers can be careless about the potential environmental impacts they can cause. For example, hiking can trample fragile vegetation, compact and erode soils, disturb sensitive wildlife, and pollute rivers and lakes with sediment and human waste. Generally, walkers should stay on maintained trails, never feed wildlife, dispose of trash in an acceptable manner (use trash receptacles or carry it out with you), and, of course, follow all posted rules and regulations.

The ethics of walking generally follow commonsense guidelines. It's reputed that American Indian Chief Seattle advised people to "Take only memories, leave nothing but footprints." That's been updated, substituting "pictures" for memories and adding "kill nothing but time." However, these old saws have been superseded by more scientifically based and professionally advanced efforts to think through these ethical considerations. These guidelines can be useful to walkers in carrying out their ethical obligations to the environment and future generations of walkers.

For example, the organization Leave No Trace has partnered with trail managers such as the US National Park Service to develop and implement a set of seven principles that should guide walkers:

1. Plan ahead and prepare.
2. Travel and camp on durable surfaces.
3. Dispose of waste properly.
4. Leave what you find.
5. Minimize campfire impacts.
6. Respect wildlife.
7. Be considerate of other visitors.

These principles are discussed and illustrated in more detail on the organization's website (www.lnt.org).

A related program of ethics for walkers has been developed in Britain and is known as the Countryside Code. A series of six principles is suggested to help walkers respect, protect, and enjoy the countryside, much of which is privately owned:

1. Consider the local community and the other people enjoying the outdoors.
2. Leave gates and property as you find them and follow paths unless wider access is available.
3. Leave no trace of your visit and take your litter home.
4. Keep dogs under effective control.

Some trails include active agricultural areas; please obey all posted signs. (Thames Path)

5. Plan ahead and be prepared.
6. Follow advice and local signs.

These principles are discussed and illustrated on the website for the organization Natural England (www.natural england.org.uk).

There are other generally accepted norms that apply to walking, particularly in natural areas. For example, when groups of hikers meet on a steep trail, the ascending group is generally offered the right-of-way. When encountering equestrians or stock, walkers should yield the right-of-way and stand quietly by the side of the trail, preferably on the downhill side. Mountain bikers should offer the right-of-way to walkers. Walkers should avoid being loud or boisterous, and refrain from using cell phones so as not to bother other walkers (though walkers are encouraged to make their presence known in grizzly bear country). Groups of walkers should not encourage slower members of the group to walk faster than they are safely able to do; one technique is to put slower members of the group in the lead so they're not left behind, and another is to place an experienced member at the end of the group to act as a "sweep."

There are also several good books that offer useful discussions of ethical practices that can help walkers be good stewards of the land. We recommend Guy and Laura Waterman's *Backwoods Ethics*, Will Harmon's *Leave No Trace*, and Rich Brame and David Cole's *Soft Paths*.

Walkers should stay on maintained trails to limit their environmental impact. (Needles)

We suggest starting your walk on the Camino Portugués in the lively city of Porto, a World Heritage Site.

Camino Portugués

As always, we'd been watching the weather report before leaving home and knew there could be showers on days one and two of our walk on the Camino Portugués. When we arrived in Porto, Portugal, the starting point of our walk, it was a beautiful day and we enjoyed sightseeing under sunny skies. However, when we checked the weather report that night, we were shocked to learn that the remnants of a strong tropical storm had changed course and the forecast for the next day—the first day of our walk—called for 50 mile-per-hour winds, heavy rain totaling 5 to 6 inches, and localized flooding. Yikes! We felt it would be dangerous to go out into these conditions, but decided to wait until the following morning, check the forecast again, and then make a decision about what to do.

Fortunately, the projection had moderated substantially by the morning—the warnings of flooding had been withdrawn—so we decided to go ahead with our walk as planned. Though it was not ideal to walk all day in a steady, driving rain (at our backs, fortunately), we were fully prepared—waterproof pants, jackets, hats, and gloves, and a substantial plastic bag lined each pack to keep everything inside dry. We saw few other pilgrims that day, most having elected to spend the day indoors, but the other walkers were also equipped for wet weather and seemed to be making the best of things. The remnants of the storm moved on quickly, and we were rewarded with near-perfect weather for the following eleven days. Our advice: watch weather forecasts carefully and never put yourself at risk, but don't be afraid of walking when the weather isn't good—hopefully, you've "practiced" walking in less than ideal conditions and are prepared.

LOCATION
Portugal and Spain

LENGTH
150 miles

ACCOMMODATIONS
Commercial: Yes
Huts/refuges: Yes
Backpacking/camping: No

BAGGAGE TRANSFER AVAILABLE
Yes

OPTION TO WALK SECTIONS
Yes

DEGREE OF CHALLENGE
Low–Moderate

SAINT JAMES WAS one of the twelve apostles, and brought Christianity to the Iberian Peninsula. After death, Saint James's remains were eventually taken to Santiago, Spain, where they've been housed since the year 841. Catholics built a large and impressive cathedral to honor his memory, and

(ABOVE) Walkers on the Camino Portugués use many of the same paths taken by pilgrims for roughly 1,000 years.

(BELOW) Most vineyards are grown and maintained at a small scale, and extended families tend the grapes.

Christians have been making their way to Santiago to pay their respects ever since. A half million or more pilgrims made the journey each year in medieval times, but the numbers dropped off substantially until quite recently; now numbers are definitely on the rise.

Santiago is considered the third most important site in Christendom (after Rome and Jerusalem), and traveling the Camino de Santiago (the Way of Saint James) is far and away the most popular Christian pilgrimage. Many pilgrimage routes throughout Europe lead to Santiago; all are considered to be the Way of Saint James. The most popular pilgrimage variation (sometimes referred to as the Camino Francés or French Way) starts on the French side of the Pyrenees Mountains and goes across northern Spain for nearly 500 miles: We describe this walk in our book, *Walking Distance*.

The second most popular route is the Camino Portugués, a wonderful walk of about 150 miles from Porto north into Spain, and on to Santiago de Compostela. There are variations of the route through Portugal, and we chose the Central Route. The walk is mostly on secondary and minor roads, farm tracks, and some walking trails. It wanders through agricultural fields, vineyards, small olive groves, patches of forest, and some of the oldest and remotest villages in Portugal. It also includes a few larger, historic cities, and crosses several major rivers on medieval bridges. The route through Portugal and then on to Santiago is intimately connected to the life and ministry of Saint James, as well as his death and burial, and has been described as "soulful." The tradition in medieval times was to carry a "passport," or credential, and have it stamped at places along the route to certify you'd completed the walk, and this tradition continues today.

We spent the day before our walk of the Camino Portugués in beautiful Porto, Portugal, and we suggest you do, too. Retaining much of its medieval flavor, this is where the country of Portugal took its name in the twelfth century. The historic and beautiful center of Porto has been designated a World Heritage Site, and we spent the day touring many of the area's attractions—the Clergymen's Tower, with its 225 steps to 360-degree views of the city; the Porto Cathedral (don't overlook its second-floor notary chamber and statue of *Santiago Peregrino*); the beautiful Ponte de Dom Luis; the impressive statue of Henry the Navigator (commemorating the importance of Portugal to exploration of the New World); and the Zona Ribeirinha (the waterfront area with its many cafes), which overlooks the iconic river barges on the Rio Douro (River of Gold).

The route of the Camino Portugués runs through a string of interesting towns, and we certainly enjoyed Barcelos, where we stopped on day two. This is an especially tourist-friendly town, and we were fortunate to have arrived on a Wednesday because there's a well-known and lively market every Thursday. (Barcelos claims it is Portugal's busiest market, and we saw no reason to disagree.) We wandered around the market for a couple of hours that morning, admiring all the regional fruits and vegetables, breads, local crafts, and even a few farm animals before we had to get back on the trail to reach our next destination.

Since it was fall, the annual grape harvest was in full swing. Most vineyards are grown and tended at a small, family scale, with extended families carefully harvesting the grapes by hand, cutting the bunches of grapes and placing them into large metal or plastic containers. Periodically, the person in charge would arrive on a tractor towing a cart and empty the containers into the cart. We were enjoying watching the process one afternoon when "the boss" dropped and spilled one of the containers, and the women who had cut the grapes laughed and teased. (No translation was needed—some things seem to be universal.)

Another favorite town was Ponte de Lima, reputed to be the oldest town in Portugal. Ponte de Lima features gorgeous gardens, and during its Corpus Christi festival in the spring, some of the streets are carpeted in designs made of flower petals. It's a dynamic place, with many of its medieval buildings remaining, and the showstopper is an especially long bridge with many graceful arches. Like many bridges we crossed, it was constructed in medieval times (the fourteenth century, in this case), but utilized Roman-era foundations; Romans sited this bridge on their road through Portugal, and we were (as usual) impressed by the evidence of their engineering skills.

The following day was a bit more challenging, with trails that were occasionally steep and rough. This led us to the highest point on the camino and then back down to the valley, where we crossed a small stream on another graceful Roman bridge. Day six of our walk was especially eventful, as it took us over the River Minho (*Mino* in Spanish), out of Portugal and into Spain. Before we crossed the bridge, we made a short detour into Valenca, an impressive medieval walled town with extensive fortifications, all of which are still intact. Many of the original structures in the village are now used

(ABOVE LEFT) The Fortaleza de Valenca is an impressive walled fortification originally designed to protect against the Spanish, just across the River Minho; today it serves as a tourist destination.

(ABOVE) Ponte de Lima, one of the lovely medieval towns along the route, has an especially long bridge with many arches; it was built in the fourteenth century on Roman foundations.

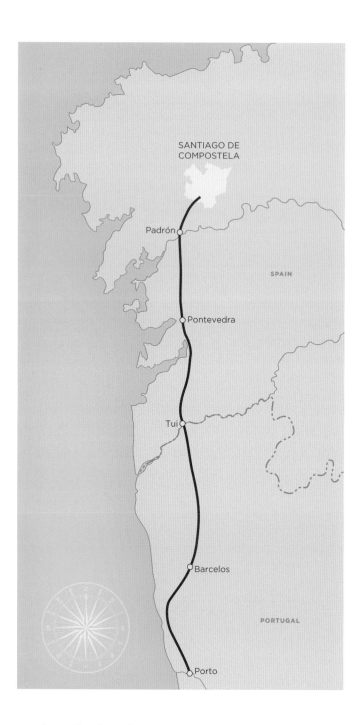

for purposes of tourism—shops and restaurants primarily. This is definitely worth the very short walk off the main track.

We crossed the River Minho into Tui, Spain, on a metal bridge constructed by Eiffel (of Eiffel Tower fame), and then had to reset our watches by an hour. Tui is an historical border city with a large cathedral and other important cultural markers. We encountered many more pilgrims in Tui because the Catholic Church requires pilgrims to walk at least the final 100 kilometers of the camino to validate that they've "completed" the walk, qualifying them to receive a *compostela*, a certificate issued by the church, to that effect; Tui is roughly 100 kilometers from Santiago.

We walked the next few days along mostly quiet country roads, enjoying the typical sounds of the rural villages—roosters crowing, dogs barking, occasional motorbikes and tractors, and families going about their business. This brought us to Pontevedra, a city of moderate size with an interesting and lively old town area. We ate at one of the restaurants bordering the major plaza, which local children use as a park, playing soccer (football!), riding bikes, etc.. The plaza had been deserted in the heat of the afternoon and couldn't have been busier at dinnertime—we enjoyed watching modern urban life in an ancient city. The old town included several significant historical buildings, including Iglesia la Peregrina (an eighteenth-century chapel constructed in the shape of a scallop shell, the symbol of Saint James), Iglesia de San Francisco, and the Basilica de Santa Maria.

The next day was an especially pleasant walk on country lanes through vineyards and on to Caldas de Reis, a town celebrated since Roman times for its spa waters. We saw hundreds of pilgrims that day, and enjoyed eating dinner that evening with a group of Germans with whom we'd exchanged greetings for several days. We noticed that our older spa hotel, in the spirit of things, offered a "Camino Refresher" foot and leg treatment.

The next day we walked on to Padrón, seeing many *horreros*, distinctive, elevated structures where corn is traditionally stored in the Galacian region of Spain. We also saw women washing clothes

The Camino Portugués offers a variety of accommodations, all welcome at the end of a day of walking.

at *lavanderias*, traditional outdoor shelters where clothes are scrubbed against large, flat stones. Padrón's entrance is along a beautiful, wide, pedestrian avenue lined with impressive poplars, and it is recognized as the starting place of Saint James's ministry.

The last day of the walk took us from Padrón to Santiago—a long walk, much of it (slightly) uphill on a warm day. But entering the old town of Santiago, a World Heritage Site, made any hardship quickly disappear (and a brief stop at a bakery didn't hurt either). Of course the cathedral is glorious, but we waited to enter it until the next day, when we planned to attend the daily pilgrim's mass at noon. Instead, we walked around town, rewarded ourselves with ice cream, and went to the Catholic Church offices to claim our *compostelas* for completing the walk.

The walk has gotten so popular (particularly on the Camino Francés), that the offices have been modernized with many counters staffed by church officials. We had to wait in line for an hour and a half to present our "credentials" (our passport with appropriate stamps) to complete the transaction. We gradually advanced to the front of the line, and then visited the next free desk when the

The well-marked trail passes many small-scale farms in the tranquil Portuguese countryside.

overhead illuminated sign indicated a free space. It was like being a delicatessen: efficient but lacking historical context.

The next day we arrived at the cathedral a half hour early to find standing-room only. But the service was moving, and included the traditional swinging of the *botafumeiro* ("smoke spreader" in Galician), an immense silver incense burner that's swung from side to side in the cathedral, nearly to the vaulted ceiling; it's a real crowd-pleaser.

The logistics of walking the Camino Portugués are relatively straightforward. The route is especially well marked with the traditional scallop-shell motif and yellow arrows. There are a few short sections of ascent and descent, but generally the walking is easy. The route can be walked from spring through fall; we walked in September and days were warm and nights cool; summer must be hot and crowded. Rainfall is generous in this region of Portugal and Spain, so be prepared with appropriate waterproof clothing. There is a range of accommodations, from *albergues de peregrinos* (hostels) to upscale hotels. Baggage transfer is available: it's easy to arrange but, in the spirit of most pilgrimages, many walkers (including us) carry their own possessions in backpacks. Many cafes and bars offer a "pilgrim" lunch and/or dinner, a low-cost meal typically with limited menu choices; normally, people in Portugal and Spain dine very late, so occasionally we made do with a large lunch and a picnic supper from a local shop. The route can be walked from Lisbon, about two-weeks-walk south of Porto, but we don't recommend it. Our research suggested that much of the route from Lisbon to Porto is on heavily trafficked roads and can be dangerous; we met a few pilgrims who had done this portion of the route and they unanimously confirmed this. Our suggestion is that walkers begin in Porto and take up to two weeks to make the journey. Walking out of a city can be confusing and unpleasant; we recommend taking a local bus or taxi to Mosteiro (near Vilar do Pinheiro in the suburbs of Porto) and starting the walk from there. Public transportation (planes, trains, buses, and taxis) serves both Porto and Santiago.

The Camino Portugués is a long enough walk to be very satisfying. It's obviously historic to the nth degree, passing through rural portions of Portugal and Spain, but also includes some towns of modest size and great cultural significance. And the route is highly spiritual for many of the people who choose to walk it; it's a great example of a trail where the journey may be far more important than the destination. In fact, John Brierley, author of the guidebook we used (and one of our very favorite travel writers) metaphysically asks readers, "Have you found the first waymark that points you in the direction of your true Destination?" Walk this route and think about some of the large and important questions and issues that we rarely make the time for in our everyday lives.

Modern-day pilgrims arriving in Santiago de Compostela are clearly identifiable by their scallop shells, the symbol of Saint James.

HEAVEN'S GAITS

Walking can have a strong spiritual dimension that is most evident in the pilgrimage. For centuries, pilgrims have been walking to holy sites around the world to seek spiritual guidance, to be healed, to carry out a form of penance, to pray for a loved one, to give thanks, or to fulfill religious obligations.

The oldest and largest pilgrimage is the Hajj; all Muslims who are physically and financially able must travel to Mecca, Saudi Arabia, to participate in this pilgrimage at least once in their lifetime. It's thought the Hajj dates to the time of Abraham, around 2000 BC, and two to three million pilgrims now participate in the Hajj each year. Most pilgrims join others in large groups on their way to Mecca, and once there follow in the footsteps of Mohammed by walking counterclockwise seven times around the Kaaba, the holy building that Muslims face during prayer. Devoted Hindus walk from the plains of India to Mount Kailash in the Himalayas; Christian pilgrimages to Rome, Jerusalem, Santiago, Canterbury, and other holy sites began in medieval times. Today, many of these pilgrimages are walked for cultural as well as religious reasons, and they are experiencing a renaissance, particularly the Camino de Santiago across northern Spain.

Mazes and labyrinths are considered by some to be a form of spiritual walking. In Greek mythology, the concept of the labyrinth was introduced as a multibranching puzzle built by Daedalus to trap the dangerous monster, the Minotaur, who was ultimately slain by Theseus. In medieval times, labyrinths were built on church floors and grounds, and were considered condensed forms of the Christian pilgrimage. The labyrinth at Chartres Cathedral in France may be the oldest of this type, dating from the third century. Labyrinths often spiral inward,

Walkers typically eat local foods along the Kumano Kodo, enhancing the immersive experience of the pilgrimage.

Regardless of religious beliefs, the passage of so many devout walkers over the centuries deepens the experience for those who follow. (Camino Portugués)

suggesting a spiritual journey into the self. However, labyrinths are increasingly being constructed and used in secular contexts, such as in public parks and gardens. Geoff Nicholson notes in *The Lost Art of Walking* that there are now a number of labyrinths in American prisons designed to instill peace and calm in those who choose to walk them.

We feature two walks in this book that are ancient and powerful pilgrimages. The Camino Portugués is the main southern approach to Santiago, Spain, and the grave of Saint James, one of the twelve apostles. (The Camino Francés is the better-known route from the east, and we describe this in our book, *Walking Distance*.) Pilgrims have walked this route for more than a thousand years. The Kumano Kodo on Japan's Kii Peninsula leads to three major religious shrines and has also been walked for centuries. It's been our experience that there's a spiritual dimension to walking traditional pilgrimage routes; regardless of religious beliefs, the passage of so many devout walkers deepens the experience for those who follow. For some people, walking any trail may have a spiritual dimension; all walks might be considered pilgrimages of a kind, a symbolic stripping away of many of the distractions and possessions of everyday life and offering the opportunity for contemplation.

Cumberland Island includes 10,000 acres of wilderness offering many hiking opportunities.

Cumberland Island National Seashore

We heard their distinctive "neigh" before we saw them. (We smelled them too, but let's talk about that in a moment.) Feral horses roam Cumberland Island and are a favorite of many visitors. Most people consider horses to be magnetic animals, and wild horses are especially romantic. But horses aren't indigenous to Cumberland Island; they were introduced by the Spanish in the colonial history of the island and were ultimately abandoned. Horses are adaptive animals and they've prospered on the island, maintaining a herd size of approximately 150 to 200 animals. They've thrived at the cost of other species, influencing the island's environment, outcompeting some of the native species, trampling sand dunes, and, as animals will, leaving their telltale droppings along trails. Wild horses provide a wonderful example of the tension that can exist between natural and cultural resources, and this is an especially rich issue at Cumberland Island. If you'd like to learn more about this, just ask a ranger . . . but be prepared for a long answer.

LOCATION
Georgia, United States

LENGTH
Variable (a few days or more)

ACCOMMODATIONS
Commercial: Yes
Huts/refuges: No
Backpacking/camping: Yes

BAGGAGE TRANSFER AVAILABLE
No

OPTION TO WALK SECTIONS
Yes

DEGREE OF CHALLENGE
Low

CUMBERLAND ISLAND is part of the extensive system of barrier islands found up and down the East Coast and along the Gulf States. Barrier islands are dynamic ecosystems just offshore that protect the mainland from the force of tropical storms and hurricanes, and they offer very specialized habitats. Only recently have we begun to appreciate the "ecological services" these islands provide. Cumberland Island is one of the few barrier islands that is mostly undeveloped, and is located in extreme southern Georgia. At nearly 40,000 acres (much of it marsh), it's a relatively large island and was set aside as a national seashore in 1972. Shortly thereafter Congress designated nearly 10,000 acres as wilderness, meaning the area could continue to be used for nonmotorized recreation, but must be left in its natural state. The island includes rich natural and cultural resources and is laced with trails, including a pristine, 17.5-mile sand beach on the Atlantic Ocean, making it an especially attractive destination for walking.

(ABOVE) The National Park Service provides a network of boardwalks to access the seashore's ocean beaches; visitors should use these facilities to avoid trampling the fragile vegetation on the park's sand dunes.

(ABOVE RIGHT) This stately lane bordered by live oaks greets visitors to Cumberland Island.

The park includes three major ecosystems: saltwater marshes, maritime forests, and sand beaches and their associated dunes. The marshes are highly productive ecologically, providing habitat for an array of sea and terrestrial animals. Flooded twice daily by the tides, the marshes are enriched by nutrients from the ocean and from rivers that flow off the nearby mainland. The dominant plant species is cordgrass, green in the spring and summer and gold in the fall and winter. The marshes are the feeding and nursery grounds for many marine species, including clams, oysters, shrimp, crabs, and flounder, as well as birdlife such as osprey, pelicans, and marsh hawks.

Maritime forest occupies the upland portion of the island. A number of tree species populate the forest but the dominant species is the beautiful live oak, which is tolerant of saltwater spray from the ocean. These trees are laced with Spanish moss (not technically a moss, but a member of the pineapple family) and resurrection fern. Most of this forest has an impressive understory of saw palmetto. This magnificent forest supports white-tailed deer, gray squirrels, raccoons, armadillos, and a variety of birdlife. Pine trees thrive in the central and upper portions of the island.

Beaches and sand dunes make up the seaward fringe of the island. The dynamic character of barrier islands is most obvious here, where the tides and wind shape the island on a daily basis, and sometimes storms make dramatic changes. Washed clean by the tides twice a day, the

beaches support a variety of animal life, including sandpipers and other shorebirds feeding in the freshly washed sand. Colonies of least terns nest on the upper beaches in spring and summer. Loggerhead turtles swim ashore at night, depositing their eggs in the sand; hatchlings emerge about sixty days later and make a beeline to the sea. Sand piles up high behind the beaches into large sand dunes that help protect the mainland from storms. Like beaches, the dunes illustrate the active character of barrier islands; notice the way in which the dunes are covering the seaward side of portions of the maritime forests. Despite their appearance, dunes are fragile and walking on them can easily disturb them and damage the vegetation that helps stabilize them. Cross the dunes carefully, finding where the National Park Service has established boardwalks and other facilities.

The human history of Cumberland Island is as rich and varied as its natural history. Archeological studies suggest the island was occupied by Native Americans over 4,000 years ago, and middens (shell mounds) are still visible. Spanish explorers arrived in the mid-1500s, named the island San Pedro, and constructed several forts and missions, but ultimately abandoned the island in the early 1700s. The English arrived shortly after, and renamed it Cumberland Island in honor of the Duke of Cumberland. They built several forts and other structures, including a hunting lodge they called

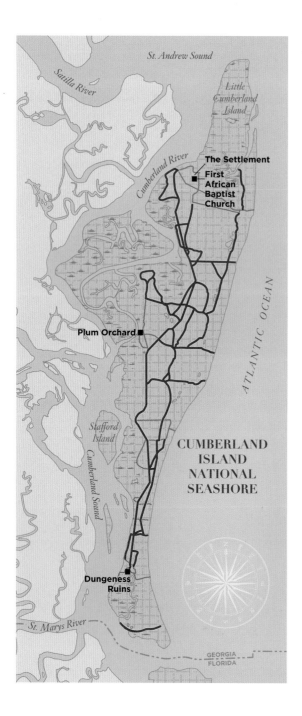

Dungeness. The English abandoned the island later in the century, and by 1774, when famous American naturalist William Bartram visited the island, it was mostly uninhabited.

Plantations were developed on Cumberland Island after the American Revolution, and the island was used for agriculture and logging. One of the most famous plantations reused the Dungeness name. Originally conceived by Revolutionary war hero Nathanael Greene and built by his widow and her second husband, Phineas Miller, this expansive home entertained statesmen and military officers. When the Civil War made plantations obsolete, the home was abandoned and the family moved away. Freed slaves established the Settlement at the northern end of the island and built the First African Baptist Church; this church drew attention in the mid-1990s when John F. Kennedy Jr. and Carolyn Bessette were married there.

The 1880s saw renewed interest in Cumberland Island, and Pittsburgh millionaire Thomas Carnegie built a fifty-nine-room Scottish castle on the old Dungeness site; it was so large and entertaining was done on such a lavish scale that a staff of 200 was necessary. You'll see the burned ruins of this final Dungeness in the island's historic district, located near the ferry dock. Carnegie's widow and heirs bought most of Cumberland Island and built other grand mansions. These include Greyfield, now a private inn, and Plum Orchard (at 20,000 square feet), administered by the National Park Service.

In 1955 the National Park Service declared Cumberland Island one of the most significant natural areas on the Atlantic and Gulf Coasts. In 1969 the developers of Hilton Head, South Carolina, made plans to develop Cumberland Island in a similar manner, but were thwarted by the establishment of the national seashore. Both the Carnegie and Mellon families contributed land, and now most of the island is part of the national park system.

Access to Cumberland Island is by a scenic 45-minute ferry ride from the mainland town of Saint Marys, Georgia (look for dolphins that often play in the wake of the boat). Several ferries run each day, and it's advisable to make a reservation as the National Park Service limits the number of visitors to the island.

Once you arrive on the island, walking is not only the best option to get around, it's really the only feasible option. A road (bureaucratically called "Main Road" by the National Park Service) runs most of the length of the island, but there are only a few motorized vehicles, used primarily for maintenance and administration. There are a handful of bicycles for rent, and there's an extensive trail system that leads to most of the island attractions, as well as the 17.5-mile ocean beach. It would take several days to walk all of these trails. The walking is generally easy, though the going on sand beaches can be slow (but we shouldn't really complain about this, should we?); there is little elevation to be gained or lost as the island rises only a few feet above the sea. Get your maps from the National Park Service visitor center at Saint Marys, and consider the possibility of doing what we call a "census hike"—walking all the trails on the island.

Most visitors start their walk at the Dungeness Dock, walk to the Dungeness Ruins, cross the island to the ocean beach, walk north to Sea Camp Beach Campground, and finally recross the island to Sea Camp Dock. From here, you can catch the ferry back to Saint Marys or walk the River Trail back to Dungeness Dock.

While most of the island is in public ownership, there are a few private estates, and walkers should be careful not to trespass. There are several options for accommodations, including a developed campground at Sea Camp and several undeveloped camping areas in the wilderness portion of the park. The only commercial lodging on the island is the grand (but a little funky) Greyfield Inn. Alternatively, visitors can stay at an inn or B&B in Saint Marys and ferry over to the island each day. There are no stores or other commercial services on the island, so bring what you'll need for the day. The National Park Services conducts guided walks and other educational programs.

Cumberland Island is a classic example of a barrier island, a diverse and dynamic landscape that plays a vital role in protecting the nation's shoreline. It's also a prototypical "cultural landscape," a unique blend of nature and culture, both of which have shaped the island into a pleasing and popular recreation resource. And that brings us back to those feral horses. Perhaps there is a place for them on the island, representing the role they played in the island's history. What do you think?

Horses were introduced to the island by the Spanish and ultimately abandoned. But horses are adaptive animals, and a herd of nearly 200 feral horses remain on the island.

FEATS OF THE FEET

There's something more than a little ironic about walking as a spectator sport. Think about it. Moreover, racewalking has to be high on the list of oxymorons. But there was a short time, a century or two ago, when Britain, the United States, and several other countries were consumed with competitive walking—called "pedestrianism"—of all permutations (as long as spectators were allowed to bet on it!). According to Matthew Algeo's entertaining book, *Pedestrianism: When Watching People Walk Was America's Favorite Spectator Sport*, it started in Britain in the early nineteenth century, probably the outgrowth of races among the footmen of aristocrats. This developed into pedestrianism, ultimately a form of endurance walking. One of the most famous pedestrians of the day was Captain Robert Barclay Allardice, who walked one mile every hour for 1,000 hours in 1809. As many as 10,000 spectators watched this feat of endurance unfold over more than a month. Another "pedestrian," Ada Anderson, walked a quarter mile in each quarter hour over 1,000 hours. Many competitors sought to walk 100 miles in less than twenty-four hours, earning the nickname of "centurions." Large cash prizes were awarded.

Interest in the sport spread to the United States, Canada, and Australia in the latter part of the nineteenth century. Due to heavy gambling, there were attempts to codify the sport with the "fair heel and toe" rule: the toe of one foot must not leave the ground before the heel of the next foot touched down. The first of the famous American pedestrians was Edward Payson Weston, who won a $10,000 prize in 1867 for walking the 1,136 miles from Portland, Maine, to Chicago in 30 days. Later, he made a bet with a friend that Abraham Lincoln would lose the presidential election in 1880. The loser of the

"Pedestrianism" was a wildly popular spectator sport.

bet (Weston, of course) would have to walk from Boston to Washington, DC in ten days to witness the inauguration—and he successfully did.

The more usual form of pedestrianism had competitors walk for six days around a short dirt track in arenas often packed with fans, many of whom wagered on the outcome. Some of the matches took place in New York City's original Madison Square Garden. The winners sometimes walked an astounding 600 miles or more. Successful competitors included Dan O'Leary, an Irish immigrant from Chicago, and Frank Hart, an immigrant from Haiti who was called "Black Dan," suggesting the democratization of the "sport." Ultimately, this kind of quirky pedestrianism declined as quickly as it evolved, morphing into racewalking, which has been an event in every summer Olympic Games since 1908.

Some people might consider walking 184 miles on the Thames Path a contemporary "feat of the feet."

At 20,310 feet, Denali caps the iconic Alaska Range and is the highest mountain in North America.

Denali National Park and Preserve

We were camped at Wonder Lake, one of Denali National Park's major attractions. The weather had been bad that day, with clouds covering the high peaks, and we were beginning to worry that we might not be fortunate enough to see the summit of Denali, from which the park takes its name. Sunrise the next day was early at this latitude, and we woke to a magical light: The weather had cleared and Denali seemed to be lit from within. This was alpenglow in the extreme. As we stood and watched, the mountain turned from yellow-orange to a rosy pink, and finally a rich purple. The mountain seemed to fill the sky. The high pressure weather system that cleared the skies overnight meant several days of good weather to fully appreciate the park, so off we went . . .

LOCATION
Alaska, United States

LENGTH
Variable (a few days to a few weeks)

ACCOMMODATIONS
Commercial: Some (nearby)
Huts/refuges: No
Backpacking/camping: Yes

BAGGAGE TRANSFER AVAILABLE
No

OPTION TO WALK SECTIONS
Yes

DEGREE OF CHALLENGE
Moderate–High

DENALI NATIONAL PARK is a "crown jewel" of the US national park system. This is one of several of the vast national parks in Alaska, but it's unusual in that visitors can reach the park relatively easily by automobile and even train. The interior of the park is accessible by buses that run along the 92-mile Denali Park Road, which penetrates deeply into the park, and this bus system facilitates hiking access to portions of the park's vast wilderness.

The park includes more than six million acres, is larger than some states, and offers nearly unlimited hiking through much of its trailless wilderness. The primary attraction of the park is Denali, the highest mountain (20,310 feet) in North America; the word "Denali" means "the high one" in the native Athabascan language. Because of the high elevation of Denali and the long and harsh winters, the park was probably not used for settlement sites by early indigenous people. Relatively few archeological sites have been found in the park, and these were probably hunting camps used on a seasonal basis. However, evidence from outside the park suggests that humans occupied this area of Alaska for 10,000 years or more.

When the park was established in 1917, it was called Mount McKinley National Park in honor of US president William McKinley. However, the name of the park was changed in 1980 to Denali

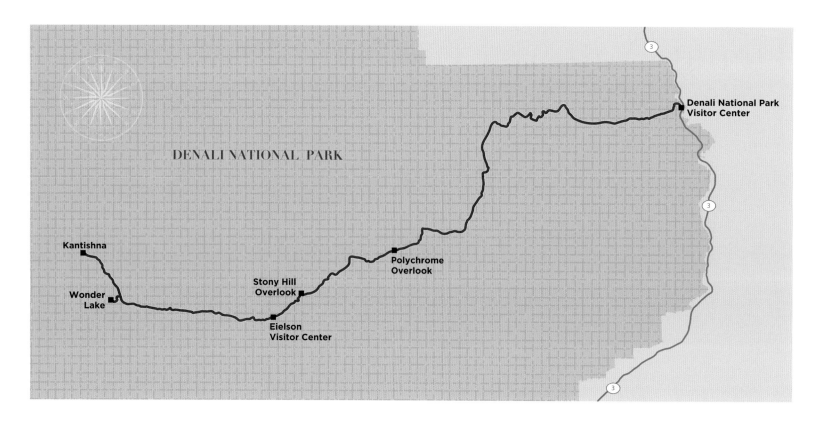

National Park and Preserve. The word "preserve" was added to note that portions of the park can be used for traditional subsistence purposes by native people. More recently, the name of the mountain itself has been changed to Denali, the name by which it was always known locally.

The park encompasses a portion of the 600-mile-long Alaska Range and surrounding areas. The elevation of Denali is 20,310 feet, but the distance from the base of the mountain to its peak (its "vertical relief") is 18,000 feet, the highest of any mountain in the world. Views of the mountain are astounding, as you have to look up as well as out to fully appreciate it. Unfortunately, the mountain is draped in clouds much of the time, at least partially obscuring the view. This is a good enough reason to spend several days at the park to enhance your chance of seeing it.

But visitors can always appreciate the remarkable wildlife; the park is sometimes referred to as the "Serengeti of North America." Iconic mammals include grizzly and black bears, herds of caribou, Dall sheep, moose, wolves, foxes, martens, Canadian lynxes, and wolverines. By riding the bus along the Denali Park Road and hiking in the park, you're sure to see many of these animals. Of course,

Denali's rivers are classic manifestations of their glacial origins, characterized by wide, braided channels and much glacial debris or sediment.

there are many migratory birds as well, including golden eagles, a variety of hawks and owls, gyrfalcons, ptarmigan, and Arctic warblers.

In the early 1970s, the first modern highway was built in interior Alaska, connecting the cities of Anchorage and Fairbanks and running near the entrance to Denali National Park. Anticipating a big increase in visitation, the National Park Service closed most of the Denali Park Road to automobile traffic and required visitors to ride buses to minimize potential disturbance of the park's iconic wildlife. The bus serves four campgrounds along the road: Sanctuary River, Teklanika River, Igloo Creek, and Wonder Lake. There are also two campgrounds closer to the park entrance, Riley Creek and Savage River, which are accessible by car. At the end of the Denali Park Road, there are several lodges in the vicinity of the abandoned mining town of Kantishna.

There are several basic options for multi-day hiking in Denali. First, there are a few relatively short maintained trails in the park—for example, several shorter trails are in the vicinity of the visitor center near the entrance to the park. The Denali Park Road travels over the Savage River at about mile 15, the point at the which the road is closed to automobile travel. From the parking lot at Savage River you can access the 2-mile long Savage River Loop Trail and the 4-mile long Savage Alpine Trail. At mile 66 along the road, there are two marked trails around the Eielson Visitor Center. The

(ABOVE) Six-million-acre Denali National Park and Preserve is virtually trailless, offering unlimited wilderness hiking.

(BELOW) Taiga, a mix of stunted trees dominated by white and black spruce, occupies the lower elevations of the park.

Tundra Loop is about a third of mile through alpine tundra, and the Eielson Alpine Trail is about 2 miles round-trip up Thorofare Ridge; this trail is steep in places. Wonder Lake is at mile 85, and the McKinley Bar Trail leads from the campground to the McKinley River, about a 5-mile round-trip.

Second, hiking is allowed in most of the park and a series of day hikes can be done in the vast trailless portion of the park. The park's shuttle bus system nicely facilitates this option. Buses will stop anywhere along the road (with a few exceptions related to the presence of sensitive wildlife) to let off and pick up hikers. Hikers can walk off into the wilderness portion of the park and return to the road to get a ride back to their end-of-the-day destination (e.g., the park entrance, one of the park's campgrounds, lodging at Kantishna). A good strategy is to consult with the park's Wilderness Access Center, located just a mile in from the park entrance; park staff there will have some good suggestions based on local conditions.

Another option is to ride on the shuttle bus until you see an area that looks intriguing, and ask the driver to stop. River valleys often make good options because the walking is relatively flat, it's easy to find your way and return to the road, and the river channels are often very wide so it may be possible to walk along the river bars. Some good options include Riley Creek, Upper Savage River, and Upper Teklanika River. Scout the terrain ahead to avoid "terrain traps," such as dense pockets of spruce forest and alder that are hard to walk through and make it difficult to see bears and other animals you'll want to avoid at close range.

Third, visitors can undertake multi-day backpacking trips in the park. In this case, you must consult with the Wilderness Access Center to receive a mandatory permit. Based on your objectives, experience, abilities, and availability of permits, rangers will suggest appealing options. The loop around Mount Eielson, the treks to Anderson and McGonagall Passes, and routes that include the Teklanika, Sanctuary, and Toklat Rivers are popular. Most hikers choose trips of 1–3 nights, though park rules allow trips of up to 30 nights!

A fourth option is to engage the services of an outfitter and fly into a remote portion of the park to do a guided or unguided hike.

This large park is comprised of several types of landscapes, including the Alaska Range with its glaciers and snowfields, vast expanses of tundra, forests, and rivers and lakes. The mountains have a complicated and varied geologic history, but result mostly from uplift caused by the collision of tectonic plates. Volcanic activity has also contributed to the underlying structure of some areas, and is very evident where the Denali Park Road travels through Polychrome Pass. Glaciers cover about 16 percent of the park and have been instrumental in shaping the landscape. Some of the existing glaciers are more than 30 miles long and nearly 4,000 feet thick. Classic manifestations of glaciation include huge cirques (amphitheater-like formations near the summits of mountains), arêtes (narrow ridges), and cols (saddles) in the mountains; moraines (piles of glacial debris) along the sides and at the terminus of glaciers; erratics (large rocks picked up by glaciers and deposited elsewhere) strewn across the valleys; wide, "braided" rivers (with multiple channels and much glacial debris); and "kettle" lakes (formed by the meltwater of large blocks of ice left behind as glaciers retreat). Large and beautiful Wonder Lake is a kettle lake that's about four miles across and nearly 300 feet deep.

Vast expanses of tundra and its low-lying vegetation are found in the middle elevations of the park, and the generally open character of these areas can make for good walking as it allows hikers to appreciate the scenery and see wildlife. The lower elevations of the park feature a mix of forests. These forests are a classic example of "taiga," a mix of usually stunted trees dominated by white and black spruce, but including some deciduous trees such as aspen, birch, poplar, and willow. Tree line in the park ranges from 2,500 to 3,000 feet. Over 450 species of flowering plants grow in the park's extensive valleys.

Hiking in Denali is exhilarating, but requires preparation. The trailless character of most of this park, its harsh conditions, and its potentially dangerous wildlife demand consultation with staff at the park's Wilderness Access Center. Moreover, overnight trips require a permit that can only be obtained at this facility. Hikers should stay at least a quarter-mile from bears, and follow all recommended procedures to disassociate food from people, including storing food and other scented items in bear-proof containers. The diligence of park managers and visitors has minimized conflict between hikers and bears. Other concerns include bad weather, cold, stream crossings, mosquitoes, and the ability to read topographic maps and use a compass while navigating off-trail. The hiking season generally runs from late May through early September.

In this book, we're deliberate in including a great range of walking and hiking opportunities. Denali National Park is clearly at the wilderness end of the spectrum. Much of the park is managed as a wilderness area, one of the largest and wildest in the United States. The objective of park managers is to provide hikers with a sense of discovery and self-reliance. This is a rare and exciting opportunity, but also comes with responsibilities. Begin your Denali experience by riding the Denali Park Road, walking the park's maintained trails, and day hiking in some of the river valleys accessible from the park's buses. If you wish, work with staff at the Wilderness Access Center to prepare yourself for the range of backpacking experiences the park offers. As always, walk *your* walk, and you'll be richly rewarded and pleased that places like Denali National Park are being preserved.

(ABOVE) The Denali Park Road runs 92 miles into the park, and buses will drop off and pick up hikers nearly anywhere along its path.

(BELOW) Caribou and other animals, such as grizzly and black bears, Dall sheep, moose, and wolves, are why Denali is often referred to as "the Serengeti of North America."

SENSE OF PLACE

"Sense of place" comes from the academic discipline of geography and is closely associated with geographer Yi-Fu Tuan. The concept refers to the characteristics that make a place special or even unique. These characteristics commonly include both natural (e.g., landforms, vegetation, animals, soils) and cultural (e.g., history, settlement pattern, foods, mythology) influences, and often include the interactions between them (e.g., the taste or terroir of local foods as derived from soil, climate, and human innovation).

Sense of place has taken on enhanced importance as the world spins more rapidly toward globalization, which is having a homogeneous effect, taking the form of suburbanization and sprawl, strip malls, industrial agriculture, and chain stores. The opposite of sense of place is "placelessness" or simply "space"—the declining presence of special natural and/or cultural features. Gertrude Stein worried about this in her assessment of contemporary tourism when she wrote that too often "there is no there there."

Pulitzer Prize–winning newspaper correspondent Paul Scott Mowrer wrote, "There is nothing like walking to get the feel of a country. A fine landscape is like a piece of music; it must be taken at the right tempo." American naturalist Edwin Way Teale observed that "It takes days of practice to learn the art of sauntering. Commonly we stride through the out-of-doors too swiftly to see more than the most obvious and prominent things. For observing nature, the best pace is a snail's pace." Bruce Feller, in his inspirational book *Walking the Bible*, writes:

As a veteran traveler, I had always believed that I left a bit of me wherever I went. I also believed that I took a bit of every place with me. I never felt that more than with this trip. It was if the act of touching these places, walking these roads, and asking these questions had added another column to my being.

Geoff Nicholson writes that walking is "a singularly unmediated and intimate form of travel, one that lets us see and taste directly." Friedrich Nietzsche wrote that "It is one of the secrets of walking: a slow approach to landscapes that

Hikers in the Maroon Bells–Snowmass Wilderness pass through groves of aspen characteristic of the Rocky Mountains.

The steep headlands and turquoise sea are classic features that contribute to the sense of place on the Abel Tasman Coast Track.

gradually renders them familiar. Like the regular encounters that deepen friendship."

And Thoreau was clearly familiar with the concept of sense of place and the ways it can affect the walker: "I feel made from the same wood as the tree whose bark I touch in passing, the same tissue as the tall grasses I brush against, and my heavy breathing, when I stop, matches the panting of the hare that stops suddenly before me."

Colorful fishing boats line Fisherman's Wharf in the San Francisco harbor.

Golden Gate Way

In what seems like a previous lifetime, we lived in San Francisco; Bob was stationed there in the US Coast Guard. We spent every opportunity exploring this remarkable city and the open lands just north of the Golden Gate Bridge. Many of our favorite places—the Presidio, the Marin Headlands, the ocean beaches—were military bases not generally accessible to the public and not designed for recreation. But since that time, many of these outdated military reserves have been transferred to the National Park Service and make up Golden Gate National Recreation Area, one of the world's largest and most beautiful urban parks. These areas have been readied for public use, and used they are! We return to San Francisco whenever we can and walk what we call the Golden Gate Way—a multi-day walk along the dramatic coast of Marin County just north of San Francisco, across the Golden Gate Bridge, and deep into the City by the Bay. We hope you'll join us on what we think of as a very personal walk.

LOCATION
California, United States

LENGTH
Variable (up to a week)

ACCOMMODATIONS
Commercial: Yes
Huts/refuges: Yes
Backpacking/camping: Yes

BAGGAGE TRANSFER AVAILABLE
No

OPTION TO WALK SECTIONS
Yes

DEGREE OF CHALLENGE
Low–Moderate

THE GOLDEN GATE WAY is the name we've given to a remarkable multi-day walk that begins at Muir Beach in Marin County, follows the coast south along high headlands and beautiful beaches, and then crosses the Golden Gate Bridge, one of the world's most iconic bridges. This portion of the walk takes two days. When you reach the San Francisco side of the bridge the route splits, with one option staying on the Pacific Ocean side of the city and the other on the San Francisco Bay side. We're often asked which of these options we like best, and our standard response is to advise that you walk both and decide for yourself. They're very different and highly appealing in their own special ways, and each option takes only a day.

Let's begin in the north and walk south, toward the city. The walk starts at Muir Beach, a detached portion of Muir Woods National Monument. The monument honors John Muir, the iconic American conservationist, and the main inland portion protects a five hundred-acre grove of coastal redwood trees. We're sure Muir would have been pleased with this forest preserve, and that

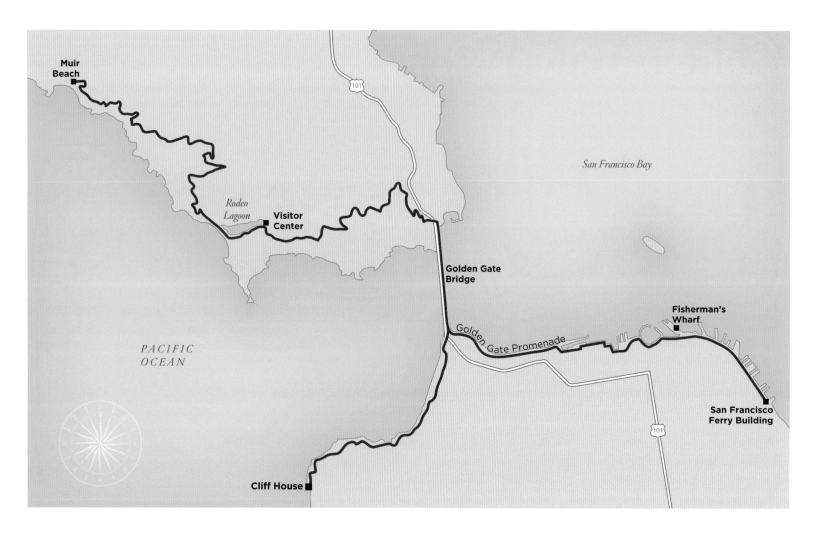

he'd be happy with so many people enjoying his namesake beach as well, especially because the beach and trail to the south have a wild feel about them.

The walk south from Muir Beach follows the undeveloped Pacific Ocean coastline, alternately rising and falling along steep headlands, darting inland to cross drainages, and occasionally descending to the sea. This walk is dramatic and remarkably lonely given its proximity to San Francisco. You'll find two major beaches along the route: Tennessee Beach (a great place for a picnic lunch), and Rodeo Beach at the end of this trail segment. You'll also see a number of smaller, more secret, pocket beaches. The landscape is generally open along the Coastal Trail; look for views of prominent and popular Mount Tamalpais and, on clear days, the Farallon Islands, a marine sanctuary in the Pacific Ocean, viewable on the horizon.

The second day's walk begins at Rodeo Beach and crosses the Golden Gate Bridge into San Francisco. Rodeo Beach is popular with surfers, and watching them is entertaining. The beach area marks the beginning of a series of former Army bases—Forts Baker, Barry, and Cronkhite—that occupy strategic headlands and once guarded the entrance to San Francisco Bay. It's unfortunate that such a military presence was necessary, but the benefit is that this area was spared commercial development and is now some of the most valuable open space in America. It's truly remarkable that all this glorious parkland is just a few minutes from San Francisco.

Inland from the beach and up a small hill is a former Army chapel that is now the visitor center for this portion of Golden Gate National Recreation Area; it's well worth a stop.

The walk from the visitor center to the north end of the Golden Gate Bridge is spectacular, and offers a number of highlights. A manifestation of the Cold War era, Nike Missile Site SF-88L has been preserved just as it looked in the 1960s. As we walked by the site and its chain-link fence, we noticed that one of the gates was open and a volunteer ranger was there to show visitors around. The highlight was a trip down the missile elevator to the underground command center, which included six Hercules missiles, radar equipment, and the launch control center. This was wildly entertaining, but a little frightening as well to think how history might have played out differently had these missiles been fired.

As you crest the last set of hills to the south, the views are astounding—across the Golden Gate to the San Francisco skyline. From your vantage point on top of the hills, the view is unusual because you are looking *down* on the towers of the Golden Gate Bridge. Just west are two sites that warrant a short walk off the main trail. Hawk Hill (Hill 129, or Battery Construction 129 in sterile military parlance) is the ideal vantage point to watch for raptors (birds of prey such as eagles and hawks). Observers have counted as many as 2,800 a day during the migration season. A half-mile walk through a tunnel and across a suspension bridge brings you to the Point Bonita Lighthouse, built in 1855 to guide ships through San Francisco Bay's infamous fog. Like the previous day's walk, this is mainly an open landscape with lots of wildflowers in the spring.

The next landmark is the Golden Gate Bridge itself. The trail brings you up to the bridge at North Vista Point, where you walk directly onto the pedestrian and bike lane on the east side of the bridge. From the span you will enjoy spectacular views of the bay and the city, including Alcatraz Island and Angel Island. Prepare yourself to share this walk with many people from around the world. It's a thrill to walk across the more than mile-long suspension bridge, one of the symbols of

A profusion of wildflowers graces the Marin Headlands portion of the walk.

(ABOVE) The long stretch of trail in Marin County follows the dramatic Pacific coastline.

(BELOW) The Ferry Building on San Francisco's waterfront houses a mix of shops and restaurants, and is a great place for walkers to refresh themselves.

San Francisco and a remarkable feat of engineering; this is surely one of the most internationally recognized bridges in the world.

Arrival at the south end of the bridge brings you onto the lands of the former Presidio of San Francisco army base, and a fork in the trail. You can continue along the Coastal Trail to the ocean, or walk along the shore of the bay and through a number of areas for which San Francisco is rightly famous. Of course, the best decision is to do both of these walks over a period of two or more days.

First, let's bear to the right along the coastal route. The trail takes you along the headlands that border the Golden Gate Strait, where you'll find the remnants of army fortifications as well as shady eucalyptus forests. You must detour inland a little to skirt Sea Cliff, one of San Francisco's most exclusive residential communities, but then you walk into heavily vegetated Land's End, where you resume walking south on the Coastal Trail. Soon you pass by three historical landmarks, the elaborate gardens of Sutro Heights (currently being restored), the ruins of Sutro Baths, and the Cliff House. The baths were constructed in the nineteenth century and included an ingenious, 25,000-person swimming facility that could fill in an hour during the Pacific Ocean's high tide. Never economically successful, the facility burned in 1966, but the foundations are still visible. The dramatic setting of the Cliff House has seen three major facilities over the last century and a half. The first two were a lavish casino and Victorian palace, but both burned. The current structure offers dinners and fabulous views out over the Pacific Ocean. Be sure to look for seals on Seal Rocks, just offshore from the Cliff House. The Cliff House is a logical ending point for this walk as there's good bus service from here into the rest of the city. However, it's tempting to continue walking south on the long stretch of Ocean Beach. The esplanade atop the seawall is ideal for walking, and you can follow it for several miles to Fort Funston, another former army base.

The second option after crossing the Golden Gate Bridge is to turn left and walk along the shores of San Francisco Bay. This way, most of which is directly on the shore, offers as rich and diverse a set of attractions as you're likely to find anywhere. You'll walk through portions of three former army bases: Fort Point, the Presidio, and Fort Mason. Crissy Field was once an army airfield, but has undergone an impressive ecological restoration that has returned the area to its native marshlands and sand beach. The Golden Gate Promenade is a wide, fully accessible trail that has been developed on the former airfield, and it's heavily used by walkers, bikers, joggers, and others, all having a grand time. The promenade connects with the Marina Green, a large open space between the bay and the fashionable Marina District, a residential and commercial area.

Farther south, you walk through part of Fort Mason and then into San Francisco Maritime National Historical Park, with its visitor center and impressive collection of ships. Continuing south, walk through the Fisherman's Wharf area, a mix of attractions popular with tourists. Finally, continue along the Embarcadero, the former bustling heart of the city's maritime industry. Now

this area is an attractive mix of residential and commercial facilities and services. The Ferry Building, with its diverse restaurants and shops, makes a logical ending point for this section of the Golden Gate Way. Refurbished streetcars and other forms of public transit can take you to wherever you're going from here, and familiarizing yourself with the options beforehand is a good idea.

The primary logistical concern for this walk is transportation for the two sections of trail north of the Golden Gate Bridge. If you have two cars, you can shuttle them between Muir Beach and Rodeo Beach, and then Rodeo Beach and the Golden Gate Bridge. Another option is to leave a car at one end of the trail and take a taxi to the other. Once you've walked into San Francisco, there are many options for public transport.

Rodeo Beach on the Pacific Ocean is a favorite location for surfers.

We suggest a minimum of four days for this walk, but this is just skimming the surface; consider taking a more leisurely approach if time allows. If you'd like to extend the walk to the north, two days of hiking will bring you to Point Reyes National Seashore, where you'll find an inviting network of trails. In fact, the coastal section of the Golden Gate Way is part of the longer (much longer—about 1,200 miles) California Coastal Trail, which is under development. A portion of the Golden Gate Way is also part of the San Francisco Bay Trail, more than 500 miles of trail encircling the bay that is also under development.

The Golden Gate Way can be walked year-round; this is a Mediterranean climate with warm, dry summers (though summer fog can be chilly, especially when combined with a breeze off the cool Pacific Ocean) and cool, rainy winters. Of course, there are many options for accommodations in this large metropolitan area—even a small campground and hostel in the Marin Headlands and another hostel at Fort Mason in San Francisco.

We feel strongly about this walk. Perhaps we're colored by our connection to the Bay Area and our affection for its natural and cultural history. However, even when viewed from the perspective of the many long-distance and multi-day walks we've done in many parts of the world, this is indeed a world-class experience. We recommend it in the strongest terms.

WANDERING AND WONDERING

While walking is thought to have contributed to development of the brain, there's no question that it has stimulated our thinking across recorded history. Aristotle is an early example, walking as he thought and taught in the Lyceum of ancient Athens. Other philosophers followed suit in what is known as the Peripatetic School (peripatetic meaning "one who walks"). Raphael captured this magical approach to teaching in his famous painting, *The School of Athens,* in which philosophers were, in the words of Frédéric Gros, author of *A Philosophy of Walking*, "upright, the tread firm, the index finger authoritative." Arianna Huffington tells the story of fourth-century BC Greek philosopher Diogenes, who, when confronted with the question of whether motion is real, got up and walked! *Solvitur ambulando:* It is solved by walking.

More recent examples of the ways in which walking has contributed to thinking include the philosophers, poets, and writers of the Romantic Movement in the eighteenth and nineteenth centuries. French philosopher Jean-Jacques Rousseau set the stage for Romanticism by questioning Western society's march toward increasing industrialization and urbanism. Joseph Amato, in his book *On Foot: A History of Walking*, calls Rousseau "the father of romantic pedestrianism." Rousseau's principal books, *The Confessions* and *Reveries of a Solitary Walker*, encouraged readers to return to nature and simplicity and were informed by his own long walks. He wrote that "[t]here is something about walking that stimulates and enlivens my thoughts," and "I can only meditate when I'm walking . . . When I stop I cease to think; my mind works only with my legs."

Similarly, French author Jules Renard wrote, "Walk. The body advances while the mind flutters around it like a bird." German novelist Thomas Mann wrote that "Thoughts come clearly while one walks." Frédéric Gros adds Friedrich Nietzsche and Montaigne to the list of walking philosophers, writing that "Nietzsche walked all day long, scribbling down here and there what the walking body—confronting sky, sea, glaciers—breathed into his thoughts," and quotes Nietzsche, who wrote that we write well "only with our feet." Montaigne wrote that "My thoughts sleep if I sit still; my fancy does not go so well by itself as when my legs move it."

Other great walker-writers of the Romantic period include William Wordsworth, Henry David Thoreau, and John Muir. Wordsworth walked extensively in England, particularly in the Lake District. His colleague Samuel Coleridge estimates that Wordsworth walked 180,000 miles over his adult life. Wordsworth had the remarkable ability to develop insights and compose his poetry while he walked. Author Christopher Morley wrote, "I always think of him as one of the first to employ

Walking while thinking and teaching was a hallmark of early Greek education, as referenced in Raphael's painting *The School of Athens*.

his legs as an instrument of philosophy." It's reputed that when a traveler asked to see Wordsworth's study at Dove Cottage, his home in the Lake District, his housekeeper replied, "Here is his library, but his study is out of doors."

Thoreau took up the Romantic mantle in America, walking extensively throughout New England and more intensively around his home in Concord, Massachusetts, and his retreat at Walden Pond. Eloquent (but often cranky), he advanced his transcendental philosophy, urging Americans to preserve remaining pockets of nature and to walk on the landscape to find manifestations of God and higher truths. His essay "Walking" is his classic statement, in which he wrote, "I think I cannot preserve my health and spirits, unless I spend four hours a day at least,—and it is commonly more than that,—sauntering through the woods and over the hills and fields, absolutely free from all worldly engagements." And in his sometimes arrogant but endearing way he wrote that "I have met but one or two persons in the course of my life who understood the art of Walking, that is, of taking walks,—who had a genius, so to speak, for *sauntering*." Summing up the importance of walking to his thinking, he wrote, "Methinks that the moment my legs begin to move, my thoughts begin to flow," and "How vain it is to sit down to write when you have not stood up to live."

John Muir carried the Romantic tradition westward, walking a thousand miles from Indiana to the Gulf of Mexico, then walking extensively in the Sierra Nevada of California throughout much of his adult life. His walks offered him deep insights into human relationships with the natural world, and he used walking as a metaphor near the end of his life when he wrote that "I only went out for a walk, and finally concluded to stay out until sundown: for going out, I found was really going in."

Throughout history, walking has stimulated a sense of wonder. (Zion Rim-to-Rim)

Many overlooks provide visitors stunning views of the natural wonder that is the Grand Canyon.

Grand Canyon Rim Trail

We were very fortunate to live at the South Rim of Grand Canyon National Park, spending a year there working with the National Park Service. In the mornings and evenings we'd often walk along the rim of the canyon, particularly along the sections of trail that extend to the east and west of Grand Canyon Village. We'd wonder why more visitors didn't take advantage of this spectacular trail, which offers so many perspectives into the canyon and its natural and cultural history. The National Park Service has upgraded the trail, extending it into the 14-mile Grand Canyon Rim Trail; we've enjoyed it on numerous occasions. It's one of the most magical walks in the national park system. Find a place to hang out at Grand Canyon Village—at the campground or one of the hotels—and spend a few days steeping yourself in one the world's great natural wonders.

GRAND CANYON NATIONAL PARK is one of the premier areas in the US national park system, and its designation as a World Heritage Site documents its global significance as well. It's a mile-deep gash in the earth that reveals two billion years of geologic history. The canyon is a staggering 277 serpentine miles long and about 10 miles wide at Grand Canyon Village, roughly the midpoint of the Grand Canyon Rim Trail. Of course the Colorado River, at the bottom of the canyon, is one of the principal erosive forces that has shaped the canyon and been the focus of so much human history and prehistory. Walking the length of the Grand Canyon Rim Trail is one of the most powerful ways to appreciate the many dimensions of the canyon.

The trail is directly on the southern rim of the canyon and extends from Yaki Point in the east to Hermits Rest in the west. It's paved for much of its length and gently graded, with some sections being wheelchair accessible. With the exception of only a few short sections, it's located away from motor vehicle traffic, and much of the trail, particularly the sections away from Grand Canyon Village and the most popular overlooks, can offer remarkable peace and quiet, even moments of

LOCATION
Arizona, United States

LENGTH
14 miles

ACCOMMODATIONS
Commercial: Yes
Huts/refuges: No
Backpacking/camping: Yes

BAGGAGE TRANSFER AVAILABLE
No

OPTION TO WALK SECTIONS
Yes

DEGREE OF CHALLENGE
Low

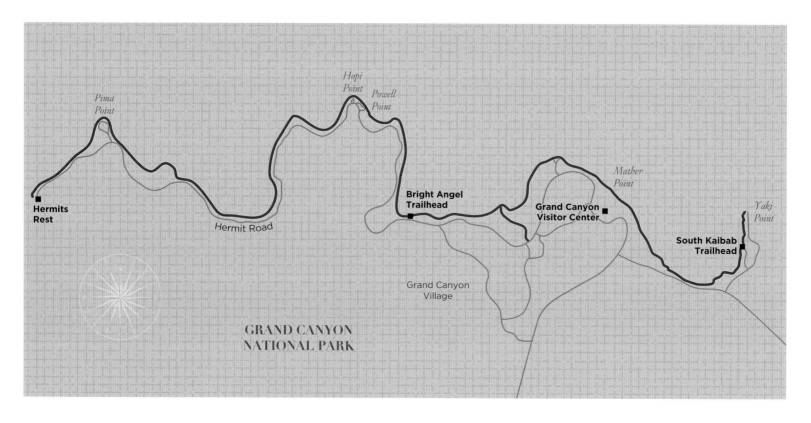

Hopi
Point

Powell
Point

Pima
Point

Mather
Point

Yaki
Point

**Hermits
Rest**

**Bright Angel
Trailhead**

**Grand Canyon
Visitor Center**

Hermit Road

**South Kaibab
Trailhead**

Grand Canyon
Village

**GRAND CANYON
NATIONAL PARK**

solitude. Following the sinuous trace of the canyon rim, the trail offers constantly changing views and perspectives that are unseen by most visitors.

The trail might best be thought of as being comprised of three sections. The middle section is closely associated with the Grand Canyon Village portion of the park and is most heavily visited. There are many important attractions along this section of the trail. For example, most visitors drive to the park and arrive at the Grand Canyon Visitor Center, a state-of-the-art facility, much of it open air. Here, visitors are advised to leave their cars and take the park's free shuttle bus system. A short walk from the visitor center takes visitors to the Rim Trail and their first view of the canyon at Mather Point. Stephen Mather was the revered first director of the National Park Service, and only the finest places in the parks use his name. Look closely and you can see Phantom Ranch at the bottom of the canyon, a little green oasis where Bright Angel Creek flows into the Colorado River, nearly five thousand feet below where you're standing.

Walk the Rim Trail to the west and you will get a sense of the magnitude and significance of the park. You'll soon reach Yavapai Point and its small but informative Geology Museum. In the 1920s, some of the most eminent geologists selected this site as the best representative view of Grand Canyon geology. Learn about how the canyon was formed and how to interpret the multicolored layers of the canyon, some formed from windblown sand dunes and others from the deposits on the bottoms of ancient lakes. With its stunning views of the canyon, this can be a great place to watch one of the many thunderstorms that gather over the canyon in summer.

A popular new component of this walk is the Trail of Time, an interpretive section that helps visitors think in geologic time. Brass markers are placed at 1-meter intervals, each representing a million years of geologic time. Viewing tubes are focused on the rock layers corresponding to these times, and rock samples are placed on the side of the trail to help visitors connect more directly with the canyon's geology. The Trail of Time won a National Park Service award for interpretive exhibits.

Farther west is the most heavily developed section of the trail, one that continues to offer striking and varied views but is also rich in the history of the canyon. El Tovar Hotel, one the great lodges of the national parks, is located here. The hotel was built by the Santa Fe Railway Company,

(ABOVE LEFT) The Grand Canyon Rim Trail is delightful in all seasons; here a gentle snowfall transforms the landscape.

(ABOVE) The Grand Canyon Rim Trail can be accessed at many points, and the park's shuttle bus system provides a convenient way to return to your starting point.

A hoop dancer performs for visitors outside Hopi House, one of the historic buildings on the developed section of the Grand Canyon Rim Trail.

borrowing architectural styles from Swiss chalets and Norwegian villas with a rustic touch. Go inside to see the impressive lobby, sit on the north-facing porch for excellent views of the canyon, and consider rewarding yourself with lunch to satisfy the hunger you've built.

El Tovar and many of the other buildings nearby are part of the cultural landscape of the park. Kolb Studio housed the enterprise of Emery and Ellsworth Kolb, pioneering photographers of the canyon. Starting in 1902, they would photograph visitors riding mules down the Bright Angel Trail, and then Emery would run four-and-a-half miles down the trail to Indian Garden to access the water needed to process the photos so they could be sold to visitors when they returned to the canyon rim. The studio operated for about 75 years and now serves as a gallery and small store. Just to the west of Kolb Studio is the trailhead for the historic Bright Angel Trail, the park's 10-mile trail from the rim to the Colorado River. (We describe hiking Grand Canyon using the Bright Angel Trail, the South Kaibab Trail, and the North Kaibab Trail in our book *Walking Distance*.) This is a well-maintained trail, but the National Park Service strongly discourages visitors from attempting to walk to the river and back in a day. However, if you are adequately prepared, you should consider hiking to Indian Garden or Plateau Point; keep in mind that both are strenuous, full-day hikes, and you'll need lots of water and sun protection.

West of this developed portion of the Rim Trail is an approximately 7-mile section that roughly parallels the park's Hermit Road. This road was built relatively early in the park's history and was touted as "a city boulevard in the wilderness." Many years ago, the road was closed to cars and is now

Mather Point Overlook is one of the most popular stops on the Grand Canyon Rim Trail; it's named for Stephen Mather, the first director of the National Park Service.

serviced by the park's shuttle bus system, keeping this portion of the park quiet and uncluttered. The Rim Trail is generally away from the road except where the bus stops to let off and pick up passengers. Both the road and trail end at Hermits Rest (named for a reclusive prospector in the late nineteenth century). Here, the Hermit Trail descends nearly 9 miles to the Colorado River. This is a relatively rough trail, but if you're prepared, consider hiking the trail for 3 miles to Dripping Springs.

The Rim Trail from the Grand Canyon Village area to Hermits Rest includes many striking overlooks. Powell Point features the memorial to Major John Wesley Powell, a geologist who organized one of the great adventures in American history, a three-month-long first descent of the Colorado River in 1869 to map the scarce water resources of the arid Southwest. The "geological section" of the canyon visible from this point was considered by Powell as the finest and most instructive view into the canyon. From Mohave Point, you can see a series of three rapids on the Colorado River—Salt Creek, Granite, and Hermit. From Pima Point, you can hear the roar of Granite Rapid on a still day.

The third section of the trail extends east of Mather Point to Yaki Point. This is also a quiet section of the Rim Trail with many nice viewpoints. The east end of the trail marks the beginning of the South Kaibab Trail that descends to the Colorado River in about 7.5 miles. Again, the National Park Service strongly discourages visitors from attempting to hike to the river and back in a day. However, walking the trail about 1.5 miles down to Cedar Point is highly recommended. There's no water along this trail, so bring plenty of your own.

Walking the length of the Grand Canyon Rim Trail is a powerful way to appreciate the many dimensions of the canyon.

The Rim Trail includes a rich stock of interpretative signs and exhibits along its length and is an excellent way to learn more about the canyon's history and natural history. Of course, you'll learn that the park is much more than geology—it includes substantive elements of biology and history as well. You'll walk through two primary types of forests: pinyon/juniper and pondersoa pine. Pinyon pines and Utah junipers are shrubby trees and grow best below 7,000 feet. However, their short stature belies their longevity—many of the pinyon pines you'll see are over 200 years old. These trees bear prized pine nuts in great quantities when the environmental conditions are right, and Utah junipers produce large numbers of blue-green berries that are eaten by birds and other wildlife. Many shrubs and flowers also populate pinyon/juniper forests, including cliffrose, sage, several species of cactus, agaves, rabbitbrush, paintbrush, and several species of penstemon. Ponderosa pines grow best above 7,000 feet and are large (100 feet or more in height) and strikingly beautiful; the bark emanates a delicious vanilla aroma when warmed by the sun. Walking in a ponderosa pine forest delights many of the senses! The diverse habitat of the park also supports a great variety of animals. Some of the glamour species you may see while walking the Rim Trail include noisy and playful ravens (watch them soar with the updrafts along the rim), massive condors (recently reintroduced to the park and a big wildlife success story), Abert's squirrels, mule deer, coyotes, elk, and lots of lizards.

What is now Grand Canyon National Park and the surrounding area was home to several Native American tribes for 12,000 years. Many contemporary Indian tribes, including the Hopi and Havasupai, maintain strong linkages to the park, and the National Park Service consults closely with several tribes regarding park management issues.

Grand Canyon National Monument was established in 1908, and elevated to a national park in 1919. But before the park was established, the Santa Fe Railway Company and the Fred Harvey Company did much to entice visitors to travel to the park, including completing a rail line into the park in 1901 and building many of the historic structures—El Tovar Hotel, Hopi House, Lookout Studio, and Hermits Rest, all of which you'll see along the Rim Trail. Many of these buildings were designed by architect Mary Colter. Later, the Civilian Conservation Corps worked in the park, including building much of the walkway and masonry walls of the Rim Trail and removing utility lines. Rail service into the park was abandoned shortly after automobiles grew popular, but was resumed in 1989 by the Grand Canyon Railway.

The Grand Canyon's Rim Trail can be accessed at many points, and the park's shuttle bus system provides a great way to walk as long and far as you want and then return to your origin by bus (or vice versa). The trail presents easy walking, and trail running shoes are fine unless you descend on the Hermit Trail, in which case lightweight boots are better. Be cognizant that the trail is at 7,000 feet, so give yourself some time to acclimate, and drink lots of water. The trail can be walked year-round. It can be hot and dry in summer, so take plenty of water and sun protection. The canyon can be snowy in the winter, adding another layer of magic. Consider walking at night as the park offers outstanding stargazing. Accommodations can be found at the campground in Grand Canyon Village and in several hotels there, as well as commercial lodging in the nearby town of Tusayan.

The Rim Trail is one of the premier walks in the US national parks; we think it's underappreciated. Most visitors to Grand Canyon's South Rim drive to a few overlooks and stop briefly in the village. Technically, they experience the Rim Trail, but they're missing an unforgettable opportunity. While walking the 14 miles of the Rim Trail can be done in one day, that's not what we're suggesting. Linger . . . soak in what you're sensing. The light over the canyon changes hour by hour and day by day. Stop to savor the views. Notice how your perspective of the canyon changes as you move along the trail. Learn from the interpretive exhibits. Experience the historic buildings. For a very different perspective of the canyon, consider dipping below the rim on one of the three trails that lead to the Colorado River. If you take a few days to walk the Rim Tail, you'll be filled with a deeper appreciation for the wonder that's Grand Canyon National Park. It's one of our favorites.

SITTING IS THE NEW SMOKING

Hippocrates of Kos was a famous Greek physician born around 460 BC and is often referred to as the "father of Western medicine." We know him best for the Hippocratic Oath, a philosophy of medical practice that doctors have sworn to throughout the ages. One of Hippocrates' most famous dictums was, "Walking is a man's best medicine." The contemporary mantra, "sitting is the new smoking," seems to validate Hippocrates; lack of physical activity leads to a host of diseases, and walking can be the ideal remedy—or even a "magic pill."

Most people are, indeed, sitting more—in the car, in the office chair, on the couch—and walking less. The US Centers for Disease Control estimate that less than half of adults get the recommended amount of physical activity, and that one out of three Americans is overweight or even obese. The US Surgeon General reports that more than half of the US population doesn't participate regularly in any type of exercise. Evolutionary biologist Daniel Lieberman writes in his book, *The Story of the Human Body: Evolution, Health, and Disease,* that "We are inadequately adapted to being too physically idle, too well fed, too comfortable." And the United States seems to be exporting this lifestyle and its associated problems around the globe.

There's a large and growing body of knowledge documenting the detrimental health effects of inactivity and the corresponding beneficial effects of physical activity, especially walking. The list of beneficial effects is astounding. A regular regimen of walking can help control weight, lower "bad" cholesterol and raise "good" cholesterol, lower blood pressure, and substantially reduce the chances of developing heart disease, strokes, diabetes, bowel cancer, and osteoporosis. Walking can even have important mental health benefits, including alleviating anxiety and depression, delaying cognitive decline, improving intellectual performance, increasing confidence, and generally boosting one's quality of life.

Long-distance walks can be good for both physical and mental health. (Camino Portugués)

Frédéric Gros sums it up simply: "Serenity comes from simply following the path."

In fact, walking is often called the "perfect exercise." It can generate enormous rewards for a modest investment. Medical and professional organizations such as the Centers for Disease Control, the Mayo Clinic, and the American Heart Association generally recommend a minimum of 30 minutes of moderate-intensity exercise at least five days a week, and brisk walking can be a good focus of this exercise program. Other guidelines suggest walking at least 10,000 steps a day—about 5 miles. Walking is a convenient activity that requires no special expertise, ability, or equipment, can take place in most locations, can be done either in a group or singly, and is inexpensive. Isn't it serendipitous that something so accessible and good for us can also be so healthy and enjoyable!

It's important to note that the opportunity to walk is not evenly distributed across the population. For example, walking can be more challenging in the high crime areas of many cities, and this tends to affect racial and ethnic minorities in particular. There seems to be growing recognition that basic health care and other societal benefits are universal rights that should apply to everyone. Shouldn't the opportunity to walk for health and pleasure be included on this list?

Walking is often called the "perfect exercise." It can generate enormous rewards for a modest investment and be enjoyed by people of all ages. (Golden Gate Way)

The Great Glen Way offers
walkers a mix of classic
Scottish forests, lakes, and
sheep-filled pastures.

Great Glen Way

We'd just finished our week-long hike of the West Highland Way, probably the most popular long-distance walk in all of Britain. This trail had been moving up our "to-do" list for several years and we weren't disappointed; in fact, we were invigorated! Scotland is an ancient country with a landscape of stark, spare beauty that is surprisingly rugged in places. We'd given ourselves another week in Scotland to see some of the usual tourist sights, but then it occurred to us: Why not walk the Great Glen Way, another of Scotland's Great Trails? This walk begins in Fort William, just where the West Highland Way ends. It was destiny. So off we went on another Scottish adventure, walking across the country in a generally northeasterly direction, arriving in Inverness six days later. It was a good choice, nicely complementing the West Highland Way and giving us plenty of time to search for Nessie, the mythical Loch Ness Monster.

LOCATION
Scotland

LENGTH
80 miles

ACCOMMODATIONS
Commercial: Yes
Huts/refuges: No
Backpacking/camping: Yes

BAGGAGE TRANSFER AVAILABLE
Yes

OPTION TO WALK SECTIONS
Yes

DEGREE OF CHALLENGE
Low-Moderate

THE GREAT GLEN is a natural feature, a major geologic fault line between Fort William and Inverness. The fault is obvious when you look at a map of the country, as it essentially divides the country in two. It's thought that the fault was created a few million years ago, and it remains geologically active, producing a number of small earthquakes each year. The trail runs along the fault line for approximately 80 miles, connecting Fort William on the west (opening to the Atlantic Ocean) and Inverness on the east (opening to the North Sea). In addition to the fault itself, major attractions include Ben Nevis (the highest mountain in Britain), Loch Ness (the most famous lake in Britain and the home of its mythical monster), and Urquhart Castle (one of the most visited castles in Scotland). In traditional Scottish Gaelic (still used in places throughout the country), the trail is known as *Slighean a' Ghlinne Mhoir*. A relatively recent addition to the Great Trails system, it was officially opened in 2002 by His Royal Highness Prince Andrew, Earl of Inverness, but it uses routes that were already in existence, some of them for hundreds of years.

Because of the prevailing winds, nearly everyone walks the trail from west to east. Fittingly, the trail begins at the Old Fort in Fort William, named for William III (William of Orange). The town is tourist-friendly and attracts lots of walkers—consider spending a day here. Another option is to take a day to climb nearby Ben Nevis.

Shortly after leaving town you encounter the ruins of Old Inverlochy Castle, which we especially enjoyed. This very small thirteenth-century castle—its courtyard is less than 10,000 square feet—was constructed at the entrance to the Great Glen. Much of the walking on the first several days is along the Caledonian Canal, built in the early nineteenth century. Because of the natural lakes along the Great Glen, only 22 miles of the canal are man-made, with the remaining 38 miles relying on three large lochs (lakes). The canal includes twenty-nine locks, which raise and lower the water level by up to 8 feet, and a system of distinctive pepperpot lighthouses and lockkeepers' cottages. Originally built for commercial traffic, today the canal is used mostly by pleasure craft. The walking is easy, and we enjoyed watching the boats maneuver through the locks. There are good views of Ben Nevis, too.

The next few days of walking is on a mostly pleasant mix of canal towpaths, forest tracks, abandoned railroad tracks, former military roads, and short stretches of motor roads. Highlights include Urquhart Castle and Loch Ness. The castle was built around 1250 on the site of an Iron Age fort and has changed hands many times, mostly by force. It was used as a fortress and residence for over 400 years, but is now mostly in ruins. The site offers fine views

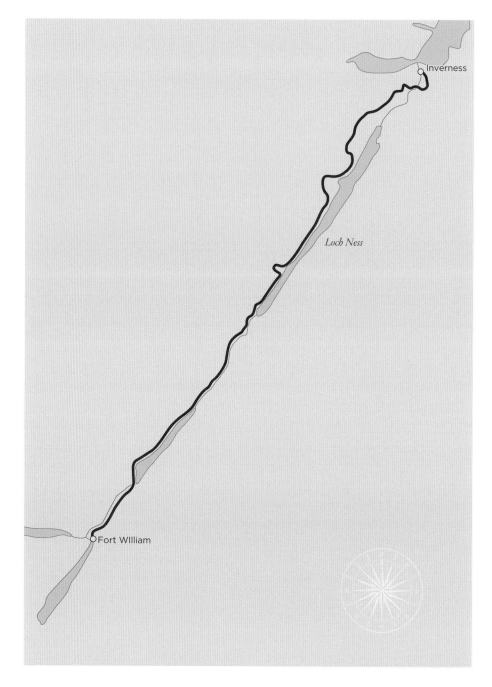

(LEFT) The upper elevations of the trail include several rivers and handsome bridges.

(BELOW) The Great Glen Way, one of Scotland's "Great Trails," features lovely views out and over the three lakes it passes.

up and down Loch Ness, and parts of the castle have been preserved, including a five-story tower house.

For most walkers, Loch Ness is the prime attraction—it's a large and fetching body of water, and the trail offers outstanding views. The length of Loch Ness accounts for more than a third of the Great Glen Way, and is located in a National Scenic Area. The trail can be occasionally steep and rough. The town of Drumnadrochit is the capital of the "monster industry" and offers two visitor centers devoted to the lake and its local mythology. You can take cruises on the lake to look for Nessie yourself (we enjoyed our boat ride, but are sorry to report that we saw no evidence of Nessie).

The legend of Nessie goes back to AD 565, but its modern era began in 1933 when sightings of a "strange spectacle on Loch Ness" were reported in the local newspaper. In 1934, a photograph of a creature with a long, serpentine neck was taken by surgeon R. K. Wilson, but has ultimately been judged a hoax. Over subsequent years, many sightings have been reported and photographs taken, but they've all been explained as mirages, atmospheric illusions, drifting logs, wakes of boats, and other phenomena (including deliberate tricks and wishful thinking). The lake has been carefully studied, including sonar sweeps and sediment analysis, and no scientific evidence supports the existence of Nessie. In fact, scientists report that the lake is relatively poor in nutrients and could not support a resident population of large predators. But all this scientific evidence doesn't seem to have

(ABOVE) Mysterious Loch Ness is the reputed home of the Loch Ness monster; the legend of "Nessie" goes back to AD 565.

(ABOVE RIGHT) Sheep farming and rock walls are common features of the Scottish countryside.

dampened interest in Nessie. In fact, Google Street Maps recently used boats and divers to enable folks to use the Internet to search the lake themselves.

The last day's hike takes you along forest and moorland tracks, and several miles of road walking. It features a mix of farmland and the striking small city of Inverness, called the "capital of the highlands." The site of Inverness has been inhabited for at least 7,000 years and offers many historic and prehistoric features. For example, neolithic stone circles and burial cairns have been found in and around the town. The town includes the handsome Inverness Castle.

The walk includes access to a number of Munros, Corbetts, and Grahams. Munros are mountains greater than 3,000 feet in height (provided the summit is adequately separated from any neighboring Munros). There are 284 Munros in Scotland, with several close to the trail. Bagging all the Munros in the country is a cult activity among many walkers and climbers. Corbetts are mountains over 2,500 feet, and Grahams are over 2,000 feet; several of each are within striking distance of the trail. You'll want to be familiar with these terms as many local walkers will be anxious to talk with you about their quests to summit them all.

Running through three types of habitats—lakes, forests, and moorlands—the trail includes a variety of interesting wildlife. Distinctive oystercatchers have long orange bills used for cracking open cockles and mussels. Larger kestrels are birds of prey that feed on small mammals. Because the Great Glen is open to the sea at both ends it attracts a variety of seabirds, such as kittiwakes, guillemots, fulmars, and shearwaters. Forests are widespread in the Great Glen and include both deciduous and evergreen types. Most of Scotland was cleared of its original Caledonian forest for agriculture, but remnants survive on the slopes above Loch Ness. Residents include pine martens, ospreys, goshawks, and deer. Moorlands support several distinctive kinds of wildlife, including buzzards, golden eagles, skylarks, curlews, grouse, ptarmigans, and mountain hares. Scots pine, the only type of pine native to Britain, grows on the moors.

The history of this part of Scotland is as complex and interesting at its natural history. Two passage graves and a ring cairn radiocarbon-dated to 2,500 to 2,000 BC are the first evidence of human presence in the area. Prehistoric hill forts show the strategic importance of the Great Glen as far back as the Iron Age. Clans feuded for centuries, as evidenced by the twelfth- and thirteenth-century castles built at Urquhart, Invergarry, and Inverlochy. The seventeenth century brought the stirrings of nationalism, growing into the Jacobite risings in the next century; the Jacobites were finally defeated in 1746. As part of the effort to "crush rebellious Scots," British General George Wade supervised the building of 240 miles of military roads in the highlands, some of which hikers on the Great Glen Way traverse today.

(ABOVE) Heathers and heaths are common along the Great Glen Way.

(BELOW) Much of the Great Glen Way follows a network of canals that join Loch Linnhe, a long sea loch that connects with the Atlantic Ocean, and the North Sea.

The Great Glen Way can be enjoyed by walkers with different levels of experience and different capabilities. For less experienced walkers, its towpaths and usually gentle forest tracks make it a good introduction to long-distance walking. For more experienced walkers, the nearby Munros, Corbetts, and Grahams offer more challenging terrain. Fort William and Inverness have good bus service to Glasgow and Edinburgh. There aren't many commercial services along the trail, so reservations for accommodations are strongly suggested. "Wild" camping is not allowed, but there are several commercial campgrounds, as well as a few hostels run by the Scottish Youth Hostels Association. The small towns along the route offer an assortment of B&Bs. You should take the cash you expect to need as there are few banks or cash machines along the route; shops are scarce as well, and only basic supplies are available.

Most people take six days for the walk. You must be prepared for the dramatic changes in weather for which Scotland is famous—good rain gear and warm clothes, including a hat and gloves, should be carried, along with bug dope for the notorious midges (we found the midges overrated and not much of a problem). The walk can be done anytime of the year, with summer quite busy; spring and fall are the best options. Baggage service can be arranged. The principles of the Countryside Code, as outlined in the essay "The Ethics of Walking," apply to this trail; it is your responsibility to know and follow these guidelines.

The Great Glen Way is a splendid walk that will appeal to many hikers—it's an interesting and beautiful walk that features a great deal of human and natural history, and world-class attractions such as Loch Ness. Moreover, it's not overly challenging and can be walked in less than a week, as well as in shorter sections. Paired with the West Highland Way, it immerses walkers in the striking Scottish countryside—or it makes a lovely, less busy, alternative.

WALKING AS THE ORIGINAL ECOTOURISM

There's a growing "greening" of many facets of life—energy production and use, small-scale housing, organic farming. This movement also has been adopted in the fields of recreation, tourism, and leisure travel. Often called "ecotourism," this expanding movement is based on principles such as appreciation of natural and cultural diversity; direct and authentic contact with people and the places in which they live; the need to slow our everyday, frantic lives; protection of the distinctive places that make our world so interesting; and investment in sustaining and stewarding special places through direct economic benefits to local residents. Moreover, many people want to introduce an element of adventure into their lives and become more active and healthy in the process.

Walking the great cultural landscapes of the world is an ideal way to pursue all these objectives. The human scale and pace of walking encourage a deep understanding and appreciation of nature and culture and ultimately lead to preservation of important cultural landscapes and the sense of place they represent. "Interpretation" in the national parks refers to educating visitors about the parks, and Freeman Tilden was a pioneering practitioner in the National Park Service. In his book, *Interpreting Our Heritage*, Tilden developed his mantra about the way to help ensure protection of special places such as national parks: "Through interpretation, understanding; through understanding, appreciation; through appreciation, protection." Understanding and appreciation of special places are essential to their protection.

Walking also contributes to personal health and fitness, and has relatively little environmental and social impact (especially when recommended "leave no trace" practices are followed). The small scale of walking makes use of facilities and services provided by local people—B&Bs, small inns, refuges, hostels, campgrounds, local foods—and the resulting economic benefits flow directly to these communities. Walking is one of the most democratic and accessible recreation activities, demanding no extraordinary athletic ability, requiring relatively little cost, and appropriate for nearly all ages. And walking is nearly always adventurous; one can never be quite sure about what's around the next bend in the trail, and every day brings new and sometimes unexpected experiences.

Walking may be the ultimate green; it's good for you and good for the earth.

Walking the world's great cultural landscapes may be the greenest form of recreation. (Pembrokeshire Coast Path)

Appreciation of special places is essential to their protection. (Queen Charlotte Track)

Walking north along the Hudson River offers great views of the George Washington Bridge and the New Jersey Palisades.

Great Saunter

It was the end of our first day on the Great Saunter, and we were bravely navigating the New York subway on the way back to our hotel. We popped out of the subway station and onto the busy street, unfolded our street map and began to consider the quickest route to the hotel. But before we had a chance to orient ourselves, a woman approached and asked if we needed directions. Well, we didn't really *need* directions—we'd successfully found our way around much of the city already that day—but a little help at the end of the day was certainly appreciated. We told her the name of our hotel, she walked us to the next street corner and pointed "that way," and off we went on the final few blocks of our day of walking. Over the next couple of days, there were other instances in which we asked for directions and found people to be uniformly pleasant and helpful. New Yorkers have a reputation as brusque, but based on our admittedly small sample size, we concluded that this criticism is undeserved.

———— ≈ ————

LOCATION
New York City, United States

LENGTH
32 miles

ACCOMMODATIONS
Commercial: Yes
Huts/refuges: No
Backpacking/camping: No

BAGGAGE TRANSFER AVAILABLE
No

OPTION TO WALK SECTIONS
Yes

DEGREE OF CHALLENGE
Low

WHEN WE READ ABOUT the Great Saunter, we were intrigued. First, the name resonated; Thoreau made this word famous among walkers when he wrote about "the art of sauntering" in his classic essay "Walking." Thoreau was smarter than most people and he knew it; indeed, his arrogant prose is one of the things that makes him so endearing. In "Walking," it's clear that he's one of the few people able to appreciate the full benefits of a good saunter. We were anxious to see if we could saunter, especially in the context of one of the world's great cities. Also, the idea of walking around the perimeter of the island of Manhattan seemed so romantic. Yes, Manhattan is still an island, though that's easy to forget as we now navigate by car, subway, and train, all of which tend to obscure the fact that the island is surrounded by the Hudson, Harlem, and East Rivers. What would New York look like from this very different perspective?

The Great Saunter is a 32-mile loop around the island, and the route stays hard on the shoreline of the three rivers throughout most of its course. Public access to the water's edge is a tribute to great, forward-thinking planners like Robert Moses and Frederick Law Olmsted, and is a gift—a

The trail passes directly under the approach to the historic Brooklyn Bridge.

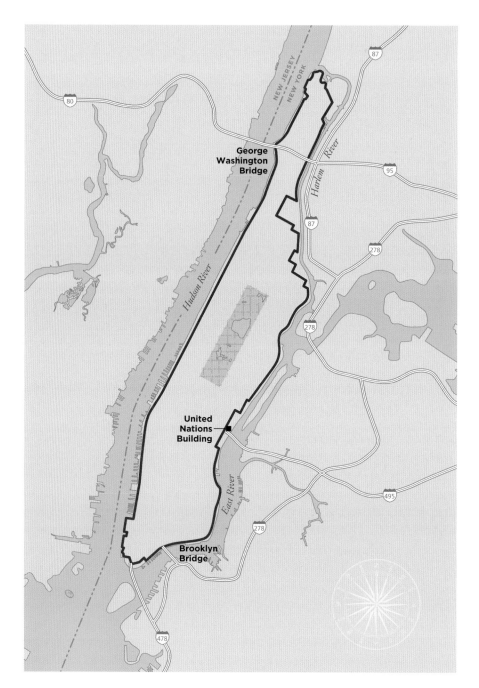

treasure, really—to the people of New York and so many millions of out-of-town visitors. The route travels through twenty waterfront parks—what has been called Manhattan's "emerald necklace"—and past innumerable and iconic attractions such as the Statue of Liberty, Ellis Island, the United Nations, and much more. Walkers share the route with bicyclists, runners, skateboarders, rollerbladers, dog walkers, anglers, commuters, sightseers, and the homeless, but it all somehow seems to work. Being on the relatively serene waterfront conveys a concomitant sense of peace and harmony among all.

Mile for mile, the Great Saunter packs more attractions and places of interest than perhaps any other walk. The route takes you through many of the city's distinctive neighborhoods, such as SoHo, Greenwich Village, Tribeca, and Harlem. Battery Park and its immediate vicinity feature Admiral Dewey Promenade, circular Castle Clinton, and views of the Statue of Liberty, along with access to ferries to the Statue of Liberty and Ellis Island (highly recommended before or after the walk). One World Trade Center (often called the "Freedom Tower") is proximate to Battery Park. The parks along the Hudson are some of the nicest, and consistently take walkers away from automobile traffic. One day of our walk was a Sunday, and we were pleasantly surprised to find the parks full of families picnicking, playing ball, and doing exactly the same things nonurban families do on weekends.

As you walk north on the Hudson, you see the George Washington Bridge, one of many icons in the city. The bridge connects Manhattan with New Jersey. Famed architect Le Corbusier called it "the most beautiful bridge in the world. Made of cables and steel beams, it gleams in the sky like an upturned arch. It is blessed." Cy Adler, in his highly recommended guide to the Great Saunter, writes that "No New Yorker should die without having first walked the great George Washington Bridge." As you approach the bridge from the south, you also get striking views of the impressive New Jersey Palisades. Other attractions we enjoyed on the Hudson side of the island include the Chelsea Piers, the waterfront from West 41st to West 47th Streets, and Fort Tryon Park and the Cloisters. Many of the great ocean liners have docked at the Chelsea Piers, and the site would have accommodated the ill-fated *Titanic*. The waterfront from West 41st to West 47th Streets draws many tourists whose cruise ships dock here, along with Navy ships whose crews seek rest and relaxation. The aircraft carrier *Intrepid* is docked in this area, and serves as a museum. Fort Tryon Park is hilly and deeply wooded, and it houses the Cloisters, a nationally prominent art and historical museum.

After we made the turn around the north end of the island and started walking along the Harlem River and then the East River, we particularly enjoyed seeing the United Nations complex of buildings and grounds, though walkers lack access to the shoreline here for security reasons. The South Street Seaport is a good example of the way in which buildings and whole neighborhoods that have decayed can be transformed into commercial and cultural hubs; the seaport is on the National Register of Historic Places. Of course, the Brooklyn Bridge is a favorite for most people, and the Empire State Building is a distinctive landmark visible from many spots along the walk. Aside from these many iconic sites, we simply enjoyed watching the busy traffic on all three rivers: ferries, cargo ships, tugboats, sightseeing boats, Coast Guard cutters, sculls, and a myriad of private boats.

As paradoxical as it may seem, there's an interesting natural history theme to this walk. Manhattan is substantially larger than it originally was due to fill dumped into shallow areas of the rivers, particularly in the downtown area. While this has added land, it has also diminished habitat for fish and waterbirds. However, the rivers still support a recreational fishery, including prized striped bass; you see lots of anglers along the walk.

Mile for mile, the Great Saunter packs more attractions and places of interest than perhaps any other walk (United Nations Building).

(ABOVE) Much of the Great Saunter runs through a series of greenways and pocket parks.

(BELOW) The frequent bridges remind walkers that Manhattan is truly an island (East River).

Native Americans called the island *Mannahatta*, which meant "hilly island," and much of this original topography is still evident in the northern, more forested portion of the island. Inwood Hill Park includes a natural salt marsh. The open area between Piers 26 and 32 is a wildlife sanctuary. Look closely along much of the shoreline and you'll see small tide pools that support marine life. Of course, the whole shoreline supports a variety of waterbirds.

Since this is a circular walk, you can start from anywhere along the route. But the conventional approach starts at the foot of the island in the vicinity of Battery Park and the South Port Ferry Terminal, and proceeds in a clockwise fashion. A first day of walking will take you along the Hudson River as far north as the George Washington Bridge. Day two might take you around the northern tip of the island along the Harlem River, and south along the East River to the United Nations. A final day closes the loop. The walk can be done relatively easily in two days, if time is short. There's even a mad-dash one-day version of the walk done every spring, organized and led by the Shorewalkers group. This might be fun, but it's not a good option for first-time walkers who will surely want to go at a more leisurely pace and enjoy the walk more fully—much like Thoreau would have preferred.

This is a relatively easy walk as it is essentially level, with the exception of the hilly northern section, and is on a paved walkway. New York's famous subway system adds to the logistical ease of the walk, as you can pick it up and be dropped off within a few blocks of nearly anywhere along the route. We were a little intimidated by the subway but caught on pretty quickly, and wound up appreciating it—it was convenient and inexpensive, but often old, loud, dirty, and gritty. But it began to grow on us. Look closely at the stations to appreciate their classic beauty in design and decoration. Be sure to load the subway app on your phone or other device. A street map of the city (paper or electronic) is useful in the several instances where the route goes "inland," around places that have no public shoreline access and inevitable construction sites. Food is readily available in many spots, either in conventional restaurants or from street-food vendors. We stumbled on a barbeque joint in West Harlem that felt authentic and funky, and the food was delicious! Most of the parks include picnic tables and benches of myriad designs. Bathrooms are a critical and limited resource. Most of the parks include these facilities, and businesses are an option if you are a customer. Bring toilet paper and hand sanitizer. Bathroom apps can be helpful to locate facilities.

The Great Saunter is great adventure. In fact, in its earlier, less formal form, it influenced the writing and thinking of Walt Whitman, who often walked in Manhattan and wrote, "Manhattan crowds, with their turbulent musical chorus!/Manhattan faces and eyes forever for me." Writing in *The New Yorker*, Adam Gopnik argues that Alfred Kazin's 1951 book, *A Walker in the City*, was influenced by Whitman and "remains the best book ever written about New York on foot." We thoroughly enjoyed the walk and came away with much better knowledge of New York, as well as a greater appreciation of one of the world's most important cities. Consider this walk a way to improve your "art of sauntering"—Thoreau would approve.

WALKING FOR OTHERS

A happy marriage of terms—"walk" and "marathon"—has given rise to the mash-up of "walkathon," a walking event designed to support a social cause. Walkathons represent a strong and growing social movement to support fighting diseases, abating hunger, raising funds for community projects, and a host of other purposes. In walkathons, participants collect donations and pledges for walking a predetermined distance, course, or time. They're typically noncompetitive, low intensity, and designed to be accessible and enjoyable.

In 1953, actor/comedian Ramón Rivero walked 80 miles in four days in Puerto Rico, raising $85,000 to help fight cancer, and this is generally recognized as the first walkathon. The first walkathon on the US mainland was held in 1968 in Minneapolis, Minnesota, sponsored by the American Freedom from Hunger Foundation. Perhaps the best-known walkathon is the Relay for Life, which benefits the American Cancer Society; each year, more than four million people in over twenty countries participate. This walkathon is designed to celebrate the lives of people who have battled cancer, remember loved ones lost, and fight back against the disease by funding research and education. Other large and well-known walkathons are the MS Challenge Walk, held throughout the United States, and the Oxfam Trailwalker, held throughout the world.

In his book *The Lost Art of Walking*, Geoff Nicholson takes issue with walking for charity, suggesting that people who wish to donate to a cause should just do it. Moreover, paying people to walk suggests that walking is somehow so onerous that people must be paid to do it. But from a more pragmatic perspective, walkathons have many benefits—raising needed funds, empowering participants, drawing together community members, and demonstrating support for those in need. They also represent an important and enjoyable way to initiate children into public service. Consider participating in walkathons as a way to contribute to your community and to prepare yourself in a supportive, nonthreatening way for long-distance walking.

We enjoyed seeing the excitement of participants in the Walk to End Breast Cancer on the Great Saunter.

Urban trails make good places for charity walks. (Sydney)

Where the Great Wall of China has been restored, the walking is relatively easy, though there are still sharp changes in elevation.

Great Wall of China

When walking on the Great Wall of China, we stayed in a guesthouse in the rural town of Gubeikou; this guesthouse was a fledgling government effort to bring tourism to rural towns. We realized we were staying in the best place in town when, on our second night there, we were joined in the dining room by a group of eight Communist Party officials. That day the community had celebrated a visit by a few buses of Chinese tourists. (All this had surely been explained over the town's frequent loud-speaker announcements but, of course, we couldn't understand a word.) The officials were obviously celebrating a successful day and certainly seemed to enjoy their dinner—in addition to a lavish spread of food, there was much drinking, more drinking than we're used to seeing in restaurants. Seven of the officials were male—and everyone smoked heavily as they congratulated each other with numerous toasts. Fortunately, our sleeping room was at some distance from the dining room, because it looked like the celebration was going to go on for a while! The evening offered insights into the local hierarchy and politics of life in rural China.

LET'S START BY getting a few facts straight about the Great Wall of China, as some of the information we learned in elementary school is not quite right.

First, there was never a single continuous wall separating China from its neighbors to the north, although archeologists have unearthed remnants of barriers along a 13,000-mile route from North Korea to Russia; walls existed before there was a China (some portions built as early as the seventh century BCE) and were used to protect states from hostile neighbors. Usually when people talk about the Great Wall of China, they're referring to the Ming Great Wall, originating in the seventh century when China first came together as a nation. The wall was designed to protect both the capital city of Beijing and the rest of the country from Mongolian invaders. Sometimes incorporating older barriers, it ran roughly 5,500 miles, and instead of one single line, it was a system of walls, and in some places several rows of walls. The Ming Great Wall follows the highest point of land, regardless

LOCATION
China

LENGTH
Variable (a few days to a week)

ACCOMMODATIONS
Commercial: Yes (nearby)
Huts/refuges: No
Backpacking/camping: No

BAGGAGE TRANSFER AVAILABLE
Yes

OPTION TO WALK SECTIONS
Yes

DEGREE OF CHALLENGE
Moderate–High

As many as 10,000 visitors a day experience the heavily restored Great Wall at Badaling, about two hours northwest of Beijing.

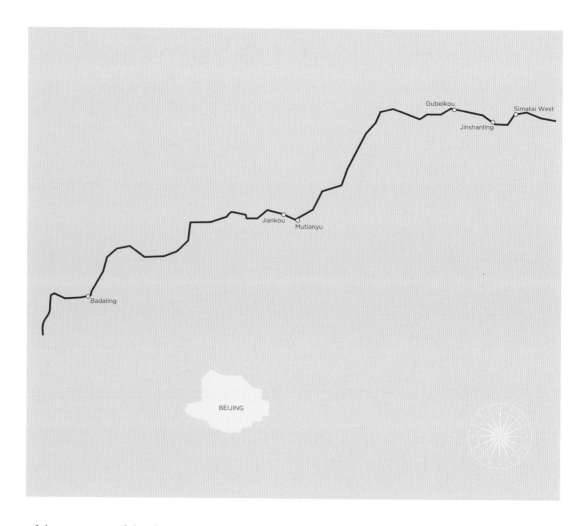

Gubeikou

Simatai West

Jinshanling

Jiankou
Mutianyu

Badaling

BEIJING

of the steepness of the slope, and we've all enjoyed photos of the "Dragon's Back" zigzagging across the landscape.

Second, you can't see the Great Wall from space with the naked eye. Although the wall is exceptionally long, it's also narrow in places, usually between 12 and 30 feet.

An immense amount of building material was used in the wall's construction, so much so that it's been estimated that the same amount of material could be used to construct a 3-foot by 3-foot wall around the earth on the equator. The style and size of the wall varied by region and by the person supervising construction, and as much as possible local materials were incorporated. Where appropriate stones weren't available, large bricks were manufactured. Understandably, much of the building material has been "quarried" over the ages, and used for homes and other buildings.

The wall was one of the grandest building projects on earth, involving millions of workers, many of whom died in the process. We were told that the wall is the largest tombstone in the world; we were also told that white mortar indicates that bones were used as a component.

Spaced along the wall are approximately 25,000 watchtowers for soldiers; we found these fascinating, and they provided the only shelter from the sun. Soldiers kept a lookout from these buildings, but mainly they were used for communication; burning wolf dung produced a thick black smoke, and messages could be passed down the wall quickly. The soldiers wore padded armor and used bows and crossbows; after the Chinese invented gunpowder in the ninth century, cannons were placed along a few strategic sections.

The wall was breached twice. In the thirteenth century Genghis Khan's forces got through, and it took the Ming Dynasty 150 years to regain control of the country. The wall was breached again in 1644 when a traitor let Manchu horsemen through; the capital city of Beijing was captured and the wall immediately became obsolete.

It's said that the Ming Great Wall was built to protect Beijing, but now Beijing (or modernity in general) is the wall's greatest threat. Although the Chinese people are very proud of the wall, highways cut through it, it's removed for communication towers, etc. The wall is a World Heritage Site, but this designation has not adequately protected it.

When people speak of walking the Great Wall of China, they're usually talking about a restored section of the wall at Badaling, about two hours northwest of Beijing. We walked there, too, and Badaling's nearly 5 miles of restored wall gives visitors an idea of what the wall was like when the protective barrier was at its zenith (assuming you mentally remove the tourist facilities at its base and the 10,000 visitors per day who pack the area.) It's quite a scene, but a less crowded experience can be had by heading west on the wall, as most tourists want to approach the watchtower on the east.

But the main event for us was a walk on the "Wild Wall" or "Wilderness Great Wall" for several days. Access to the wall is restricted; you're not supposed to walk on the wall without a guide. We contracted with a guide who took us a few hours northeast of Beijing to explore sections of the wall not often visited by outsiders. We walked a rough uphill track for nearly an hour, and then mounted the wall and walked for the rest of the day. (On subsequent days we were able to get on the wall more directly.)

It was thrilling to see the remains of the Great Wall rising in the midst of a sea of limestone mountains. We walked on unrestored sections of the wall, with no paving stones at all on the walkway, following informal paths on the top of the wall through the bushes and trees that have taken over. Some areas had been neatened up a bit—the surface we walked on was rough, the steps broken, parapets

In places the walking is challenging; the slopes can be as steep as 60 degrees, the footing is rough, and the drop-offs are precarious.

(ABOVE) Spaced along the wall are approximately 25,000 watchtowers; they provided a place for soldiers to eat and sleep and were important defensive positions.

(ABOVE RIGHT) A brief detour off the Wall because of a military installation provided the opportunity to observe life in a rural farming valley; we met an older lady in a Mao jacket who was farming with a wooden hoe.

missing, etc., but the basic integrity of the structure was still there. A few miles were restored, looking more like the Badaling section; this is where we encountered other walkers, exclusively Chinese. The restored sections also featured gift shops, toboggan slides, gondola rides, and other attractions at their approaches, but we much preferred the wilder areas.

There are no facilities on the wilder sections of the wall, although we did encounter a lone vendor selling sodas in the shade of one of the crumbling watchtowers. The allure of something other than water couldn't be ignored but, looking around, we couldn't figure where he had come from. Our guide spoke with the enterprising vendor and told us he walked three miles uphill (steeply uphill on a tiny path he'd worn) from his small village every morning with a case of assorted drinks to sell. At the end of the day, he took the unsold drinks and empty containers back home. It was humbling to be reminded what a privileged life we lead.

In places the walking is challenging—the slopes can be as steep as 60 degrees, the footing rough, and the drop-offs precarious. Some people have suggested that walking on the wall is like being on an unending StairMaster; others describe it as walking laps on the track of a roller coaster. We each carried a single hiking pole, using our free hands to grab onto support when necessary. A few places were vertigo-inducing, but generally it was just uphill and downhill in the hot sun.

Although we walked for several days, we probably didn't cover all that many miles because the going was slow. We experienced sections of the wall in the Jiankou, Mutianyu, Jinshanling and Simatai West areas. When we were walking to Jinshanling from Gubeikou, we had to get off the wall and walk beside it for about an hour and a half because of a large military installation. This detour provided the opportunity to observe life in a rural farming valley, and we met an older lady in a Mao jacket who was farming with a wooden hoe. This was an interesting journey back in time.

As at Hadrian's Wall in England, we wondered at the xenophobia that makes walling out a people necessary—or should we be thinking of the enemy forces that must be defended against? We saw examples of horse barriers below the wall; the terrain in those places was so steep that we couldn't imagine riding a horse there, but we all know the Mongols were renowned for their horsemanship.

The views are breathtaking as the wall crawls along the ridgelines from peak to peak. It's just like in *National Geographic* magazine . . . only better! We saw few animals—cuckoos, magpies, squirrels, chipmunks, and a few lizards, but we really weren't there for the fauna. Both oak and peach trees seem to find the remains of the watchtowers good habitat, but we weren't there for the flora either. This walk is all about the cultural landscape . . . both past and present.

We spent several weeks in China and had a variety of experiences, but our time on the Wild Wall was the highlight. As we walked along, we tried to imagine being a forced laborer enslaved to work at the seemingly endless task of building an impregnable barrier, or being an enemy invader and encountering the wall, or being a soldier stationed at one of the towers, or being a peasant living in the shadow of the wall . . . The Great Wall of China is truly a cultural resource for the whole world.

(ABOVE LEFT) The Ming Great Wall follows the highest point of land, regardless of the steepness of the slope.

(ABOVE) The shady (sometimes ruined) watchtowers provide the only shelter from the sun.

GLOBAL TO LOCAL, LOCAL TO GLOBAL

Deciding where to walk is an important part of the walking experience—will you make a pilgrimage to Santiago; walk with John Muir in his beloved High Sierra; explore the great coastlines of California, Britain, Australia, and New Zealand; circumnavigate the island of Manhattan; scale the Great Wall of China; stroll through the neighborhoods of Paris; or perhaps just explore your own neighborhood a little more closely?

In fact, researching and choosing a place to walk can be one of the most enjoyable parts of a walking adventure, considering the many alternatives that are available, reading guidebooks, consulting maps, making travel arrangements, and anticipating the walk. This book addresses long-distance and multi-day walks primarily, but also offers encouragement to walk more in everyday life as a way to prepare for more

In this book we describe thirty of what we consider the world's great long-distance trails and multi-day walks; these are many of our favorites. (Grand Canyon Rim Trail)

Walk more in everyday life as a way to prepare for more ambitious walks, to adopt a healthy lifestyle, to add interest to life, and to lessen your impact on the environment. (Golden Gate Way)

ambitious walks and to adopt a healthy lifestyle, add interest to life, and lessen your impact on the environment.

"Think globally, act locally" is an old environmental adage that suggests we inform ourselves about global environmental issues and then act accordingly in our everyday lives and in our home communities. Perhaps there's an analogous way of thinking about walking: you appreciate the idea of long-distance walking, so consider how you might walk more in your daily activities as a way to add enjoyment to life and to prepare yourself for long-distance walks. Is it feasible to walk to and from your place of work? Or to the market? How about a stroll around your neighborhood (or someone else's neighborhood) in the morning, in the evening, or on the weekend? When possible, take the stairs instead of the elevator. Explore your local parks. Walk outside whenever you can, even when the weather's less than ideal, as this will prepare you for the eventualities of long-distance walking. Carry a pack to get used to it and to enhance the aerobic quality of walking. Current medical guidelines suggest you walk at least 10,000 steps a day—about 5 miles. Consider using a pedometer and make a game of it.

By walking locally, we follow in the footsteps of great walkers like Henry David Thoreau. Thinking about his native Concord, Massachusetts, Thoreau wrote, "My vicinity affords many good walks; and though for so many years I have walked almost every day, and sometimes for several days together, I have not yet exhausted them." He continued:

> *An absolutely new prospect is a great happiness, and I can still get this any afternoon. Two or three hours' walking will carry me to as strange a country as I ever expect to see. A single farmhouse which I had not seen before is sometimes as good as the dominions of the King of Dahomey. There is in fact a sort of harmony discoverable between the capabilities of the landscape within a circle of ten miles' radius, or the limits of an afternoon walk, and the three score years and ten of human life. It will never become quite familiar to you.*

Beyond the local is the global. States, provinces, regions, and countries have extensive systems of parks, trails, and other reserves that offer many lifetimes of walking adventure. Many countries have national-level trail systems and participate in international trail networks.

That brings us to the long-distance trails and multi-day walks we recommend in this book. We've taken this assignment seriously and devoted ourselves to a decade of "field work." In this book we describe thirty of what we consider the world's great long-distance trails and multi-day walks; these are many of our favorites. We've included a table at the end of the book that we hope will help you decide which trails and walks you'd like to explore. We've been deliberate about including a great spectrum of long-distance trails and multi-day walks that vary in length, geography, and challenge.

In many parts of the world people have integrated walking into their daily lives. (Amalfi Coast)

Most of the route to the village of Supai is through a beautiful dry wash in Hualapai Canyon.

Havasu Canyon

The end of the day found us in Supai, tired but exhilarated from our day of scrambling along magical Havasu Creek and seeing its iconic waterfalls. Supai is the small village in the middle of the Havasupai Indian Reservation and one of the most isolated settlements in the Lower 48 states. Eight miles from the nearest road, Supai is the only place left in the contiguous United States where mail is still delivered by pack train. We sat on the bench outside the general store and enjoyed just watching the world go by—other hikers coming and going from the cafe, local residents running errands or simply milling about, and a parade of animals, mostly dogs of all shapes and sizes and the occasional stray horse or mule. Just as the canyon itself was otherworldly, so was the culture. And then it occurred to us: Not only did this seem like another country, but in many ways it is. From a legal standpoint, Indian reservations are autonomous nations; the residents have their own rich histories and often ascribe to very different worldviews and associated values. We began to more fully appreciate that our hike into Havasu Canyon, while initially focused on its distinctive and stunning beauty, had an important cultural component as well.

LOCATION
Arizona, United States

LENGTH
22+ miles

ACCOMMODATIONS
Commercial: Yes
Huts/refuges: No
Backpacking/camping: Yes

BAGGAGE TRANSFER AVAILABLE
Yes

OPTION TO WALK SECTIONS
No

DEGREE OF CHALLENGE
Moderate

OF COURSE, EVERYONE KNOWS about the Grand Canyon, the mile-deep gash in the earth that is one of the world's great geological features. Most of the canyon is protected as a national park. But relatively few people know that a portion of the canyon—Havasu Canyon, one of its most appealing areas—is part of the Havasupai Indian Reservation. Thanks to the Havasupai people, visitors are welcome to walk the nearly 20-mile trail that follows the canyon down to the village of Supai and on to the Colorado River. Visitors can stay in a large campground below the village or in a lodge in Supai.

The hike begins where the road ends on the rim of the canyon at Hualapai Hilltop; views into the canyons below are striking. The elevation is 5,200 feet. There's a sprawling, busy parking area where backpackers organize their gear, Havasupai horsemen prepare their pack trains to deliver supplies to the village, and helicopters land and depart as they, too, deliver supplies and ferry visitors. The

Havasupai Tribe has erected a number of homemade signs that set forth their rules for visiting the reservation, and some visitors might find them less than welcoming. But remember, this is a different culture, and we found all residents we met to be friendly and helpful.

The trail to Supai drops steeply by means of about a mile-long series of switchbacks, then levels out and

Hiking through Hualapai Canyon offers iconic views of western canyon country.

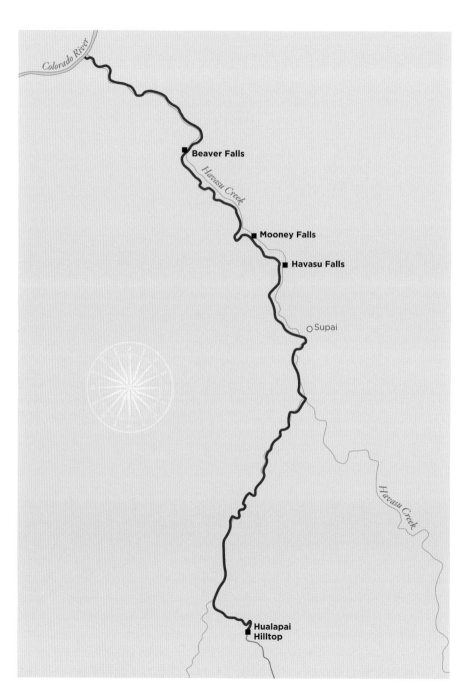

descends gradually through long, winding, and beautiful Hualapai Canyon. Here, you pick your way through a series of dry washes, occasionally scrambling around large rocks.

As you approach Supai you reach Havasu Creek, and the excitement picks up. The creek is laden with the mineral travertine, which precipitates out of the water and coats the bottom of the stream; refraction of light turns the water a distinctive and appealing milky blue or turquoise. The creek is perennial and supports lush riparian vegetation. The combination of these features makes the canyon a true oasis in the midst of arid surroundings. At the village of Supai, you'll find a cluster of houses and small farms and ranches, as well as a school (through eighth grade), a tourist office, a cafe, a general store, a lodge, and a church. The population of Supai is around 300.

The hike beyond Supai is the main event. Follow the creek for a few miles as it descends toward the Colorado River through a sprawling linear campground. Here you'll find a series of three dramatic waterfalls: Havasu, Mooney, and Beaver. Havasu drops 100 feet from the cliff tops into a stunning, deep, turquoise pool. The surrounding cliffs are cloaked in large sheets, or plates, of brown travertine. Below the falls, travertine also forms low, curving dams that create a series of steps with blue-green pools that continues for miles, all the way to the Colorado River. It's a scene that could easily be from another planet. Mooney is just as dramatic, dropping nearly 200 feet (it's higher than Niagara Falls). The trail in this section is more demanding, sometimes descending very steeply, with steel stanchions and chains for assistance, but the view is more than worth the effort. Two miles farther down the trail is Beaver Falls, only a little less dramatic and much less visited. And several miles

(ABOVE LEFT) Havasu Creek is laden with the mineral travertine, which precipitates out of the water and coats the bottom of the stream; refraction of light turns the water a distinctive and appealing milky blue or turquoise.

(ABOVE) Havasu Falls plunges from the cliff tops into a stunning, deep, turquoise pool. The surrounding cliffs are cloaked in large sheets, or plates, of brown travertine.

(ABOVE) Supai is the small village in the middle of the Havasupai Indian Reservation and one of the most isolated settlements in the Lower 48 states.

(ABOVE RIGHT) The Havasu people are skilled horsemen, and most supplies are delivered to the remote village of Supai by pack stock.

beyond Beaver Falls is the end of the trail, as Havasu Creek empties into the Colorado. This last section is more a cross-county route than a maintained trail, and several crossings of Havasu Creek are required, some of them deep if the water is high. No camping is allowed along this stretch of trail, so it must be completed as a day hike.

A variety of plants and animals are drawn to this area. Huge Fremont's cottonwood trees are scattered along the creek, in addition to mesquite and acacia trees. Large groupings of sacred datura, with its showy, white, trumpet-shaped blossoms are scattered around the creek. This plant blooms at night and its flowers wither the next morning; be careful because the plant is poisonous. Mule deer and desert bighorn sheep inhabit the canyon. Watch for the American dipper as it feeds on the bottom of the creek, and listen for the canyon wren, with its distinctive, descending series of calls. On the higher, more arid sections of the trail familiar desert vegetation predominates, including yucca, agave, and squawbush.

The cultural history of this area is equally interesting. The Havasupai have lived in this canyon for more than 800 years. "Havasu" means blue-green and "pai" means people. The native people farmed in canyons with perennial streams and also hunted animals and gathered plants. The Havasupai Indian Reservation was established in 1880 on lands bordering Havasu Creek, and was expanded in 1975 to nearly 200,000 acres. In addition, 95,000 acres of Grand Canyon National Park are reserved for traditional uses of the Havasupai. It's estimated that there are about 650 members of the tribe, nearly half of whom live in Supai. The Havasupai have a reputation as skilled horsemen

and it's interesting to watch them ride and manage the pack trains that ply the trail. (Be sure to give the right-of-way to horses on the trail.) The Havasupai are also known to be warm and generous and like to live in harmony with the land.

This hike can vary from as little as three days to a week. It's 8 miles from Hualapai Hilltop to Supai, and another 2–3 miles to the campground and the Havasu Falls and Mooney Falls area. This includes a drop in elevation of more than 2,000 feet. It's another 8 miles to the Colorado River. Most visitors hike to the campground on their first day, spend a day or two seeing the falls and surrounding area, and then hike back up to Hualapai Hilltop. Very few hike to the Colorado River as it's a long and challenging journey.

It's a long drive to Hualapai Hilltop from just about anywhere—nearly 200 miles from both Grand Canyon Village and Las Vegas. The nearest commercial services are 68 miles away in Peach Springs, where there's a motel and gas station. The best times to make this hike are spring and fall when temperatures are mild; summer is hot. Hike during the week and it will be less crowded. You must get permission to enter the reservation (which requires a fee) and you must have a reservation for the campground or the lodge. You'll need to plan your trip well in advance to make these reservations. There is little water available between Hualapai Hilltop and Supai, so take plenty of water with you. We used hiking poles and found them helpful, especially where the trail is more of a cross-country route. Of course, it's uphill as you hike back to Hualapai Hilltop, so factor that into your planning. As your trip approaches, watch the weather forecasts closely. Like all canyons in the Southwest, Havasu Canyon is subject to flash floods, and the trail should not be hiked if thunderstorms are likely. A historic flood occurred in 2008, causing a great deal of damage. If you hike all the way to the Colorado River, don't be tempted to swim in the river—the water is cold and the current strong.

Havasu Canyon is an enchanted land, and this hike offers an intimate experience in a place unlike any other. It's a part of the Grand Canyon landscape that few people see, and offers insights into how one group of Native Americans has lived in relative isolation for centuries, and how they are adapting to life in the modern world.

The hike into Havasu Canyon starts at Hualapai Hilltop and offers dramatic views into Hualapai Canyon.

THE ART OF WALKING

Walking has achieved recognition, even a certain status, as manifested in its portrayal in art, where it is both subject and medium. Of course, artists have included representations of people walking for centuries, but walking is usually incidental and not the focus or message of the artist. But as Rebecca Solnit points out in her book *Wanderlust*, there are important exceptions to this generalization, such as nineteenth-century Japanese printmaker Hiroshige's *Fifty-Three Stations of the Tokaido Road*, a series of images along the 312-mile walk from what is now Tokyo to Kyoto. Solnit describes the prints as "a road movie from when roads were for walkers and movies were woodblock prints."

We encountered this interactive piece at a recent art show, where visitors were invited to make their own cairns.

Geoff Nicholson, in his engaging book *The Lost Art of Walking*, cites the "motion studies" of photographer Eadweard Muybridge, from the late nineteenth century, as an early representation of walking as art, though this was not necessarily Muybridge's objective. Muybridge was principally interested in using photography to study human motion (and the motion of other animals). He presented his series of photos of a naked man walking (the photographer himself) using what he called a "zoopraxiscope," which allowed him to show the photos in a way that created the illusion of movement. The result was both a scientific and artistic revelation. Nicholson writes that the photographs are highly aesthetic and fascinating "because they reveal the magical nature of something we take so much for granted."

A more conscious artistic focus on walking is evident in the postmodern period, starting in the 1950s and '60s. This is a time when painters such as Jackson Pollock repositioned the emphasis of art away from the "object" and more on the "process" of creation. Moreover, artists began to more consciously address the myriad of ideas associated with the relationship between people and their everyday world, ultimately evolving into "conceptual artists." Practitioners such as Richard Long used walking to address this change in emphasis. For example, one of his earliest pieces, *A Line Made by Walking*, was a photograph of a path he made in a meadow by the simple act of walking it; in other words, he "drew" the line with his feet. He and other artists elaborated on this approach to develop a subgenre of walking-related art.

Of course, art takes many forms, including literature, poetry, and music. We've already noted Thoreau's essay "Walking," a thoughtful and well-crafted philosophical statement that many would judge as having artistic merit; certainly, it's a form of conceptual art. Charles Dickens's extensive walks through London informed his novels, and Wordsworth's poetry was inspired by his walking in England's Lake District.

Nicholson recounts many songs in which walking plays an important role, from twelfth-century troubadours to Robert Johnson's "Walkin' Blues," to Patsy Cline's "Walkin' After Midnight." And who could forget Nancy Sinatra's "These Boots Are Made for Walkin'?" (Remember, art is a relative term!)

Conceptual artist Richard Long made a series of art pieces focusing on walking; this is his *Line Made by Walking* created by the author by walking in a meadow. In other words, he "drew" the line with his feet.

Large and beautiful Tenaya Lake is between May Lake and Sunrise High Sierra Camps and offers stunning views into the glacially carved High Sierra.

High Sierra Camps Loop

Okay, we admit it, we're biased—the Sierra Nevada are our favorite mountains. There, we've said it. There's just nothing not to like about these mountains, with their high granite peaks and domes, plentiful streams and lakes, lush flower-filled meadows, ancient trees, and the powerful aura of John Muir. Here's where we took our very first backpacking trip so many years ago, using borrowed equipment and relying on frighteningly little knowledge. We made lots of mistakes, but the experience was mesmerizing, and we've been coming back pretty regularly. We've known about the High Sierra Camps for many years, hiked past them on a number of occasions, and recently decided to give them a try. They offer a way of enjoying and appreciating the mountains that is more characteristic of Europe, with its hut systems. We thoroughly enjoyed our hike and suggest you consider this an option for immersing yourself in "our" Sierra Nevada.

———— ≈ ————

YOSEMITE NATIONAL PARK was one of the first national parks in America and is widely considered one of the "crown jewels" of the national park system. Its more than four million annual visitors are a testament to its place in the minds of those who appreciate the national parks. Yosemite Valley is generally considered the heart of the park, a dramatic 7-square-mile, glacially carved valley with some of the world's highest waterfalls. But for those who really know the park, hiking through its vast, nearly three-quarter-million-acre wilderness is the only way to truly appreciate all Yosemite has to offer. It's here, as he "tramped" through the park's high country, that John Muir formulated much of his original philosophy about the relationship between humans and nature.

The High Sierra Camps Loop offers access to some of the most strikingly beautiful portions of the Yosemite wilderness. The park provides a series of six "camps"—clusters of large, semipermanent tents and common areas—spaced an easy day's hike apart. The camps are located such that they offer a six-day loop that totals about 50 miles (though you can easily tack on extra mileage on some very tempting side trails). Each tent has four to six dormitory-style beds with mattresses

LOCATION
California, United States

LENGTH
50+ miles

ACCOMMODATIONS
Commercial: No
Huts/refuges: Yes
Backpacking/camping: Yes

BAGGAGE TRANSFER AVAILABLE
No

OPTION TO WALK SECTIONS
Some

DEGREE OF CHALLENGE
Moderate

(ABOVE) A short (and worthwhile) detour takes walkers along the John Muir Trail through gorgeous Lyell Canyon.

(ABOVE RIGHT) Trails connecting the High Sierra Camps are well marked and maintained.

and pillows, and a wood stove. Employees, most of them energetic young men and women, prepare family-style dinners and breakfasts and serve them in large, canvas-sided structures. Showers are available at three of the camps (May Lake, Sunrise, and Merced Lake, if the water supply is sufficient), though a dip in one of the many (admittedly icy) lakes and streams along the trail may be an even better alternative. All camps have restroom facilities. By using the camps, you can backpack through the Yosemite wilderness without having to carry a backpack! Of course, you'll need a day pack for essentials such as a rain jacket, warm outerwear, lunches (you can ask the camps to pack one for you each day), maps, snacks, etc.

The classic High Sierra Camps Loop starts at Tuolumne Meadows Lodge, the largest of the camps and the only one accessible by car. The trail crosses Tioga Road and enters the wilderness, going northwest through spectacular Tuolumne Meadows with views to the south of the dramatic Cathedral Range. The trail then follows the Tuolumne River as it descends to Glen Aulin High Sierra Camp. Glen Aulin means "beautiful valley," and the camp is adjacent to a waterfall and pool on the Tuolumne River. Portions of this section of the hike are on the John Muir Trail and the Pacific Crest Trail.

The hike to May Lake High Sierra Camp is varied, sometimes passing deep in the coniferous forest and often crossing open granite expanses with breathtaking views of the High Sierra peaks to the south and west. When we reached May Lake after a long walk, we revived ourselves by soaking our feet in the lake's cold waters. (Cold water and tired feet make an unbeatable combination!)

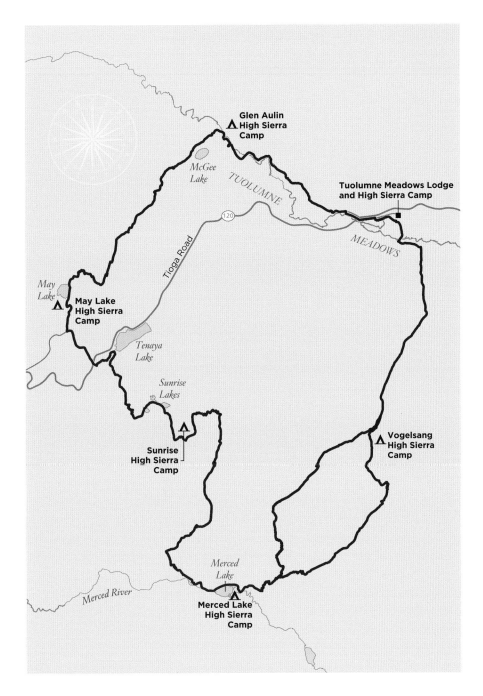

The hike to Sunrise High Sierra Camp offers marvelous views of large and beautiful Tenaya Lake as the trail descends to cross the Tioga Road. The trail then climbs, steeply in places. While you pause to catch your breath, take a moment to appreciate the art of trail-making, and admire the rock steps you're using. At the junction with the trail to Clouds Rest, take a short, informal trail to the west that dead ends and offers unusual and striking views of Half Dome and Yosemite Valley. Back on the main trail, pass several lakes and you'll soon reach Sunrise High Sierra Camp, perched on the edge of vast, alpine Sunrise Meadow.

The walk to Merced Lake High Sierra Camp descends for much of its distance, eventually joining the Merced River and following it to the outlet of Merced Lake. The camp, the oldest and remotest of those in the High Sierra, is located on the northern shoreline of the lake. Of course, the descent to Merced Lake suggests the climb that's needed to reach Vogelsang High Sierra Camp, located at the base of Vogelsang and Fletcher Peaks. This is the highest of the camps and is known for the sunset alpenglow on its surrounding summits.

The final day of the six-day loop descends by Evelyn and Ireland Lakes, and then offers views into serene Lyell Canyon as it returns to your starting point at Tuolumne Meadows Lodge. But before you walk the last mile or so, take at least a little time to walk up Lyell Canyon, one of the truly magical places in the park.

The landscape of the High Sierra Camps Loop is classic high-country Yosemite: mountains approaching 14,000 feet, smooth granite domes, spacious meadows that support a rich stock of wildflowers, and deep pine forests. This is a textbook illustration of glaciers making landscapes—see the evidence for yourself in the granite domes, the smooth glacial polish on many of the rock

The High Sierras are justifiably famous for wildflowers.

surfaces, the U-shaped valleys, glacial lakes, glacial erratics (large rocks that have been dropped by the glaciers in their retreat), and in the striations on the rocks made by the glaciers as they advanced. Visitors enjoy seeing black bears, mule deer, marmots, pikas, and a variety of birds. Common showy flowers include alpine columbine, Indian paintbrush, and snow plant.

The history of the High Sierra Camps is closely tied to the National Park Service. The NPS's first director, Stephen Mather, established the camps in 1916; Mather negotiated an agreement with a private company to build a series of mountain "chalets" in the high country of Yosemite with the objective of providing wider public access to this area of the park. The company was not financially successful, and in 1918 closed the three locations it had built. The 1920s saw the building of additional camps, and the last one was added in 1961. The High Sierra Camps are controversial because some wilderness advocates think their comfort and convenience are anathema to the ideal of wilderness. Moreover, pack stock handle resupplying, causing environmental damage to the trails and meadows and conflicting with hikers. These issues must be balanced against the value of the camps in providing access to the park and building a strong constituency for the national parks. Today camp management works to limit environmental impacts. For instance, social trails are being restored to their natural states, recycling and composting are being used where possible, solar-powered composting toilets have been added at some locations, and the use of linens has been discontinued to reduce the number of mules needed to carry items in and out of the camps.

The High Sierra Camps are so popular that there's a lottery for their use. Entries must be made in November and results are released in January. However, there are often cancellations and open reservations start in April. We didn't enter the lottery the year we walked the loop, but found enough openings to patch together an itinerary as long as we started at the first available camp and used the shuttle bus along Tioga Road to reposition ourselves. Because the cost of operating the camps is high, so are the fees—over $150 per person per night (in the early days, the cost was $1 per night and $1 per meal). If you prefer to do a more conventional backpacking trip around the loop, you must reserve a permit from the National Park Service, and a limited number of backpackers can arrange to eat meals in the dining tents. This part of Yosemite is not called the "high country" for nothing—elevations along the trail range from 7,800 feet to 10,300 feet, making the season for the camps short, usually from mid-June to mid-September. A free shuttle bus runs along the Tioga Road and this enables walkers to do section hikes.

We've already admitted our love of the Sierra, and we have a special place in our hearts for Yosemite. Walking the wilderness portions of the park (nearly 95 percent of the park) can be life-changing; it was for us. The High Sierra Camps Loop is an unusual opportunity to walk some of Yosemite's most beautiful landscapes in a way that is less taxing than conventional backpacking. If using the camps is not appealing or you're not able to book the dates you need, then the loop can be done as a marvelous backpacking trip. In either case, we're confident that this loop will wind up at or near the top of your list of best hikes.

The High Sierra Camps are clusters of semipermanent tents that sleep four to six people; each of the six camp locations includes a large dining area.

MADE FOR WALKING

Where do trails come from?

As Robert Macfarlane notes in his book *The Old Ways; A Journey on Foot*, some trails are artifacts from quite a long time ago: the tracks of wildlife or the travel routes of indigenous people, explorers, and settlers. Macfarlane writes that "Many regions still have their old ways, connecting place to place, leading over passes or round mountains, to church or chapel, river or sea."

Trails often represent the "least cost" route between destinations—shelter and food, for example, or connections among settlements. However, most of the trails we now use were built explicitly for walking (and other uses as well—more about that in a moment). And they've been remarkably successful in offering access to many millions of walkers each year. But to accommodate large numbers of walkers, a science and art of trail-building and maintenance has developed, along with a very large network of agencies, organizations, and volunteers that have built and maintain the trails we describe in this book—and the hundreds of thousands of miles of other trails all over the world.

Trails must be carefully designed, built, and maintained to ensure they're sustainable—that they can withstand the footsteps of many walkers over a long period of time. Good trail design and layout are imperative. Of course, a good trail connects important points of interest (e.g., natural features, historic sites) and associated views. Attractive trail locations include along ridgelines, on the tops of bluffs and cliffs, and on naturally occurring benches along streams. Other types of locations should be avoided if possible, including very rocky or steep slopes and wetlands. Stream crossings should be considered carefully to determine if they're needed, feasible, and safe. Road crossings also need careful consideration; they

can be useful for access, but also dangerous to walkers and can diminish the quality of the walking experience.

Of course, many trails must address changes in elevation; this change in topography adds interest, but also creates challenges in controlling erosion. Trails on grades of less than 5 percent (a rise of 5 feet over a horizontal distance of 100 feet) probably need no special design features. Trails with grades of 5 to 10 percent need special attention to keep water from draining along the trail tread and causing erosion. If the trail is on a side slope, the surface of the trail can be "outsloped" to discourage water from collecting on the trail. Otherwise, short grade dips can be constructed at periodic intervals, or a system of water bars can be installed. Generally, trails should not exceed a 10-percent grade. Switchbacks can be used to

Trails must be carefully designed, built, and maintained to ensure they're sustainable—that they can withstand the footsteps of many walkers over a long period of time. (Zion Rim-to-Rim)

keep grades low even when the trail must climb a steep slope, and short, steep sections of trail often include rock or wooden steps. Generally, trails should not be flat, as this allows water to collect on the trail, saturating soils and making them susceptible to erosion. Flat sections of trails often are surfaced with rocks, or wooden planking.

Walkers have a responsibility to keep trails sustainable. For example, walkers should generally stay on maintained trails to avoid unnecessary trampling of soil and vegetation. It's best not to walk around wet areas and widen the trail. Moreover, walking off trails leads to networks of "social trails" that encourage other walkers to follow. Walkers should refrain from "shortcutting" switchbacks and tampering with trail blazes, cairns, and other trail markings.

Many trails are used by a variety of recreationists, including mountain bikers and equestrians. We encourage you to be as tolerant of other users as possible. Most are there to enjoy many of the same benefits as you—to enjoy the out of doors, to get some exercise, to be with their families and friends, etc. Try to accommodate other types of users—step off the trail for stock and don't "spook" them, don't block the trail for faster-moving bikers, etc. Hopefully, they'll respect you as well. We're likely to have more trails if all trail users can cooperate and speak with one voice.

You can do a great deal of good by directly supporting sustainable trails. The reality is that much of the work necessary to build and maintain trails is done by volunteers and nonprofit organizations such as the Appalachian Mountain Club, the Student Conservation Association, American Trails, the American Hiking Society, Ramblers, and many others.

There are a number of folk heroes in trail-building history. For example, Bill Bryson, in his wildly popular and funny book, *A Walk in the Woods*, pays tribute to Myron Avery and his work to make the Appalachian Trail a reality:

He mapped it out, bullied and cajoled clubs into producing volunteer crews, and personally superintended the construction of hundreds of miles of path. He extended its planned length from 1,200 miles to well over 2,000, and before he finished he had walked every inch of it. In under seven years, using volunteer labor, he built a 2,000-mile trail through mountain wilderness. Armies have done less than this.

Alfred Wainwright enjoys a similar legendary status in England.

Consider joining trail organizations, donating to them, and even working on trail crews. It's hard but satisfying work. At the very least, when you pass people doing work along the trail, be sure to thank them for their good service.

Volunteers and nonprofit organizations such as the Student Conservation Association and the American Hiking Society do much of the work necessary to build and maintain trails. Consider joining trail organizations, donating to them, and working on trail crews. (High Sierra Camps Loop)

The Kii Peninsula is isolated and filled with mountains, making the area ideal for self-reflection.

Kumano Kodo

Japanese has the reputation of being one of the most difficult languages on earth, and reading it is challenging for people used to a phonetic alphabet. We had to be especially careful when reading Japanese signs to make sure that the characters matched the ones in our guidebook. We thought we might have some special challenges navigating on the Kumano Kodo once we reached the small towns where we would spend the night, but we had no problem at all as local people were so helpful. For example, when we entered Takahara, where we had our first lodging, we passed a small group of older women who were socializing and enjoying the late afternoon sun. We exchanged greetings, continued on, and then realized two of the women had broken off from the group and were gently "herding" us toward our guesthouse. With a few hand gestures and much smiling and bowing, they gracefully helped us find our way . . . even though we hadn't indicated that we needed assistance. This was just an example of the kindness Japanese people show to visitors (or perhaps it's simply a more pragmatic solution to getting tourists to the correct spot initially, rather than dealing with them later on). But these women knew where we should go and adroitly helped us make a few turns to assure success. Fortunately, we knew how to say *arigatou* (thank you), as this was a phrase we used often.

~

THE CAMINO DE SANTIAGO across northern Spain has become increasingly popular thanks to several successful books and films showcasing the route. Because we'd enjoyed walking it so much (and described it in our book *Walking Distance*), we were pleased to learn of the Kumano Kodo, another important pilgrimage route on the other side of the world. In fact, the Camino and Kumano Kodo are the only pilgrimage routes to have received World Heritage Site status.

Despite their obvious differences in geography, culture, and religious doctrine, the two routes share much in common, including a history of a thousand years or more, the universal search for

LOCATION
Japan

LENGTH
Variable (up to two weeks)

ACCOMMODATIONS
Commercial: Yes
Huts/refuges: No
Backpacking/camping: No

BAGGAGE TRANSFER AVAILABLE
Yes

OPTION TO WALK SECTIONS
Yes

DEGREE OF CHALLENGE
Moderate

Much of the walk traverses magical-seeming cedar forests with pockets of bamboo.

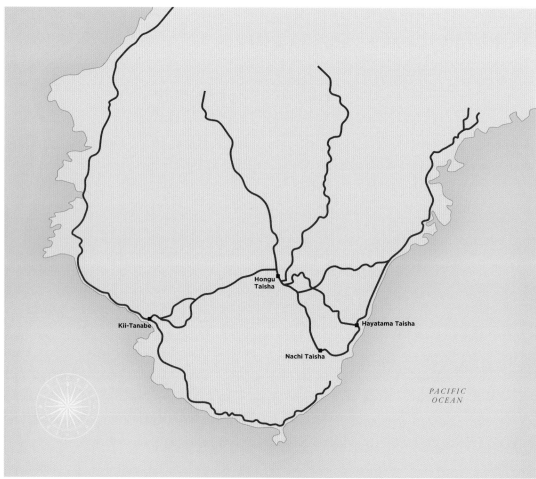

PACIFIC OCEAN

Hongu Taisha

Kii-Tanabe

Hayatama Taisha

Nachi Taisha

spiritual meaning, and an opportunity to test oneself against physical hardship (well, not so much nowadays) and solitude. Both offer rewards far beyond what is asked. In fact, we were especially intrigued at an interpretive sign at one of the Kumano Kodo visitor centers that addressed the similarities of these ancient pilgrimage routes, suggesting that "Perhaps the simple process of walking these trails and sharing fundamental human experiences can bring cultures together and offer hints of how to reach the elusive goal of world peace."

The Kumano Kodo is a 200-mile network of pilgrimage routes through the mountains of Japan's Kii Peninsula, about 120 miles south of Kyoto, and traverses one of the remotest and most mystical areas of Japan. The area is sparsely populated, heavily forested, and includes deep valleys, rivers, waterfalls, hot springs, agricultural areas, and rural villages. But most importantly it includes three major shrines: Hongu Taisha, Hayatama Taisha, and Nachi Taisha. Seven routes can be taken to visit some or all of these shrines, the most popular of which is Nakahechi, the approximately 55-mile route that we chose.

Though visiting the shrines is a vital element of the pilgrimage, the walk itself is equally important. The spiritual heritage of Japan is rich and complex, including elements of Buddhism, Confucianism, Taoism, and native Shintoism. The resulting Shugendo borrows from these and can be translated as the "path of training to achieve spiritual powers." It's a form of nature worship that's centered on an ascetic, mountain-dwelling practice that's at least partly derived from the sacrifice and hardships associated with being in nature. The steep, isolated mountains of the Kii Peninsula are an ideal place to practice this worldview.

The Kumano Kodo has been a major center for pilgrimage for centuries, first by Imperial and aristocratic families beginning at the end of the eighth century. Pilgrims traditionally left from Kyoto with support parties numbering in the hundreds and walked for a month or more. After a few centuries, the pilgrimage evolved into a sharply more democratic phenomenon, open to all levels of society, regardless of gender, class, or sect.

As with the Camino de Santiago, the Kumano Kodo is experiencing a contemporary revival. However, we saw very few walkers, though the shrines were crowded with mostly Japanese visitors traveling by bus and private vehicle. Just as it was conventional for pilgrims on the Camino to be dressed in a robe and carry a staff, a gourd to hold water, and a scallop shell signifying they were religious travelers, pilgrims on the Kumano Kodo dressed in white coats, wore large straw sun hats, and carried bamboo walking sticks. Some modern-day walkers continue this tradition (though no one wears the traditional straw sandals). Contemporary pilgrims on the Kumano Kodo carry passports (similar to the credentials carried on the Camino), stamping them at major and minor shrines along the way to validate completion of the journey.

In addition to the three main shrines, the Nakahechi route includes roughly one hundred diverse *oji*, smaller shrines that often required pilgrims to purify or test themselves, perhaps by bathing in a nearby cold mountain stream. Modern pilgrims generally skip the purification and testing, but usually leave a small offering, often a coin or two.

To position for the trip, walkers can take the famous Japanese trains from any metropolitan area to Tanabe. Pilgrims on the Nakahechi route then take a short bus ride from Tanabe to a small visitor center; here we purchased conventional bamboo walking sticks for a nominal fee (we found these useful), acquired our passports, and looked at the interesting exhibits.

The walking route officially starts at Takijiri-oji, a nearby shrine. We walked up into the forest for a few hours; the trail was rough (the only rough stretch we encountered) and steep at times. The

Small fields of rice are planted in openings in the forest.

(ABOVE) Many steeper stretches of the trail are artfully stepped with local stones.

(BELOW) The Kumano Kodo is well-maintained thanks to help from many volunteers.

small village where we spent the night consisted of scattered homes and some active rice fields. We had seen only one other walker that day, but that night encountered a guided group of pilgrims at dinner. Dinner consisted of many small dishes that were even more beautiful than they were tasty, and it was a good thing we'd practiced our chopsticks skills (though we never did learn how to eat the soft tofu). As always, our room had traditional *shoji* (screens) and two futons on *tatami* (straw mats), and we slept soundly on the floor in the traditional manner.

We walked most of the next day through dramatic cedar forests, often with a rich understory of ferns and occasional patches of bamboo. There was much climbing and descending, and steps eased the steepest places. The trail from this point to the end was in beautiful condition thanks to the efforts of local volunteers. That evening we stayed in a modest guesthouse and visited a separate public bath that was segregated by sex. Our dinner was taken at a traditional low table, where we kneeled on the floor and were offered lots of fish dishes, both cooked and raw. We saw fewer than ten pilgrims that day.

The next day was foggy at first, then clear, with more forest walking that ultimately took us to Hongu Grand Shrine. The impressive shrine has been rebuilt several times over its long history due to fires and floods, and is now situated on a hill. Visitors who come by car or bus must ascend a long set of steps leading to the shrine and its multiple buildings. The pavilions are excellent examples of traditional Japanese shrine architecture, including use of natural, unfinished materials, intricate joint work instead of nails, and a gracefully sweeping roof that extends out over the front of the shrine. The site also includes a contemporary visitor center that calls attention to the Kumano Kodo's designation as a World Heritage Site and its spiritual connection to the Camino de Santiago.

From the shrine, we took a local bus to our evening stop, the small town of Yunomine Onsen, with its historic natural hot springs. Yunomine Onsen is a popular tourist destination with multiple options for bathing, as well as cooking eggs, sausages, or vegetables in the thermal waters.

We walked through large and beautiful cedar forests again the next day. The trail included extensive steps, water bars, and retaining walls artfully crafted from local river cobbles. We spent the night in the modest home of a Japanese family. Our final day on the Kumano Kodo included a full day of walking through the forest, with occasional views out to the sea of mountains. We continued to pass by more *oji* and the ruins of several historic teahouses. Toward the end of the day, we got our first views of the Pacific Ocean and walked on to the Nachi shrine and the town of Nachi-Katsura, where we spent the night. The shrine consists of several buildings constructed using traditional Japanese shrine architecture, along with the striking, 436-foot Nachi Waterfall, the highest single-drop waterfall in Japan. There are many guesthouses and restaurants in the town a short walk away.

Our pilgrimage completed, we took a local bus the next day to Katsuura, where we boarded a train for the long ride to Tokyo.

Hikers face a number of logistical considerations in walking the Kumano Kodo, the first of which is language. We had only a few basic words of Japanese and, this being a very rural part of Japan, we encountered almost no English. Japanese characters made reading signs challenging, to say the least. We found only a few signs in English, the principal one being "Not Kumano Kodo" on several potentially confusing side trails; we found this warning cheerfully useful. Despite not sharing a language, we found people to be kind and helpful, and always managed to make our way along the well-marked route without difficulty.

The walk might be best described as moderate in difficulty. Except for the first few miles, the trail is well groomed, but the Kii Mountains range from 3,000 to 6,000 feet in elevation, and there are some sustained climbs. Although the route passes through some small villages, there is little opportunity to resupply. Some accommodations will prepare lunches for walkers if asked; otherwise you should bring some food with you. There is good train service to this region of Japan, and reasonably good local bus service that allows for walking the route in sections. We suggest you make sure you know where you're going each day before setting out, because you'll generally be on your own, unable to ask for directions. We used the services of a local hiking company that made our lodging arrangements and provided a cell phone for questions, but we found we didn't need the phone.

We enjoyed this walk, as it was rich in both nature and culture—the combination of spiritual shrines embedded in the surrounding mountains and forests is powerful. In fact, the document that describes the Kumano Kodo's designation as a World Heritage Site emphasizes the area as an important "cultural landscape," stating:

> ". . . [I]t is not enough to preserve only the shrines and temples; it is also necessary to maintain the surrounding nature in good condition . . . and to conserve the cultural landscape, which has been inherited and nurtured from generation to generation, as part of our proud heritage to be presented to the world."

We appreciate the way in which the Japanese have conserved this natural and cultural resource, and we're glad we experienced it in such an intimate way.

(ABOVE) Along with its three major shrines, the Kumano Kodo also includes nearly a hundred *oji*, or minor shrines.

(BELOW) The Nachi Shrine and its associated waterfall mark the traditional end of the Kumano Kodo.

JOURNEY VERSUS DESTINATION

All walks have two fundamental components: the journey and the destination. But which is more important? Like many seemingly simple questions of this kind, the answer can be complicated. In a strictly practical sense, of course it's important, maybe even imperative, to reach your destination. We've walked many long-distance trails where much depended on reaching the end point of our walk, both on a daily basis and for the trail as a whole. For example, travel arrangements—a reservation for an overnight stay in a hut, catching a flight back home—demanded that we not only arrive at our destination, but that we do so in a timely way. Moreover, it can be immensely satisfying to walk a long-distance trail in its entirety, and that usually means starting at one end and finishing at the other.

But a little research suggests that the journey trumps the destination in many (maybe even most) cases. Many writers have expressed this point of view in eloquent terms. For example, Ernest Hemingway wrote, "It is good to have an end to journey toward; but it is the journey that matters, in the end." Contemporary musician Drake writes, "Sometimes it's the journey that teaches you a lot about the destination." Buddhist monk Thich Nhat Hanh uses a short verse to express this idea powerfully: "I have arrived/I am here/my destination/is in each step." Arianna Huffington writes, "Often by 'taking a walk' we mean that we're not walking to get anywhere in particular. But even when we are walking toward a destination, when we're walking to connect two places, the in-between—the space, the interval—can be more important."

Sometimes this idea is applied more broadly, to happiness and to life in general. "Happiness is a direction, not a place." (Sydney J. Harris); "There is no way to happiness, happiness is the way." (Thich Nhat Hanh); "Focus on the journey, not

Ernest Hemingway wrote, "It is good to have an end to journey towards; but it is the journey that matters, in the end." (Zion Rim-to-Rim)

the destination. Joy is found not in finishing an activity, but in doing it." (Greg Anderson).

Perhaps the best example of the vital importance of the journey is the religious pilgrimage. For example, we recently walked the Camino de Santiago (described in our book *Walking Distance*) and the Camino Portugués, the route to Santiago that starts in Portugal, and the Kumano Kodo (both described in this book). Sure, reaching Santiago is an important marker of success—just ask the hundreds of walkers at the daily pilgrim's mass in the great cathedral that houses the remains of Saint James. But for many people this walk is more about the journey than the destination, and we think that's the way it was intended. This long walk is a test of one's devotion and an opportunity—really an obligation—to think through many of life's more basic and important questions. We met a number of pilgrims along the trail who were at a moment of transition in their lives—graduation from college, loss of a loved one, a change in careers, retirement—and this long walk, this journey, was mostly about finding themselves in the world. When we were at the church offices in Santiago to receive our *compostelas*, we saw a sign on the bulletin board that read, "The longest journey is the journey inward," a quotation from Dag Hammarskjold, Pulitzer Prize-winner and former Secretary General of the United Nations. Walking offers rare opportunities for such inward journeys.

A lot of attention is focused on the destination in the contemporary world, even in the backpacking community. Writer Matt Colon notes the growing emphasis on completing super long-distance trails, such as the Appalachian Trail, in the fastest time. And if that weren't enough, there's also the "triple

After a long journey, pilgrims queue up in Santiago de Compostela to get their certificates of completion from the church offices. (Camino Portugués)

crown"—completing the Appalachian Trail, the Pacific Crest Trail, and the Continental Divide Trail within a calendar year. Colon suggests that this approach to walking, putting more emphasis on pace than place, may be missing the mark, and also "the subtle virtues of slowing down and submitting to the earth-driven cadences of wild places."

So is it mostly about the journey or the destination? Of course the answer is some of both, depending on the context. Why *not* rejoice in reaching your destination? But we think it may be a mistake to get so wrapped up in the destination that you don't enjoy and appreciate the journey.

Maroon Lake reflects the images of 14,000-foot-plus Maroon Peak and North Maroon Peak; perhaps this is the most photographed scene in the Rocky Mountains.

Maroon Bells–Snowmass Wilderness

For a variety of reasons, we were happy to receive an invitation to a wedding in Aspen, Colorado. We were delighted to share in the festive weekend itself, and excited that the celebrations were to be in such a beautiful part of the country. To put the icing on the (wedding) cake, so to speak, Aspen is the gateway town to the Maroon Bells–Snowmass Wilderness, famous for its wildflowers and 14,000-foot peaks. Why not stay on after the wedding to walk in this place, which had been on our "to do" list for so long? It worked out beautifully—we thoroughly enjoyed the wedding and then went off to do our wonderful four-day backpacking trip. We tell this story because it's a good example of how we try to take maximum advantage of travel. We encourage you to look for opportunities to add on walks when you're traveling for pleasure or work, as our walk in the Maroon Bells–Snowmass Wilderness exemplifies.

LOCATION
Colorado, United States

LENGTH
27+ miles

ACCOMMODATIONS
Commercial: No
Huts/refuges: No
Backpacking/camping: Yes

BAGGAGE TRANSFER AVAILABLE
No

OPTION TO WALK SECTIONS
Some

DEGREE OF CHALLENGE
High

THE MAROON BELLS–SNOWMASS WILDERNESS includes what may be the most photographed mountains in North America. Yes, that's a big statement, but so are the mountains; six peaks rise above 14,000 feet, and nine passes are over 12,000 feet. This is quintessential Colorado Rocky Mountain high country. The Maroon Bells are part of the Elk Mountain Range, which, in turn, is part of the Rocky Mountains. The Maroon Bells–Snowmass Wilderness totals nearly 200,000 acres and is managed by the US Forest Service; its designation as wilderness ensures that the area is protected from development. This area has nearly all the elements that exemplify the Rockies—high, rugged peaks, an exuberant display of wildflowers (perhaps the very best in all the Rocky Mountains), long, glaciated valleys, forests of spruce and aspen, glistening alpine lakes, rushing creeks with waterfalls big and small, an appealing array of wildlife, and a network of trails with five-star campsites.

The area takes its name from distinctive, bell-shaped Maroon Peak and its twin, North Maroon Peak, both more than 14,000 feet, and from the massive snow accumulations characteristic of the higher regions of the Rockies. The mountains contain an iron-bearing mineral that oxidizes (rusts)

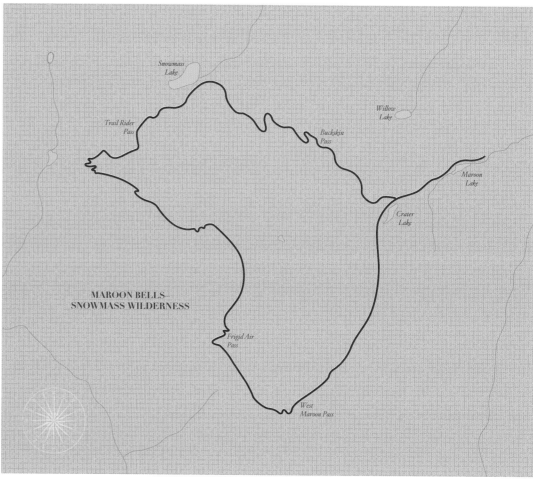

The Maroon Bells–Snowmass Wilderness features many high-elevation lakes that are ideal for camping.

when exposed, and this gives them their characteristic reddish-brown color. As in many mountain ranges the geology is complex, including deposition of 10,000 feet of sediments from ancient lakes and seas, geologic uplift and faulting, and then erosion from weather and water. More recently, glaciers formed as the climate cooled, and these glaciers flowed and ground through the mountains, giving form to the characteristic U-shaped valleys.

The wilderness includes a network of 175 miles of trails, offering an array of hiking itineraries. Since this was our first hike in the area, we chose what's called the Four Pass Loop. This 27-mile trail leads over four 12,000+-foot passes and showcases many of the attractions for which the Rocky

Mountains are justly famous. This backpacking trip takes about four days, though a layover day or two is well justified because the hiking is challenging, because there is so much beauty to behold, because there are several interesting side trails, or because of all of the above.

The hike starts at the end of Maroon Creek Road, a short drive from Aspen. Maroon Lake is a five-minute walk from the parking area and was formed by rock slides and a giant beaver dam. Sitting up straight and proud behind the lake are Maroon Peak and North Maroon Peak, their reflections glistening on the surface of the lake. The mythology suggests that this is the most popular scene to photograph in the Rocky Mountains, and you'll understand why. Wow! Early morning and the end of the day are the best times to capture this image as the wind is less likely to wrinkle the surface of the lake.

Follow the trail around the right side of the lake for almost 2 miles to enter the wilderness and reach Crater Lake, which demands more photographs. This is an easy, popular walk. At Crater Lake it's decision time; the Four Pass Loop can be done in a clockwise or counterclockwise direction. To the right you pass through Minnehaha Gulch, then above tree line, and finally steeply up to Buckskin Pass at 12,500 feet, the first of the four 12,000+-foot passes. The last mile or two takes you through large expanses of alpine meadow and tundra carpeted with flowers and cut by small mountain streams. Tree line is about 11,400 feet—this is the point at which cold temperatures, drying winds, and a short growing season don't allow for growth of trees. There's often a large snow cornice

(ABOVE) Note the classic U-shaped valley, which is characteristic of glaciated landscapes.

(ABOVE RIGHT) The four 12,000-foot-plus passes along the Four Pass Loop offer long and inviting views of the Maroon Bells–Snow Mass Wilderness.

blocking the very top of the pass, so look for a smaller side trail that bypasses this obstacle. The views from the pass are worth the climb.

If you decide to go left at Crater Lake, it's a longer hike to West Maroon Pass at 12,500 feet. Once again, the views of the surrounding mountains and lakes are worth the burning in your calves (and lungs).

Once you crest either Buckskin Pass or West Maroon Pass, the route that connects them is a brilliant mix of rugged mountains, rich meadows, mountain streams, and beautiful lakes that encircle the Elk Mountains. There are lots of good campsites, and large Snowmass Lake offers some of the best spots. Of course, there are still two more passes to negotiate, Trail Rider Pass at 12,400 feet, and aptly named Frigid Air Pass at 12,380 feet.

Black bears inhabit these mountains, but they are rarely seen. Other iconic animals include bighorn sheep, mule deer, elk, coyote, beaver, marmot, and pika. You'll see many species of birds, including golden eagles and red-tailed hawks; Steller's jays will want to share your campsite with you—resist the temptation to feed them. Common and showy wildflowers include the Colorado blue columbine (the state flower), paintbrush, fireweed, cinquefoil, chiming bells, and many more. Many types of trees grow here, depending on water and elevation. Riparian zones support willows, alder, river birch, and the stands of aspen for which Colorado is famous. Higher elevations include spruce and fir.

This area was explored for minerals in the late nineteenth century, with a silver boom starting in 1879. A railroad reached Aspen in 1887, but the silver market crashed in the early 1890s and most people abandoned the area. Contemporary hikers are likely to come upon the ruins of prospectors' cabins and other evidence of this colorful period. After World War II, Aspen developed into a major ski resort, and each year attracts hundreds of thousands of skiers as well as the rich and famous.

This is a challenging hike due to altitude and substantial climbs over 12,000+-foot passes. It's wise to spend a few days in the vicinity to acclimate to the altitude. This a backpacking trip only, though some of the nicest portions of the hike (from Maroon Lake to Crater Lake, and then on to either Buckskin Pass or West Maroon Pass) can be done as day hikes. The trail can be rough and rocky and there are several creeks to be forded—these can be dangerous if water levels are high so exercise caution. The hiking season is short—usually from mid-July to late September. The Maroon Bells are rightly a popular tourist attraction, so don't expect much solitude until you're over the first of the high passes. This is a fragile natural area that accommodates a lot of use, so it's especially important to employ low-impact hiking and camping practices, including storing food in bear canisters. Afternoon thunderstorms are frequent; a good strategy is to cross high passes early in the day to avoid exposure to lightning. Mosquitoes can be annoying in the early summer.

Due to the popularity of Maroon and Crater Lakes, the Forest Service has established a mandatory free shuttle bus system that connects Aspen and the Maroon Lake parking area; it runs from mid-June to October. Backpackers are allowed to drive their cars and leave them at the Maroon Lake parking area, but the shuttles make this unnecessary. There are lots of accommodations in the town of Aspen, but they tend to be expensive: the town of Glenwood Springs is farther from Maroon Lake, but accommodations are more affordable. Less expensive still are several drive-in campgrounds in the area operated by the Forest Service. Information about hiking in the Maroon Bells–Snowmass Wilderness can be obtained from the Forest Service by phone, over the Internet, and at the Aspen and Carbondale ranger stations.

This is a world-class hike through the essence of the famous Rocky Mountains. Like many things in life, it requires some preparation and effort, but the rewards are ample; this is a hike you'll celebrate for the rest of your life. Prepare yourself with physical training and backpacking experiences, then relish in this unforgettable wilderness trip.

The Maroon Bells–Snowmass Wilderness is nearly 200,000 acres of classic Rocky Mountain scenery that includes high rugged peaks, exuberant displays of wildflowers, long glaciated valleys, forests of spruce and aspen, glistening alpine lakes, rushing creeks, an appealing array of wildlife, and a network of trails with five-star campsites.

"SINCE YOU ASKED . . ."

We're often asked how to do a long-distance or multi-day walk: how to prepare, make arrangements, select clothing and gear, find commercial services if needed, and so forth. Like walking itself, most of it's pretty straightforward, and preparing for a walk is a vital and enjoyable part of the walking experience.

Prepare for a long-distance walk by practicing walking—more often and farther. But not necessarily faster: as Frédéric Gros writes, "The lesson was that in walking the authentic sign of assurance is a good slowness." Avoid the too-common rationalization that you'll undergo most of the needed physical training en route, preparing for day two by walking day one, etc. By walking more in your everyday life, you'll gain the ability and confidence that comes with knowing that by continuing to place one foot in front of the other you *will* reach your destination. Better yet, you'll enjoy the journey.

Increase your daily walking slowly; be patient—it's much better to have small improvements from week to week than to overdo it at the beginning and end up discouraged or injured. When the situation allows, carry a pack to get used to it and enhance the aerobic quality of walking, and include some walking on varied terrain. Walk in all sorts of weather to get used to the experience.

Choosing which trail (or portion of trail) to walk can be engaging and enjoyable, and sometimes we're asked, "How do you know about all these trails?" The answer is simple: The more you involve yourself in the walking/hiking community, the more "plugged in" you become. Everyone loves to talk about where they've been . . . including us! This book offers thirty long-distance and multi-day walks (and our book, *Walking Distance*, suggests thirty more). See, you're already gathering a list.

When we're in the early planning stages, we look online for the walking options in the area we're planning to visit; words such as "walk," "hike," "long-distance" are useful search terms. For well-known trails, there are a plethora of companies that conduct and support walking trips, offering a variety of options from budget to upscale. Some simply provide the "missing pieces"—a ride to the trailhead, for example; others do all the planning for you, offer a guide, and even supply daily snacks. Simply reading what is available commercially helps if you're planning to walk independently. As you begin to focus in on a few alternative walks, then it's time to gather materials (guidebooks, maps) to get more detail.

We wear lightweight, multiuse clothing on our walks; we want to be comfortable but carry as little weight as possible

Nearly all gear you might need for walking trips is subject to the lightweight revolution—packs, sleeping bags and pads, tents, stoves, and even walking shoes. (Cumberland Island National Seashore)

in our packs. And we want our clothes to be field-tested before a trip. The most important item of clothing is boots/shoes. If your feet are happy, chances are the rest of you will be too. Although some outdoor outfitters still push heavy-duty, expedition-type boots made of leather, we don't recommend them (unless you're going on an expedition!). The trend is toward lighter footwear, and we endorse this, often walking in trail running shoes. Wear your new boots/shoes on your training walks; if anything needs to be adjusted, it's best to deal with it at home.

Nearly all the gear you might need for walking trips is subject to the lightweight revolution—packs, sleeping bags and pads, tents, stoves, etc. We highly recommend you consider the lightweight versions of this type of equipment, but be aware it can't be treated with the disregard often shown to heavier, "bulletproof" gear. Avoid the pitfalls of famously overweight packs. Telling the story of her sometimes misadventurous hike on the Pacific Crest Trail in *Wild*, Cheryl Strayed reveals that she called her pack "Monster," while in his book on walking the Pennine Way, *Walking Home: A Poet's Journey*, Simon Armitage calls his "Tombstone."

Even though walking is pretty basic, long-distance and multi-day walking need some preparation and care, and we've developed a more detailed set of guidelines in our book *Walking Distance*. We hope you find it helpful.

We'd like to emphasize two final bits of advice here. First, walk *your* walk—tailor walking to your individual needs and interests. Some people get great satisfaction out of testing themselves, walking challenging trails in long days. But others prefer to linger and stay closer to developed areas, and

Prepare for a long-distance walk by practicing walking, going more often and farther. (Acadia Carriage Roads)

this is just as valid. Some people backpack while others enjoy local inns and B&Bs. Some enjoy planning the logistics of their walks and others prefer to leave the details to commercial companies. How do you want to walk? We find that our tastes change from time to time and from trip to trip, and we've wound up doing many kinds of walks. You'll find this reflected in the trails we describe in this book.

Finally, the most important thing you can bring on a walk is a sense of curiosity about the beautiful and interesting world in which we live. See places and meet people in the intimate way that only walking allows. We've found this wonderfully enjoyable and rewarding, and hope you will too.

The Needles is a rugged place, but trails lead walkers safely and surely through this remarkable landscape.

Needles

We'd arrived the night before in Moab, a tourist-friendly town we like in southeast Utah. Moab serves as the jumping-off point for Canyonlands National Park, our destination. We were up early the next morning—well before the sun—because it's a long drive of about 75 miles to the Needles section of the park, and we wanted to get in a full day of hiking. We drove south for a while, then turned west onto UT 211 for the last 35 miles, traveling one of the most striking drives in the American Southwest. We stopped briefly at Newspaper Rock to see its exuberant display of petroglyphs, and then headed on toward the park. But we just couldn't resist stopping regularly to admire and photograph the dramatic scenery in the rich early-morning light. It was glorious! We passed a series of large, inviting canyons, a few historic ranches with horses grazing in extensive pastures, small streams lined with large cottonwoods that were glowing in yellow and gold fall colors, and iconic geologic formations with colorful names like Sixshooter Peak, Molly's Nipple, and Wooden Shoe Arch. We arrived at the park a few hours later (!) to spectacular views of the spires for which the Needles are named, framed by a classic, deep-blue western sky. We reached our trailhead about midmorning, much later than we'd anticipated, but tingling from the approach to the park. Fortunately, we'd scheduled several days to explore the Needles on foot.

———— ≈ ————

IF THE US NATIONAL PARKS are "America's crown jewels," then Canyonlands National Park is surely a gem. This national park in southern Utah is composed of vast, high desert split into three geographic "districts" by the Colorado and Green Rivers, the two longest and most historic rivers in the American Southwest. One of these districts, the Needles, is known for the colorful Cedar Mesa sandstone spires rising out of the desert floor, along with a labyrinth of entrenched canyons, stone arches, potholes, remnants of Native American occupation, and vast expanses of slickrock. With

LOCATION
Utah, United States

LENGTH
Variable (up to a week)

ACCOMMODATIONS
Commercial: No
Huts/refuges: No
Backpacking/camping: Yes

BAGGAGE TRANSFER AVAILABLE
No

OPTION TO WALK SECTIONS
Yes

DEGREE OF CHALLENGE
Moderate

its nearly 75 miles of trails, this is a hiker's paradise that demands several days (some might say years) of exploration. The spires that characterize this area were formed by fractures in the sandstone caused by movement along a deep, underlying layer of salt. Erosion of these fractures by rain and snow has resulted in the present-day pinnacles.

Many of the trails in the Needles form a dense network of interconnected routes that climb in and out of canyons and along slickrock benches and ridges. This system of trails offers a great variety of options, all beautiful. Nearly everyone would agree that the loop trail to Chesler Park is the glamour hike. Chesler Park is a large grassy area ringed by the area's iconic spires, and the combination is especially dramatic. The Joint Trail forms part of this loop, a quarter-mile walk through a deep and narrow fracture; in places, you may have to squeeze your way through, but it's lots of fun. Even though this is a fairly long hike (about 11 miles), we recommend adding a short side trail to Chesler Park Overlook, as it offers an impressive elevated perspective of Chesler Park and the variety of sandstone formations around it. There are several designated campsites in this area.

Another favorite walk connects Big Spring Canyon Trail and Squaw Canyon Trail. This 7.5-mile loop is relatively easy and offers a great introduction to the Needles landscape. Highlights include walking over great expanses of slickrock, two beautiful canyons that often have flowing streams, especially in the spring, and great views of the surrounding landscape. Another alternative in the same area is the 10.8-mile hike through Big Spring Canyon to the Elephant Canyon parking area, but you'll need transportation to get from one trailhead to the other. Much of this walk is on slickrock benches

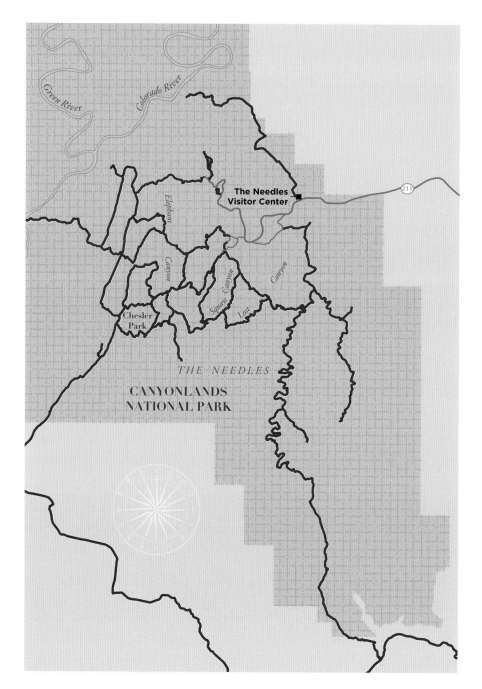

and mesa tops that offer views down into several attractive canyons. You have to climb two ladders to get over the pass that separates Big Spring Canyon and Elephant Canyon; most people would probably rate this trail as at least moderately difficult.

Other distinctive hikes include those to Confluence Overlook and Druid Arch. The trail to Confluence Overlook is a little less interesting than many of the other trails in the Needles, but the destination is awe-inspiring—the trail ends at a steep, thousand-foot cliff with striking views of the point at which the Green River flows into the Colorado River. Be careful—the viewing area is not fenced. The view includes parts of the remote Maze district of the park and the popular Island in the Sky district. The trail passes over some slickrock areas, but most is more ordinary dirt path. You'll encounter some "Canyonlands mushrooms," huge rocks that erosion has shaped into this classic form. This out-and-back trail is 10 miles round-trip over dry, open country, and probably not suitable in the heat of summer. The 11-mile trail to Druid Arch combines portions of the trail to Chesler Park and goes through Elephant Canyon, but adds another few miles to get to impressive Druid Arch, a rare double sandstone arch. The last half-mile is steep, and requires climbing one ladder and doing some scrambling over loose rock. Druid Arch is spectacular and, despite its challenging terrain, this trail is one of the most popular in the park.

This part of Utah receives an average of only 8 inches of rain a year, making it very arid. Despite this, plants and animals are diverse and interesting. Many of the flat, open areas are covered in grasses (some areas have been taken over by invasive cheatgrass) and sagebrush. Dominate trees include shrubby pinyon pines and Utah junipers, and big cottonwoods in canyon bottoms. Trees in this environment must be resilient, some growing out of the smallest cracks in the sandstone. Junipers have

(ABOVE LEFT) Chesler Park is a large area ringed by iconic Needles spires, and the combination of grassland and these geologic features is especially dramatic.

(ABOVE) An ancient granary is a manifestation of Native American occupation of this area.

(ABOVE) The unusual Joint Trail is just wide enough for hiker and backpack.

(ABOVE RIGHT) A network of trails invites walkers into the beautiful and interesting Needles section of Canyonlands National Park.

adapted to periodic drought by limiting growth to a few branches, letting others die. You'll find lots of prickly pear cactus and narrowleaf yucca, as well as large patches of cryptobiotic soil crust, a complex groundcover that binds the soil together and fixes nitrogen, contributing to fertility. This dark soil crust is an important ecological component of the landscape that takes hundreds of years to develop, but that can be destroyed by just a few footsteps; be sure to recognize this biologic soil and walk around, not through it. In years that have more precipitation, wildflowers decorate much of the park. Animals include bighorn sheep, peregrine falcons, squirrels, several kinds of snakes, and lots of lizards.

Archeological evidence confirms that the present-day park was home to Native Americans known as the Ancestral Puebloans. It's thought that these people migrated to this area about AD 950, grew corn, beans, and squash and supplemented this diet by hunting and gathering, and then left the area in the late thirteenth century, probably because of prolonged drought. You can see a granary where they stored corn on the short Roadside Ruin Trail; this interpretive trail identifies plants and explains how they were used by Native Americans. Though Newspaper Rock, one of the largest known collections of rock art in the world, is not in the park, it's worth a stop on the road that leads to and from the Needles.

There are two visitor centers that can be very useful to hikers, one just off the main street in Moab (this is a multiagency center that offers advice about recreation opportunities in the larger region) and the other just beyond the official entrance to the Needles. We've found the rangers and volunteers to be very helpful and knowledgeable about local conditions. Hiking in the Needles can be challenging due to soft sand in some canyon bottoms and the need to scramble in some places, including using ladders that have been placed by the National Park Service. As the word "slickrock" implies, these areas can be slippery when wet. Trails are usually well marked by cairns. Elevations in the park are high, frequently over 5,000 feet, so it might take some time to become acclimated. Be liberal in estimating hiking times so you don't get caught out after darkness sets in. Water is very scarce in the Needles so you'll need to take ample water with you on your hikes—a few quarts per day per person—more in summer.

There are three basic ways to do multi-day hikes in the Needles. The first is to backpack, for which you'll need a permit from the National Park Service; there are many designated campsites. The second is do a series of day hikes while camped inside or just outside the park. Squaw Flat Campground is one of the sweetest in the national parks, but there are only 26 campsites, so you better be there early; some of the hikes described above start from Loop B of the campground.

Because there are few large trees in the arid Needles, cairns are used to mark the trails.

The funky Needles Outpost is just outside the park's boundary, and offers both camping and the only commercial services around. The third option is to do a series of day hikes while staying the night in either Moab or Monticello. You'll wind up doing a lot of driving on this alternative, but remember that the drive is spectacular. Best times to hike in the Needles are spring and fall; summer can be very hot, and winter cold and snowy

The Needles is a world-class landscape of canyons, spires, and slickrock, overlaid with a dense network of nearly 75 miles of hiker-friendly trails. We've hiked in the Needles on several occasions and can't seem to get enough of it. We recommend it in the highest terms—just allow plenty of time for the scenic drive in and out of the park.

TRAILBLAZING

Everyone knows the fairy tale of Hansel and Gretel, and the clever way they made a trail using white pebbles and bread crumbs to find their way back through the forest. But the idea of marking a trail didn't originate with Hansel and Gretel. Humans have been using this basic technique—using markers other than bread crumbs, of course—for thousands of years. Most trails are marked in some way to assist hikers. In fact, trails that are part of the US national trails system are required to be marked. There are three basic types of markers: blazes, cairns, and posts.

Blazes are marks on trees and can be of three types. Most of the original blazes were vertical cuts made with a hatchet or ax through a tree's bark, and these can still be seen on many older trails. However, increasing concern for the health of trees has led to the predominance of painted blazes. Typically, tree bark is smoothed (but not breached) and a vertical rectangular mark is painted on the surface. The third type of blaze is a metal, wooden, or plastic insignia that's used in place of (or sometimes in addition to) a painted blaze. For example, national trails in Britain are marked with the symbol of an acorn. Painted and insignia blazes can be applied to any handy surface, including trees, utility poles, fences, and buildings.

The Camino Portugués is liberally blazed with yellow arrows.

Blazes can have many properties that enhance their usefulness. For example, the color of blazes can signify important information. Many long-distance trails in the United States are blazed in white, and this differentiates them from side or other connecting trails that might be blazed in blue, orange, or some other color. Long-distance trails in Europe and elsewhere may use multicolored stripes as blazes—these blazes are associated with particular trails and are used consistently along the trail.

Blazes can also be presented in alternative configurations as shown in the accompanying illustration; these configurations convey important information. Most blazes are simply vertical rectangles and merely mark the trail. However, other blazes mark the beginnings and endings of trails, turns in the trail, and spur trails. Generally, a double blaze (one beside or sometimes on top of the other) suggests that hikers look ahead carefully as something—a turn, an adjoining trail, etc.—is about to happen. Paying attention to blazes can make wayfinding much easier and contributes to hiker safety.

CONTINUE STRAIGHT	START OF TRAIL	RIGHT TURN
SPUR LEADING TO A DIFFERENT TRAIL	END OF TRAIL	LEFT TURN

The configuration of trail blazes offers useful information for wayfinding.

The second basic type of trail marker is cairns. Not all trails are in forests, and so small piles of rocks are often used to mark routes above tree line or in open landscapes such as areas of bedrock, meadows, moors, and tundra. In his fascinating book, *Cairns: Messengers in Stone*, David Williams outlines the very long history of human use of cairns as one of the earliest forms of communication.

The question of which way to go is one of the central reasons that humans have mounded up rocks for thousands of years. We have done so to let others know where we were going, to enable others to follow or find their own way, and to provide information for returning.

For example, the Inuit people of the Arctic used the distinctive *inuksuk* (often appearing in the shape of a human) to mark their routes of travel. The word *cairn* originated in sixteenth-century Scotland and was derived from the Gaelic *carn*, referring to a heap of stones. American poet William Cullen Bryant immortalized the cairn in his poem "Monument Mountain":

And o'er the mould that covered her, the tribe
Built up a simple monument, a cone
Of small loose stones. Thenceforth, all who passed,
Hunter, and dame, and virgin, laid a stone
In silence on the pile. It stands there yet.

Like blazes, alternative configurations of cairns can offer useful information. For example, a stone placed at the side of a cairn is a signal that the trail turns in that direction. A very large cairn often marks the summit of a mountain or the highest point on a trail. Very small cairns—one rock placed on another—are sometimes called "ducks" and simply mark the progress of the trail. Bates cairns are a particular type of cairn that features a "pointer" stone on top, signifying the appropriate direction of travel.

The third type of trail marker is a post set in the ground. These tend to be used sparingly, usually in open country and where there are few stones available to build cairns. The three types of trail markers—blazes, cairns, and posts—are sometimes used together, for example, painted blazes on rocks and posts in forests to mark major trail junctions. Marking systems can vary somewhat from place to place, so pay careful attention to them.

Trail markings help hikers find their way, though the ability to read a map and use a compass and/or GPS is still a useful skill. Of course, you need to pay attention to trail markers, maps, and guidebooks to stay on the trail. John Brierley, author of widely used guidebooks to the Camino de Santiago, wisely advises readers: "When the mind wanders, the feet will follow." It's always a good feeling to see a blaze, cairn, or post when you're not quite sure whether you're on the trail. That's

For centuries, people have been using cairns to mark trails. (Needles)

Posts mark all the national trails in England—note the acorn symbol. (Pennine Way)

why these markings are often called "confidence markers." Simon Armitage expressed the depth of feeling about finding one of these confidence markers while stumbling through the mist on the moors of England's Pennine Way when he wrote, "A minute later, when I find a marker post with the initials PW on it, I don't just want to hug it, I want to marry it and have its children. Being able to put a finger on the map and say with

absolute confidence I AM HERE makes the air smell sweeter and the sandwiches taste fresher." If you haven't seen a trail marker for a while and think you may have wandered off the trail, it's generally recommended that you return to the last trail marker seen and try again.

Trail markers are an important part of hiking, and we should be thankful for them (both literally and sometimes figuratively). However, trail markers are not without some controversy. By definition, trail markers suggest a human presence, but some people hike to escape many of the artifacts of civilization; this is particularly the case in wilderness areas. Trail markers—their type, location, and frequency—should be used thoughtfully to achieve the right balance between convenience and sensitivity to keeping areas natural where appropriate. This issue seems to be particularly challenging as it applies to cairns. It seems to be human nature to add stones to existing cairns, or even to build more cairns. In fact, there's a myth that adding stones to a cairn will bring good luck. But too many cairns can become unsightly, even representing a form of graffiti. Moreover, gathering stones from off the trail can cause impacts to the environment. And improperly located or constructed cairns can lead hikers astray, creating a safety hazard. It's probably best to leave trail marking to the experts who do this good work.

Walkers in Paris pass many traditional businesses, such as this flower shop on Ile de la Cité.

Paris

We'd just returned home from our trip to Paris, where we had walked the city for ten days, enjoying its architecture and monuments and exploring its diverse neighborhoods. Our friends asked us if we had visited the Louvre, gone up the Eiffel Tower, toured Notre Dame, etc. They seemed a little taken aback when we told them how much we'd appreciated the city, but that we hadn't actually gone *in* any of these world-famous attractions. We'd taken a different approach, experiencing these places from the sidewalks, including their natural, historical, and cultural contexts (and avoiding the painfully long lines to enter the attractions as well). At first, we were a tad defensive about our unconventional visit, but then decided we'd spent our time very productively: We walked for ten days, deeply immersed in the "living museum" that *is* Paris.

———— ≈ ————

For centuries, Paris has been "the walking city." Nineteenth-century intellectual and writer Walter Benjamin richly described the life of the *flaneur,* or bohemian, who famously explored the city's nooks and crannies and who went "botanizing on the asphalt." Frédéric Gros, in his book, *A Philosophy of Walking,* writes of the stylish form of urban walking that emerged in Paris and other cities at the time.

With this history in mind, we fashioned a plan to walk Paris. We decided to deepen the experience by living as Parisians, renting an apartment in a residential area, using public transport, shopping at neighborhood stores. Since we speak little French, it may have been more logical to stay in a hotel where the front desk could have helped us with our plans. But being on our own seemed more freeing, and we're glad we made this choice. We never did get the hang of our apartment's combination clothes washing/drying machine, but we did make friends with the owners of the local *boulangerie.* We may not have always been efficient when using public transit, but we were able to use it to get to and from our daily walks. We enjoyed our daily rambles so much we'd sometimes go out again after dinner to experience the city by night.

LOCATION
France

LENGTH
Variable

ACCOMMODATIONS
Commercial: Yes
Huts/refuges: No
Backpacking/camping: No

BAGGAGE TRANSFER AVAILABLE
No

OPTION TO WALK SECTIONS
Yes

DEGREE OF CHALLENGE
Low

(ABOVE) The 70-ton head-and-hand, *L'Écoute* (*Listen*), by Henri de Miller, rests in front of Saint-Eustache Church near Les Halles shopping center; this modern sculpture is popular with both adults and children.

(BELOW) Paris's iconic sidewalk cafes offer thirsty walkers both rest and refreshment—and the opportunity to observe other walkers.

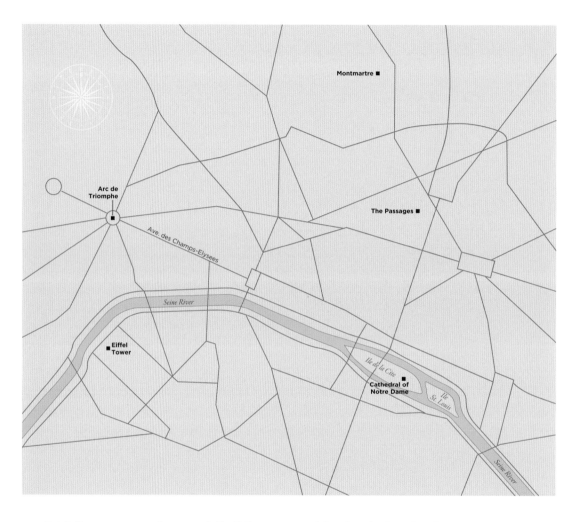

Initially, we expected to carefully follow our guidebook, which offered a series of suggested walks with detailed maps and comprehensive information. But we found this to be too confining—we felt we were spending too much time on the sidewalks reading the book rather than paying attention to what was all around us. A new plan emerged—in the evening we'd select a neighborhood for the following day, rough out the route on our map, and mark the places where we wanted detailed information. We'd reread the general information about the area the next morning, get ourselves to our starting point, and then wander, checking the map and book occasionally so we didn't miss significant buildings or other attractions. One warning: There is so much to see and do in Paris that

it's impossible to cover everything. It's best to start with a general idea of the kinds of things that interest you (arts? buildings? history? parks?) and try to include your "must sees" at the beginning, because we found the more we explored, the more we wanted to explore.

So where did we go? Of course, like most tourists we enjoyed the significant landmarks of Paris, but we appreciated them in a different fashion. And everything in between contributed to the fabric of our walks.

Here's one day: the Louvre is one of the largest museums in the world, and everyone agrees it is absolutely marvelous. We exited the subway at the Louvre stop, where the platform itself showcases impressive artworks. Aboveground, we were able to appreciate (on several occasions and from very different vantage points) the striking setting of the Louvre on the banks of the Seine. The museum is housed in a former palace, the I. M. Pei–designed glass pyramid is featured in its courtyard, and,

(ABOVE LEFT) Walkers can appreciate Norte Dame's flying buttresses, used to support the cathedral's thin walls in the French Gothic style.

(ABOVE) Modern day *flaneurs* can experience all of the iconic monuments of Paris.

(ABOVE) The Seine runs through the heart of Paris, and walkers enjoy the vantage points its banks provide.

(BELOW) Walkers sometimes encounter surprises, such as this tiny pocket park at the very end of the Ile de la Cité.

as we strolled past the *long* lines waiting to get in, we realized the pyramid is viewable through the Arc de Triomphe du Carrousel, which is itself framed by the Louvre. Turning around we enjoyed the Grand Basin, where Parisians were soaking up the sunshine, the Luxor Obelisk on the Place de la Concorde, and the Arc de Triomphe at the top of the Champs-Élysées. The same day included Christmas markets in the Tuileries, strolling past the Eiffel Tower and through its gardens, exploring the embassy area near our apartment, and stumbling upon a sidewalk vendor selling rotisserie chicken and potatoes (our dinner that night). What a grand day!

Another morning we explored the arcades of Paris, covered passages built in the 1820s and 1830s. These "Cathedrals of Commerce," built of iron with glass ceilings, offered heat, light, and shelter to shoppers seeking a variety of goods and services, and all modern-day shopping malls owe their existence to these early precursors. The heyday of the arcades ended with the advent of the department store, but these covered passages remain, most refurbished and again offering their charms to Parisian shoppers (and modern-day *flaneurs*). While walking from one arcade to the next we watched roofers removing historic clay tiles as they remodeled a building; we asked permission to take one of the tiles from the pile of construction debris and have used it as the base for a candle ever since. Its patinated surface speaks to its urban history, it delights more than any candleholder we've ever bought, and reminds us of our good walks through Paris.

Montmartre is the historic arts district. Topped by the white Basilica of the Sacred Heart, this large hill in the eighteenth *arrondissement* (one of many numbered neighborhoods in Paris) has been famous since the latter half of the nineteenth century, when Impressionist painters were attracted to the low rents and congenial atmosphere. In Montmartre's golden days, Picasso, Matisse, Monet, Van Gogh, and many others lived their often colorful lives here. Their works are now formally displayed in the Musée d'Orsay, a grand, refurbished train station on the banks of the Seine. While the museum is undoubtedly worth the wait in line, we experienced the places where these great artists lived and worked. The views over the city are impressive, and we understand why they were such an inspiration—and it was fun to encounter an informal arts market where (perhaps) the next great artists were showing their work.

In the early nineteenth century, parts of Paris were crowded, unhealthy, and dangerous, and these poor conditions served as the crucible for unrest. Napoleon III, self-declared emperor of France, challenged Georges-Eugène Haussmann, prefect (chief administrative officer) of Paris and the surrounding area, to unify and beautify the city, bringing in air and light. Much of what everyone loves about Paris (the wide boulevards, large public spaces, grand buildings, and monuments) are thanks to Haussmann's ambitious plans. By walking so much of the city we were able to appreciate just how grandiose, successful, and enduring Haussmann's plan was.

Sometimes our walks rewarded us with pleasant surprises. After we crossed Pont Neuf, the oldest extant bridge in Paris (1607), we enjoyed the street scenes of the only two natural islands left in the city, Ile de la Cité and Ile Saint-Louis; this was one of our most stunning walks. Avoiding the long queues of visitors waiting for admission, we strolled around the full perimeter of Notre Dame and appreciated its early use of flying buttresses to support the thin walls needed to achieve the French Gothic effect. We enjoyed the sense of history this area evoked. Ile de la Cité is the oldest part of Paris where Romans camped in the third century BC and where Vikings attacked in the mid-ninth century. But we didn't expect to encounter the entertaining street performers, nor did we expect the tiny pocket park at the very end of the island where folks were waiting their turns to be photographed in front of a stunning ginkgo tree in its full fall mantle of gold.

We had another pleasant surprise when walking in Saint-Germain-des-Prés, a tony Left Bank neighborhood with homes and stores for the truly wealthy (with a good dose of the historical mixed in). It was midafternoon on a chilly day and we were debating going in one of the ubiquitous sidewalk cafes for which Paris is famous when we stumbled on a street vendor making crepes. Two warm, chocolate-filled crepes later, we were "good to go," feeling both refreshed and authentic.

As with any walking adventure, the more prepared you are beforehand, the more successful you'll be, but be sure to leave some time in all your walks in Paris for extemporaneous straying. We came to Paris with our guidebooks and maps and walked with them constantly, finding the laminated "Streetwise Paris" map especially useful. If there are museums or other buildings that you want to enter, it's often possible to arrange a ticket ahead of time, and this tactic puts you in a *much* shorter line; check online about availability. We used the metro system, purchasing *carnets* of ten tickets at a time; they are economical and can be used on the bus, too. When nature inevitably calls, there are street-side public toilets in some areas, and restrooms in cafes are usually accessible, too (if you're not a patron, it's customary to leave a euro on the bar). Paris is walkable any season of the year, though it would be crowded in some areas at the height of summer. We visited in late November and early December, and days were cool to cold, but generally temperatures were good for long walks.

In many ways, sauntering Paris turned out to be like the more conventional trails we describe in this book; we just had the luxury of taking a more free-form approach to our walking. We were surprised by how much we could see and understand in an urban environment by doing one neighborhood at a time; in addition, we really enjoyed the interconnectedness of the culture of Paris, and its landscape and built environment. The success of this trip led to more urban walks for us, with still more in the planning phase. Walking *in* a living museum was wonderful!

The arcades of Paris, built in the 1820s and 1830s, provided Parisians with heat, light, and shelter as they shopped; they're being restored and offer their charms to walkers today.

"BOTANIZING ON THE ASPHALT"

Many people think of walking as an activity that's done primarily in parks, wilderness, and other natural areas, and many of the walks we recommend in this book are good examples—hiking in California's Sierra Nevada, walking the Pennine Way in England and Scotland, walking through the Val d'Orcia in Italy's Tuscany.

But don't forget that the world's great cities—perhaps even the one you live or work in—can also be rewarding walking destinations. Think of their sidewalks as a vast network of trails offering a wealth of walking adventures. Pay close attention to historic canals and railways, as many have been converted into appealing trails that cover large areas of geography. Increasing numbers of "greenways" now form linked systems of trails that connect home, work, parks, and other attractions.

Walk the Great Saunter around the island of Manhattan to get a deep sense of the diversity of the city and to see how the three rivers that bound it have contributed to the sense of place.

In fact, walking in cities has a rich history. Charles Dickens walked as far as 20 miles a day in his native London, giving him welcome respite from his writing desk and enriching his stories with observations on the sometimes grim details of urban life. Phyllis Pearsall obsessively walked 3,000 miles on the 23,000 streets of London in 1930s. But it was in Paris that the art of urban walking reached its zenith. Nineteenth-century intellectual and writer Walter Benjamin richly described the life of the *flaneur*, or bohemian, who famously explored the city's nooks and crannies and who went "botanizing on the asphalt." Benjamin wrote:

> [the] signboards and street names, passers-by, roofs, kiosks, or bars must speak to the wanderer like a crackling twig under his feet, like the startling call of a bittern in the distance, like the sudden stillness of a clearing with a lily standing erect at its center. Paris taught me this art of straying.

Frédéric Gros, in *A Philosophy of Walking*, writes of the stylish form of urban walking that emerged in Paris and other cities at the time:

> Walking through these great megalopolises (Berlin, London, Paris), you passed through districts that were like different worlds, separate, apart. Everything could vary: the size and architectural style of the buildings, the quality and scent of the air, the way of living, the ambiance, the light, the social topography. The flaneur *appeared at a time when the city had acquired enough scale to become a landscape. It could be crossed as if it were a mountain, with its*

passes, its reversals of viewpoint, its dangers and surprises too. It had become a forest, a jungle.

For centuries, Paris has enjoyed the reputation of being "the walking city." In more contemporary terms, cities support a variety of walkers and walking, including those who are window-shopping, people-watching, strolling and promenading, and of course "street walking." In a seemingly perverse way, writers have likened the city to a different type of wilderness—a mysterious and adventurous place that must be experienced on foot.

We're anxious to advance walking in cities and to bring long-distance and multi-day walking "to the people." Consequently, we've included several of the world's great cities in this recommended group of "trails." Of course Paris is on the list—gawk at its stately monuments and buildings, stroll its historic boulevards, walk its distinctive neighborhoods to sense its rich history, beauty, and culture. Walk in Sydney and see firsthand how reserving pedestrian access to the area's foreshore has contributed to the city's attractiveness and vitality. Walk the Great Saunter around the island of Manhattan to get a deep sense of the diversity of the city and how the three rivers that bound it have contributed to its sense of place. Walk the Golden Gate Way in the San Francisco Bay Area and the Backbone Trail in the Los Angeles Basin, and deepen your understanding of the ways in which parks and walking trails can contribute to the quality of life. Follow the Thames Path from river's source through London to read the history of the English people as written on the landscape. We hope you'll consider this type of walking and appreciate the rewards it offers.

For centuries Paris has enjoyed the reputation of being the walking city.

Along the Pembrokeshire Coast Path, the Irish Sea takes on a sparkling turquoise color in the sunshine.

Pembrokeshire Coast Path

We were about halfway along on our two-week thru-hike of the Pembrokeshire Coast Path in Wales. We'd just rounded the last bend in the trail as it traced the shores of beautiful St. Brides Bay and there it was—the dramatic St. Davids lifeboat station at St. Justinian's, the place we'd seen in so many pictures. But the reality of the site was even more impressive than we'd expected. The building housing the 35-foot lifeboat was perched on a platform well above the high tideline, and a steep ramp connected it to the water. A greased track down the middle of the ramp helped ensure a quick launch (and an adrenaline-laced ride!) in the case of emergency. And emergencies are not uncommon along this stretch of coastline. The Royal National Lifeboat Institution (RNLI) was founded in 1824 and maintains several hundred lifeboat stations in the United Kingdom and Ireland. It's estimated that this heroic group of mostly volunteers has saved nearly 140,000 lives. We enjoyed a quick tour of the lifeboat station, and it reminded us of a firehouse in its preparedness—boots and helmets arranged at the ready and the lifeboat polished to a fire engine-quality shine. The RNLI is an important manifestation of the ways in which the people of Wales (and the British Isles more broadly) have adapted to their island environment, and the St. Davids lifeboat station is an especially dramatic example.

LOCATION
Wales

LENGTH
186 miles

ACCOMMODATIONS
Commercial: Yes
Huts/refuges: No
Backpacking/camping: Some

BAGGAGE TRANSFER AVAILABLE
Yes

OPTION TO WALK SECTIONS
Yes

DEGREE OF CHALLENGE
Moderate

PEMBROKESHIRE IS A LARGE PENINSULA in southwest Wales, bordered on three sides by the sea. This dramatic, historic, and remarkable coastline is readily accessible by means of the Pembrokeshire Coast Path, running from Amroth in the south to St. Dogmaels in the north. Though these communities are only about 25 miles apart as the crow flies, the Pembrokeshire peninsula juts far to the west, into the Irish Sea, and the undulating nature of the coastline extends the trail to 186 glorious miles.

The trail opened in 1970 and is the centerpiece of Pembrokeshire Coast National Park and one of Britain's national trails. Nearly all of the trail is directly on the coast, following the tops of cliffs that drop steeply to the sea or crossing ocean beaches and estuaries. However, the trail offers access to a great variety of related landscapes and features, including sand dunes, sea stacks, coves and bays, intertidal flats, sea caves, blowholes, arches, lighthouses and beacons, agricultural fields, quaint harbors, historic villages, numerous islands, and much more. There's nothing dull about the Pembrokeshire Coast Path!

As with all natural history, the story of Pembrokeshire begins with geology, and this story is as complex and convoluted as the coastline itself. All three of the major types of rocks are seen along the trail: sedimentary (limestone, sandstone, slate, and shale), volcanic (in the form of intrusions), and metamorphic (granite and coal). Moreover, these rock layers are often violently twisted and tortured by massive earth movements, including continental drift and collision, uplift, erosion, and glacial action. The record of this geology is vividly presented for close inspection to walkers in the sheer cliffs along the trail. Geologists theorize that many of the mountains of western Europe, including Wales, were once part of the Central Pangean Mountains, as were the Appalachian Mountains in North America. This ancient landform was broken apart by tectonic forces some 250 million years ago. In recognition of this common geologic heritage, the Pembrokeshire Coast Path has been designated an official part of what has recently grown to be the International Appalachian Trail.

This complex geology has resulted in many diverse habitats, including cliff faces, intertidal zones, cliff-top expanses of gorse, brackens, and ferns, agricultural hedgerows, patches of forest, isolated islands and, of course, the vast sea. Terrestrial mammals include rabbits, foxes, and badgers, but the glamour species are marine mammals and seabirds. Hikers often see (and hear) grey seals sunning themselves on the rocks and beaches of inaccessible coves. You're less likely to see porpoises, dolphins, and whales. The trail is considered a hot spot for seabirds, including gannets, fulmars, cormorants, kittiwakes and other gulls, terns, guillemots, puffins, and razorbills (the symbol of Pembrokeshire Coast

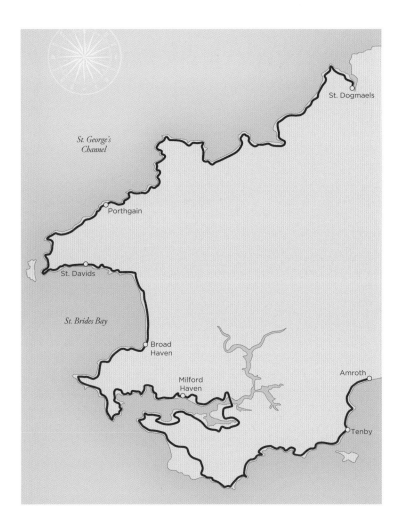

National Park). Wildflowers are abundant in spring and summer, with heather and foxglove especially showy. Summer brings many species of butterflies. The sea is especially clear, often an appealing turquoise.

The Pembrokeshire coast is subject to extreme tidal fluctuation as the powerful North Atlantic Ocean pushes vast quantities of water through the relatively narrow channel between Ireland and Wales. This results in large intertidal zones and wide beaches.

It's common to see boats moored in harbors sitting on extended mudflats, waiting for the tide to float them once again in the eternal, twice-a-day cycle.

The culture and human history of the Pembrokeshire region is also highly diverse. The trail passes around and through many Neolithic hill forts, barrows (ancient burial chambers), stone circles, and standing stones. For example, Carreg Samson, the remains of a burial mound between the towns of Trefin and Abercastle, is estimated to be about 5,000 years old and is comprised of large stones reminiscent of Stonehenge. In fact, some of the stones comprising Stonehenge are thought to have been quarried in the nearby Preseli Hills. We especially enjoyed the roughly two-thousand-year-old Sacraus Stone, preserved in the church in St. Dogmaels, on which a short passage has been written in both Latin and the local ancient language of Ogham, making this a sort of "Rosetta Stone."

The long recorded history of Pembrokeshire includes a medieval period in which walled towns and Norman churches were constructed. The town of Tenby, retaining many of its original walls, and the impressive cathedral at St. Davids, sited to have a low profile to conceal it from Viking raiders, are good examples of this period. Saint David is the patron saint of Wales, and pilgrimages to St. Davids Cathedral are an important tradition in the Christian church.

Fishing, agriculture, and trade are the traditional forms of economic development, and evidence is found in abundance in the villages and harbors along the trail and in the surrounding farms, where

(ABOVE LEFT) The RNLI lifeboat station at St. Justinian's is an iconic sight along the Pembrokeshire Coast Path.

(ABOVE) Swimmers should use caution; the Irish Sea is cold and the currents strong.

(ABOVE) Extreme tidal fluctuations characterize the Pembrokeshire Coast.

(BELOW) Cliffs get higher as you approach the northern end of the Pembrokeshire Coast Path.

sheep, cattle, and crops are raised. Quarrying and mining have been important in some areas; the small village of Porthgain, for example, retains remnants of this activity.

The most obvious manifestation of the culture of the Pembrokeshire region is the Welsh language, which is still in use by many residents. Most signing and place-names are given in both English and Welsh. *Llwybr Arfordir Sir Penfro* is Welsh for Pembrokeshire Coast Path and on all the signs marking the trail.

More modern history has brought military bases to the Pembrokeshire region because of its strategic importance. While some of these are still in operation, others have been abandoned and are part of Pembrokeshire Coast National Park. Over the past several decades, energy development has sprung up in the Milford Haven area because of its excellent deepwater port. Several large oil refineries have been constructed and, while these have provided needed employment, they are visual and potential environmental intrusions. Perhaps the most important natural resource of the Pembrokeshire region is its stunning beauty and this is protected in perpetuity by the Pembrokeshire Coast Path.

We enjoyed many highlights of our walk on the Pembrokeshire Coast Path: beautiful and tourist-friendly villages like Tenby, Dale, Solva, St. Davids, and St. Dogmaels. The castles at Manorbier, Pembroke, and Newport. The expansive beaches at Freshwater West, Newgale, Broad Haven, Musselwick Sands, and Poppit Sands. The lily ponds on the way to Bosherston. The lighthouse at Strumble Head. The boat tour around Ramsey Island. The local foods, including fish and chips, goat's cheese, regional beers, *cawl* (a hearty local soup that comes in many varieties), lamb, sausages, laverbread (a seaweed pancake), and Welsh cakes (a variant on English scones—or is it the other way around?). But most of all we remember with great fondness the wild-seeming, rugged, and often deserted coastline that comprises the Pembrokeshire Coast Path.

The Pembrokeshire Coast Path is ideally suited to meet the logistical needs of thru, section, and day hikers. There's a ready and regular string of communities, from tiny fishing villages to larger towns, poised to accommodate and resupply walkers. Small hotels, B&Bs, and ubiquitous pubs offer hospitality and rewarding opportunities to meet local people. A number of companies offer booking services (reservations at accommodations are desirable in the peak months of July and August), and will arrange baggage transport if desired. There are only a few hostels along the route, and camping is generally only by permission of local landowners. Regional bus companies—the colorfully named Strumble Shuttle, Coastal Cruiser, Poppit Rocket, and Puffin Shuttle—offer great ways to shorten long days if needed, and return walkers to their origin. This "Walk by Bus" program is a model for other long-distance trails.

Most walkers will want at least two weeks to thru-hike the trail, but this doesn't allow much time for leisurely exploration of beaches, hidden coves, historic sites, and colorful villages. If time is tight, consideration should be given to skipping the two to three days of walking around Milford Haven, and to bussing around the active military bases if they are currently in use (chances are you'll hear the firing if they are).

Though the trail is open all year, most walking is done in the spring, summer, and fall. We walked in the latter part of June and early July and found use to be generally low, with the exception of fair-weather weekend days. Walking can be done in either direction, though starting in the south can be a good way to prepare yourself for the more challenging sections (higher cliffs, fewer services) in the north. The trail is well marked with the acorn motif of all national trails in Britain.

We found thru-hiking the Pembrokeshire Coast Path to be challenging in several ways. Most importantly, the trail is directly exposed to the often wet and windy weather that blows in from the North Atlantic Ocean. Walkers must be prepared with serious rain gear: jacket, pants, hat, gaiters, and waterproof boots. Moreover, when the trail is wet and muddy, progress can be slow. We strongly recommend hiking poles on this trail. Some sections include high grass and other vegetation (including briars and stinging nettles) that make long pants and gaiters desirable. The trail also involves substantial elevation gain and loss on most days. While this may seem paradoxical for a trail that runs hard on the edge of the sea, the landscape includes high headlands (the highest is nearly 600 feet) that are regularly cut by valleys, rivers, and other small drainages. Walking the length of the trail includes more elevation gain than climbing Mount Everest!

Walkers need to respect several considerations that apply to this trail. Much of the trail is perched on the tops of high cliffs; walkers should stay on the trail and not approach cliffs too closely. In some areas, the trail itself is very close to the cliff tops and special care should be exercised. This is an active landscape where cliffs continue to be undercut by the sea, and this can present a danger to walkers (you'll be reminded of this by the many "slumps" along the route). Some walking can be done directly on beaches, but walkers should be wary of waves and tides; don't find yourself stranded and vulnerable on a long stretch of beach with the tide rising. Tide tables are readily available and easy to read; carry and use them. Exercise care in swimming, as the water is cold and subject to currents and strong tidal action.

The Pembrokeshire Coast Path is part of the Wales Coastal Path, which covers all of the country's 870 miles of coastline. Moreover, Offa's Dyke Path, another national trail, marks the land-based border between Wales and England. Walking all of these trails allows a complete circumnavigation of the country, perhaps the only such walking opportunity in the world. Add that to the remainder of the International Appalachian Trail, which extends to multiple continents, and there are many months of profitable walking to be done, indeed.

The Pembrokeshire Coast Path is one of the great coastal walks in the world, making many "best of" lists, and for good reason. However, it also has a reputation in the walking community as a trail that can "kick your butt" if you let it. Prepare yourself with the proper gear, knowledge, and mindset, and you'll be richly rewarded.

(ABOVE) Grey seals sun themselves in inaccessible coves; you'll often hear them barking before you see them.

(BELOW) Fields of heather are common along the Pembrokeshire Coast Path.

ADVENTURES (AND MISADVENTURES)

We look forward to our long-distance and multi-day walks because they're always adventures, big and small. They allow us to explore places we haven't been, and to appreciate these places at the human scale and speed that's offered only by walking. Despite the research and planning we do, the trails we walk and the cultural landscapes they traverse are never quite like we imagined. Even when we read guidebooks describing the trails and follow detailed maps, we're never quite sure what's around the next bend. Every day on the trail is an adventure.

We've found it interesting that there's a strong movement in society toward "adventure tourism," a type of travel with an emphasis on exploration and being physically active. We think this is a reaction to the increasingly sedentary lifestyles that many of us lead, along with a search for more new and "authentic" experiences in a world that seems to be increasingly homogeneous. We think a little adventure in life is a good thing, and our walks have given us more than our fair share.

But we were a little surprised when we read the common dictionary definition of the word "adventure": "an unusual and exciting, typically hazardous, experience or activity." Of course, it was the reference to "hazardous" that caught our attention. Our walks aren't designed to be hazardous—in fact, just the opposite.

On the other hand, we have to admit to having had some "misadventures" sprinkled in with our adventures (could this be "misadventure tourism"?). But most were pretty tame, though they may not have seemed that way at the time. For example, our walk on the Pembrokeshire Coast Path took us two weeks. It was a glorious walk, but it rained thirteen out of fourteen days! To be fair, most days it just showered on and off, but it was a wet walk that was part adventure and part misadventure. We laugh now about our unfortunate timing, but this walk confirmed that, with proper clothing and gear, rain doesn't have to ruin the experience of walking (though

Although it rains quite a bit on the Pembrokeshire Coast Path, the weather can't ruin the experiences of those who are prepared.

we generally prefer sunny skies). Moreover, the ways in which we adapted to the rain, both physically and psychologically, turned out to be an important part of the adventure.

And now that we think about it, we've had plenty of misadventures—space doesn't allow a complete accounting—but none could be classified as hazardous.

We write about this to encourage you to embrace the misadventures that are inevitable in walking long distances. We came across a commentary piece in the *New York Times* recently describing the experience of a father and daughter who did a two-week backpacking trip on the Pacific Crest Trail. They wrote:

> *We hiked 145 miles, and it was typical backpacking bliss: We were chewed on by mosquitoes, rained on and thundered at, broiled by noonday sun, mocked by a 20-mile stretch of dry trail, and left limping from blisters. The perfect trip!*

In a seemingly perverse way, a few misadventures can actually heighten the intensity of adventure travel. And that has led to Manning's dictum: you can't have any real adventures in life without some misadventures along the way. Maybe Helen Keller said it better: "Life is either a daring adventure or nothing."

Walking the world's great trails can add just the right measure of adventure to life. (Great Wall of China)

Consider pushing your perceived limits just a tad: walk a little farther in your everyday life at home, try some modest long-distance walks, embrace some walks you think might be at the margins of your ability. Of course, you should never knowingly put yourself at risk in the process.

Sheep are ubiquitous at lower elevations in Peak District National Park at the southern end of the Pennine Way.

Pennine Way

We started our walk of the Pennine Way on a warm weekend in July, and were pleasantly surprised to see a number of groups of teenage boys and girls hiking the trail; they carried full packs and were obviously camping along the way. At rest breaks, we took advantage of the opportunity to talk with them and learned that they were engaged in the Duke of Edinburgh's Award program. To receive an award, participants must demonstrate certain skills, do volunteer work, and take part in an "expedition" that includes hiking and at least one night of camping. We enjoyed the enthusiasm of these young people (well, some of them were more enthusiastic than others) and admired their public spirit. We couldn't help but think that Britain is doing a good job encouraging its youth to appreciate and steward their natural and cultural heritage.

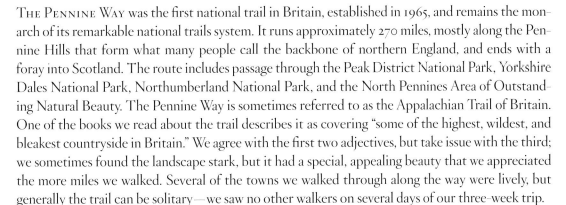

THE PENNINE WAY was the first national trail in Britain, established in 1965, and remains the monarch of its remarkable national trails system. It runs approximately 270 miles, mostly along the Pennine Hills that form what many people call the backbone of northern England, and ends with a foray into Scotland. The route includes passage through the Peak District National Park, Yorkshire Dales National Park, Northumberland National Park, and the North Pennines Area of Outstanding Natural Beauty. The Pennine Way is sometimes referred to as the Appalachian Trail of Britain. One of the books we read about the trail describes it as covering "some of the highest, wildest, and bleakest countryside in Britain." We agree with the first two adjectives, but take issue with the third; we sometimes found the landscape stark, but it had a special, appealing beauty that we appreciated the more miles we walked. Several of the towns we walked through along the way were lively, but generally the trail can be solitary—we saw no other walkers on several days of our three-week trip.

The trail has great cachet in Britain as the most challenging of the national trails. Part of its reputation is based on its length, remoteness, and many climbs (walkers gain approximately 40,000 feet in elevation over the course of the trail). But the reputation is also based on the peat

LOCATION
England and Scotland

LENGTH
270 miles

ACCOMMODATIONS
Commercial: Yes
Huts/refuges: No
Backpacking/camping: Some

BAGGAGE TRANSFER AVAILABLE
Yes

OPTION TO WALK SECTIONS
Yes

DEGREE OF CHALLENGE
Moderate–High

bogs—described as "appalling" and "spirit sapping"—
that must be traversed on the trail's many high moors.
The peat is a manifestation of the history of the British Isles. The land was once covered in forest, but early
inhabitants cut the trees for building material and to
clear the land for agriculture. Many of the trees rotted
in place, no longer absorbing and evaporating rainfall.
Since much of the underlying bedrock is largely imper-
meable, the rotting trees were transformed into massive
peat bogs, requiring walkers to make their way through
what is described as "cold, black porridge."

Much of the challenge of the bogs is now diminished through an ongoing program of "slabbing" the trail
with large, flat stones from the nearby abandoned mill
buildings of the Calder Valley, where the Industrial Revolution was born. This process is controversial among
walkers; some prefer that the trail be maintained with
its original character, but others counter that the stones
reduce erosion caused by people searching for the best
route through or around the bogs, and that the stones
add an important element of accessibility. At any rate,
the stones are an inventive and adaptive reuse of materials from the outdated mills, and we appreciated the
efforts to attract more walkers to the trail.

The trail is also a favorite because of what it's done
for walking in Britain. In reaction to the "enclosures" of
much of Britain's open lands by the rich and powerful
in the nineteenth century, hundreds of walkers staged a
"mass trespass" on popular Kinder Scout in 1932. Pro-
testors from the neighboring towns of Manchester and
Sheffield asserted what they felt was their right to walk
in this area. Several were arrested, but the demonstra-
tion and continued protests ultimately led to Britain's
"right to roam" laws, as well as establishment of national
parks and trails. It was truly stirring to ascend Jacob's

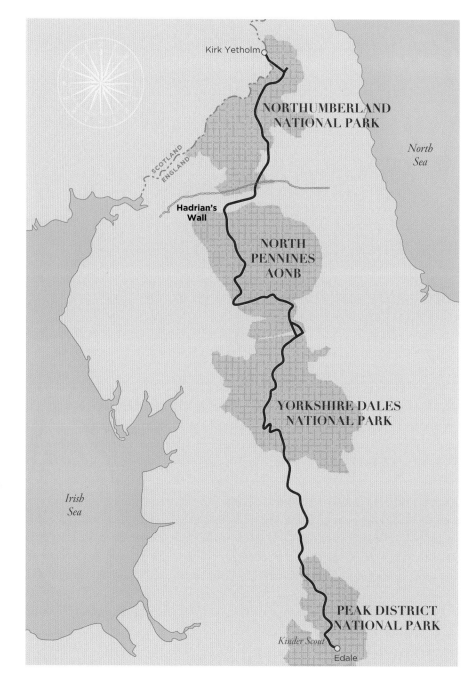

Ladder (a long series of gentle steps) to the top of Kinder Scout and see for ourselves the site of this historic, grassroots movement that has had such a lasting and expansive affect for the universal rights of walkers.

The Pennine Way is a long and diverse walk, and we experienced many highlights. It begins in the lovely English village of Edale and runs north to Kirk Yetholm, Scotland. We were filled with excitement as we started our walk in Edale, with its Peak District National Park Visitor Center (where a quote from American nature writer John Muir is featured). We walked north out of the village, passing through quintessential fields of sheep and the official sign that stated we had 275 miles to go! (The "official" distance of the trail ranges from 265 to 275 miles, depending on the source.)

On day three we reached stately Stoodley Pike, a 121-foot monument completed in 1856 to mark the end of the Crimean War; the monument can be seen for miles in the Southern Pennines, and the view was even better after climbing the stairs to the top.

The trail skirts the fringes of the town of Haworth and what is popularly known as "Brontë country," the home of the three Brontë sisters, Emily, Charlotte, and Anne. All three wrote enduring novels that were informed by the austere landscape of the area's extensive moors. The trail passes directly by the ruined farmstead called Top Withens, which many associate with Emily Brontë's *Wuthering Heights* (though this connection is disputed). We enjoyed the town of Malham as well, with its Yorkshire Dales National Park Visitor Center and bustling tourist facilities and services. Just outside town, and along the trail, is the interesting Malham Cove, a huge natural amphitheater.

(ABOVE LEFT) The Swaledale is the picturesque center of the Yorkshire Dales National Park, with its extensive system of small field barns.

(ABOVE) Several miles of the Pennine Way parallel Hadrian's Wall, built in AD 122 to discourage raids from the north into Roman-occupied territory.

The Swaledale is the picturesque center of the Yorkshire Dales National Park, with its extensive system of small, plain, field barns, so numerous it seems like every field has its own. Along with miles of stone walls dividing the fields and the ubiquitous sheep, the scenery is magical, and the villages of Thwaite and Keld are idyllic. We spent the night in Keld, which is at the intersection of the Pennine Way and the well-known Coast-to-Coast Trail, which we'd walked several years earlier (and describe in our book, *Walking Distance*). Pen-y-Ghent, a distinctive mountain that requires a short but steep climb, is an important natural feature in this area. Descending from Pen-y-Ghent, the trail leads into the town of Horton in Ribblesdale, where you'll find the Pen-y-Ghent Cafe, nearly as old as the trail. Be sure to stop and talk with other walkers, shop for any needed outdoor items, and sign the Pennine Way logbook, which goes back to 1966. High Cup Nick is another interesting natural feature along the trail, a classic and impressively steep U-shaped valley characteristic of glaciation; it's a textbook example of this geologic process and we were impressed with its scale.

Low Force Waterfall on the River Tees near Middleton-in-Teesdale sparkles in the sunshine.

All Pennine Way walkers will remember the climb over Cross Fell; at nearly 3,000 feet it's the highest point along the trail and carries the distinction of having some of the worst weather in England (including more than one hundred days a year of gale-force winds). We're pleased to report that our walk over the summit was truly authentic in this way; we huddled in the lee of one of the large summit cairns for a quick lunch and then headed off on our descent. The trail over the fell connects the towns of Dufton and Alston. Dufton is a small, sweet village and we were there on a Saturday night; the town green was the setting for an art fair with live music by talented locals. We had dinner at the Stag Inn, a pub that was hosting a birthday party for an older man; the group referred to themselves as a "bunch of old boogers." Lots of local color. The long climb down from Cross Fell led us to Alston, a larger, hilly market town with a range of stores and several welcoming teashops.

One of our favorite sections of the trail was the several-mile stretch that paralleled Hadrian's Wall. Built by the Romans at the direction of Emperor Hadrian in AD 122, this coast-to-coast fortification was designed to discourage raids from the north into Roman-occupied territory. The original wall is 8 feet deep and 12 feet high, and it includes periodic forts and more frequent mile castles and turrets. The wall is a World Heritage Site, and Pennine Way walkers experience one of the best-preserved sections. We suggest you also visit the nearby Roman Army Museum in Hexham, just off the route.

After Hadrian's Wall, the trail heads toward Scotland, where we saw relatively few walkers. Over the course of the last two days, the trail led over the stark and dramatic Cheviot Hills and danced along the border between England and Scotland, delivering us to Kirk Yetholm, Scotland, where a sign on the Border Hotel officially announced the end of the trail. Other attractions along the trail include several impressive waterfalls, and portions of two long-distance canals, now used primarily for recreation.

Along its nearly 300-mile length, the trail includes a great variety of interesting and attractive plants and animals. Though much of the trail is treeless, we walked through several beautiful groves of beech and several large evergreen plantations, portions of which were being harvested. The moors were cloaked in heather, showy cottongrass (actually a sedge), rushes, and sphagnum (moss). Common animals included rabbits, red and black grouse, curlews, snipe, and deer.

Some of our memories are of the interesting places we stayed and the meals we enjoyed (and felt we had so richly earned). The Tan Hill Inn is the highest pub in England and deserves a visit, if just for a pint. We devoured welcome lunches at the Wensleydale Cafe, where we ate the local cheese made famous by the Claymation figures Wallace and Gromit, and at the Conduit Cafe in Middleton-in-Teesdale, where the sign reads "Friendly dogs and muddy boots welcome." We enjoyed traditional fish and chips with mushy peas on more than one occasion, though England's pubs have diversified their menus over the last decade or two. Perhaps our favorite overnight was spent at Clove Lodge, a small B&B. The oldest part of the house was built in 1302, and we were housed in the original (now remodeled) piggery. We feasted the next morning on eggs gathered in the barn just before breakfast.

This is a trail for experienced hikers. Walking the Pennine Way requires substantive planning as it's a long trail and there are lots of logistics to tend to. We took three weeks to complete the journey, though frequent road crossings make it relatively easy to do the hike in sections (as most Brits seem to do), or to take a "best of" approach. Most of the track is on open moorlands fully exposed to the weather, so industrial-strength rain gear is a necessity, along with warm clothes and sun protection. Summer and early fall are the prime walking seasons. Most people walk south to north to put prevailing winds and the sun at their back. The trail is marked with the national trail acorn symbols, with cairns at higher elevations, but wayfinding can occasionally be challenging, especially in the mist that can settle over the moors. Knowing how to read a map and use a compass and/or GPS are essential. In the more lonely sections of the trail, accommodations and other services can be scarce, so plan your walk carefully. Though a few hardy walkers camp, most use B&Bs.

Completing the Pennine Way is a remarkable experience—historic, beautiful, and challenging—and it will initiate you into the ranks of elite walkers. But don't forget, this trail offers dramatic section hiking as well—the only problem is deciding which sections to hike!

(ABOVE) Lower elevations of the southern and middle portions of the Pennine Way traverse typical English farms with their unending drystacked stone walls.

(BELOW) The Pennine Way is approximately 270 miles long and runs through the "backbone" of northern England, ending with a foray into Scotland.

The rich set of ideas associated with walking, along with the very act of walking itself, have advanced an array of political causes. For example, the Romantic philosophy of Rousseau, informed by his long walks, suggested an inherent value in the individual, and this, in turn, offered a powerful argument against the tyranny of a wealthy majority. These ideas helped inspire the Women's March on Versailles in 1789 to protest the scarcity and price of bread, and this was an important precursor of the French Revolution.

Another prominent example is Mohandas Gandhi's 240-mile Salt March in 1930 to protest British taxes on traditional salt-making by Indian people (and British colonialism more generally). Marches were an important component of Gandhi's philosophy of *satyagraha*, or nonviolent resistance to unjust laws and treatment. Frédéric Gros describes the power and devotion of Gandhi's walking:

The enduring image is that of an old man of nearly seventy-seven, walking all day leaning on the shoulder of his young niece, holding his pilgrim's staff in the other hand, going on foot from village to village, from massacre to massacre, supported by faith alone, dressed like the poorest of the poor, underlining everywhere the reality of love and the absurdity of hatred, and opposing the world's violence with the infinite peace of a slow, humble, unending walk.

Other more contemporary examples include Dr. Martin Luther King Jr.'s 54-mile march in 1965 from Selma to Montgomery, Alabama, to protest unjust voting laws (this route is now memorialized as the Selma to Montgomery National Historic Trail, and Cesar Chavez's 340-mile March

A neighborhood group in Sydney came together to save their foreshore walking area.

for Justice in 1966 in California to protest poor treatment of farmworkers.

More recent pedestrian-led demonstrations include the protest in Tiananmen Square, China, and Czechoslovakia's Velvet Revolution, both in 1989. It's no coincidence that the autobiographies of King and Nelson Mandela are titled *Stride Toward Freedom* and *Long Walk to Freedom*, respectively.

The marches noted here are a few of the many that have taken place over a long history of protests, demonstrations, and parades with strong political agendas—peace, civil rights, cultural pride, freedom from sexual violence, and much more—and demonstrate the potential power they can exert. There have even been walks to protect walking, as when several hundred people staged a mass trespass in 1932 on Kinder Scout (now part of the Pennine Way) in the Peak District of England, ultimately leading to legislation to assure the historic "right to roam." Joseph Amato suggests that walking in this way adds important elements of "earnestness," "solemnity," and "humility" to help advance political causes, and that walking is thus "a form of public discourse." Rebecca Solnit says that "walking becomes testifying."

One of the political causes closest to many walkers is conservation. The prophets of Romanticism sent legions of walkers out of their gardens and into the wider and wilder landscape, where they searched for beauty and solitude. In this way, walking evolved into an attraction, not just a means to an end. Of course, this meant that walkers needed wild places to walk in. Walkers banded together in what have become powerful social forces, such as the Scottish Rights of Way & Access Society (founded in 1845), the Commons Preservation Society (founded in England in 1865), the Appalachian Mountain Club (founded in America in 1876), the Sierra Club (founded in America in 1892), Wandervogel (founded officially in Germany in 1901), and the Ramblers' Association (founded in England in 1935, now known simply as Ramblers). These organizations have been instrumental in environmental conservation and preservation and organize trips for millions of walkers each year. Consider joining your national or local hiking group and bearing witness to the importance of walking.

Kinder Scout on England's Pennine Way was the site of a mass trespass in 1932 to promote the "right to roam."

Climbs to the higher passes offer sweeping views of the big landscapes of the Popo Agie Wilderness.

Popo Agie Wilderness

They typically sensed us well before we saw them, and we knew we'd been spotted when we heard their sharp whistles warning others of potential danger. Marmots and pikas aren't among the glamour species of the northern Rocky Mountains, but they're certainly two of the most interesting and entertaining. Both species live in rocky meadows and talus slopes at very high elevations. Marmots are large members of the squirrel family and have reddish-brown fur and a yellow belly. They live in colonies, and one marmot stands guard while others are feeding in the open. They've adapted to the cold of high elevations by hibernating for more than half their lives; during hibernation, their body temperatures drop as low as 41 degrees, and they take only one or two breaths per minute. Pikas are smaller mammals with brown and black fur, and they are especially appealing. They also live in colonies and warn of danger using high-pitched calls. However, pikas don't hibernate—they harvest grasses and other plant material, dry this vegetation on rocks, and store it away in "hay piles" for the winter. Though it's difficult to get very close to either marmots or pikas, many enjoyable hours can be spent watching them from afar as they go through their daily routines of feeding, interacting, and sunning themselves, much like the hikers in this area!

LOCATION
Wyoming, United States

LENGTH
Variable (a few days to a few weeks)

ACCOMMODATIONS
Commercial: No
Huts/refuges: No
Backpacking/camping: Yes

BAGGAGE TRANSFER AVAILABLE
No

OPTION TO WALK SECTIONS
Yes

DEGREE OF CHALLENGE
Moderate–High

THE VAST SHOSHONE NATIONAL FOREST, nearly 2.5 million acres (larger than Yellowstone National Park), was the first national forest in the United States, established in 1891. The forest was named in honor of the Shoshone tribe of Native Americans, one of several tribes—including the Lakota, Crow, and Northern Cheyenne—in this region of Wyoming. The national forest borders Yellowstone National Park and, together with a suite of other protected lands, comprises the Greater Yellowstone Ecosystem, an area of approximately 20 million acres that offers the opportunity to take a large, landscape-scale approach to conservation.

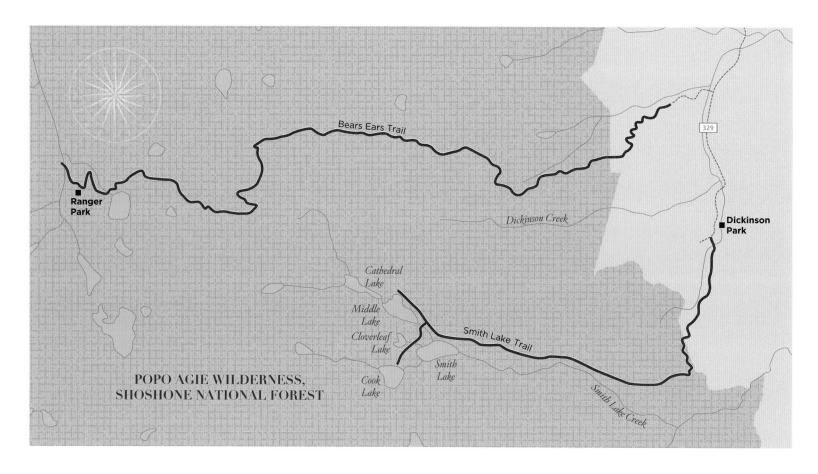

The Shoshone National Forest includes four large wilderness areas that occupy more than half the forest. The hundred-thousand-acre Popo Agie (pronounced po-PO-zsha) Wilderness is located in the Wind River Range in the southern portion of the forest. Popo Agie means "beginning of the waters" in the Crow language and refers to the area's high-elevation watersheds. As a wilderness area, it's managed according to the 1964 Wilderness Act, which prohibits most forms of economic development and requires that the area be preserved in its natural state and provide for recreation, including opportunities for solitude.

Most of the Popo Agie Wilderness is very high elevation, ranging from around 8,000 feet to 13,255-foot Wind River Peak; twenty mountains exceed 12,000 feet. The wilderness features picturesque jagged peaks, deep valleys and canyons, nearly sheer granite walls, huge cirques, talus slopes, extensive forests at lower elevations, vast areas of flower-filled meadows and tundra, and many

(ABOVE LEFT) Colorful wildflowers carpet the meadows and alpine tundra in the Popo Agie Wilderness.

(ABOVE) High-elevation trails present dramatic views down to the area's many lakes.

large, perennial snowfields; it's the quintessential mountain landscape. The area includes more than 300 alpine and subalpine lakes and ponds, many filled with trout, and miles of clear, cold mountain streams, all tributaries of the Little Wind River. The fishing is so good that many folks hike and camp primarily to access these waters (a fishing license is required).

There are many lifetimes of walking to be done in the Popo Agie Wilderness, and we've hiked in the area several times. Our two favorite routes are accessed from the Dickinson Park Trailhead, one of the remoter trailheads. (The word "park" is a geographical term that means a broad flat valley.) Driving to this trailhead is part of the adventure. The closest town is Lander, Wyoming, about 35 miles away. Lander is a good place to purchase last-minute supplies and has a US Forest Service office that's a great place to get up-to-date information on conditions in the wilderness. Much of the road to Dickinson Park is on the Wind River Indian Reservation and a permit (available in Lander) is needed from the Shoshone and Arapaho Tribes. The road is rough in places (one guidebook calls it "long and tortuous"), but we haven't encountered any problems—just allow sufficient time. The road is passable with a standard automobile except during very wet weather. The drive offers time to enjoy the exposed geology of the area, including the many layers of sedimentary rock that are tilted, broken, and exposed due to uplift and erosion by glaciers and streams. The scenery is very different from the granite core of the Wind River Range, where you'll soon be hiking.

(ABOVE) High elevation snowfields in the Popo Agie Wilderness may not melt until mid-to-late summer.

(ABOVE RIGHT) Trails in the Popo Agie Wilderness rise to over 12,000 feet.

Dickinson Park is a lovely area, and you'll find a small Forest Service campground here, as well as two trails leading directly into the wilderness. At the end of the road is the Smith Lake Trail, which leads to a cluster of eight sparkling lakes with a stunning background of three large cirques and the deep blue western sky. This is only 12 miles round-trip and could be done as a long day hike, but that would be a shame as the trail and the lakes near its terminus are an ideal base camp. Set up your tent at one of the lakes (Middle Lake is a favorite) and enjoy a few leisurely days exploring the area, maybe fishing, and taking in the area's spectacular views.

Along the trail, you'll see several of the area's iconic peaks, including Wind River Peak, forests of spruce, fir, and lodgepole pine, and evidence of glaciation—the cirques that frame the lakes, erratic boulders, expanses of granite that shine with glacial polish, and, of course, the area's many lakes and ponds. The Smith Lake Trail is relatively easy and an especially good option if you have only a few days for hiking; we also suggest it as a great choice for families with children.

Just north of the campground at Dickinson Park is the trailhead for the grand Bears Ears Trail. This longer trail—a little more than 12 miles one way—is more suited to a multi-day backpacking trip. The trail climbs and traverses many of the environments characteristic of the Wind Rivers, including evergreen forests, high mountain lakes, rugged peaks, and large meadows and tundra. Much of the trail is above tree line, offering stunning views of the surrounding mountains. The trail climbs

to nearly 12,000 feet, rising almost 3,000 feet in the first 8 miles. Early summer flowers are spectacular, as are views into the dramatic Cirque of Towers, a world-class rock climbing area. Popular and beautiful Valentine Lake, at well over 10,000 feet, offers a number of idyllic campsites and (more) good fishing. An out-and-back hike to Valentine Lake should take a few days. However, a network of trails can be added to this route and beckon hikers into longer and more adventurous trips.

The natural history of the Wind River Range starts with the complex geology of the area. The underlying granite bedrock was slowly uplifted over a period of millions of years. Three periods of global cooling over the last 250,000 years covered the area with ice as much as 1,000 feet thick, eroding and shaping the mountains into their contemporary form. A variety of trees, shrubs, and flowers cover much of the area, depending on the wide range of elevations. Deciduous trees include aspen at lower elevations and cottonwoods along lower stretches of streams. Coniferous trees dominate, including lodgepole pine, Engelmann spruce, whitebark pine, and subalpine fir. Iconic mammals include elk, mule deer, pronghorn antelope, bighorn sheep, and moose. Grizzly bears and wolves have been reported, but are rare. There are a variety of birds, including bald and golden eagles, red-tailed hawks, falcons, trumpeter swans, and sage and ruffed grouse.

The human history of the area is also rich. Evidence suggests that Native Americans used this area for hunting as many as 10,000 years ago, and some of the current trails in the Wind Rivers are

Rocky meadows and talus slopes make ideal habitat for marmots and pikas, two of the more interesting and entertaining species in the Popo Agie Wilderness.

probably derived from prehistoric routes. The Wind River Range was so named by the Crow because there was always a wind coming off the mountains. Colorful mountain men such as Jedediah Smith and Jim Bridger and rugged employees of the Hudson's Bay Company explored the region. The Lewis and Clark Expedition, accompanied by Sacagawea, traveled through the area, and covered wagons heading to the West Coast also used Wind River passes. The US Forest Service designated the Popo Agie a Primitive Area in 1932, and Congress designated it a Wilderness Area in 1984.

Because it's wilderness, hiking here demands good planning and relative fitness, and use of a detailed guidebook and maps is advised. Trails can be rough, but are generally easy to follow. Because of the high elevation and perennial snowfields that clog the passes, the hiking season is short—usually early July to early September. The high elevations also suggest hikers take some period of acclimatization. Some of the steam crossings do not have bridges and may require fording; high water levels early in the season can make this challenging and dangerous—be careful and turn back if necessary. Occasional afternoon thunderstorms make rain gear a necessity, and warm clothes are a requirement; daytime temperatures often reach into the 70s, but frost and even snow can occur in all months. All hiking parties should store their food in bear-resistant canisters (which can be borrowed from the Forest Service in Lander); some hikers choose to carry bear spray. Drinking water is plentiful, but must be treated. And, lastly, some folks find that all those lakes and streams provide ideal habitat for mosquitoes, especially early in the season. We found them to be problematic only for an hour or so at dusk, and were happy to have our head nets in addition to repellant.

We think the beauty of the Popo Agie Wilderness rivals that of some of the better-known national parks in the northern Rockies, such as Yellowstone and Grand Teton. Yet the area is relatively lightly used, no permits are needed, and camping is generally "at large," allowing for an increasingly rare opportunity to enjoy pristine nature, freedom, and solitude. Hiking in this wilderness is a bit of an adventure, but that only adds to the fun.

WORLD WIDE WEB

The last several decades have seen development of remarkable systems of national and international trails throughout much of the world, and these trails represent many lifetimes of walking adventures. For example, the US Congress passed the National Trails System Act in 1968 "to promote the preservation of, and access to, travel within, and enjoyment and appreciation of the open-air, outdoor areas and historic resources of the Nation." Several categories of trails exist, including national scenic trails, national recreation trails, national historic trails, national geologic trails, and national connecting and side trails. Typically these are long-distance trails, most of them very long distance.

The Appalachian National Scenic Trail (about 2,200 miles) and the Pacific Crest National Scenic Trail (about 2,700 miles) were the first components of the National Trails System. Today there are more than 60,000 miles of national trails (more miles than the interstate highway system), though portions of many of these trails are still under development. These trails introduce walkers to the great diversity of American landscapes, including most of its major ecosystems, as well as the nation's rich history. This book includes descriptions of all or part of three national trails: the Presidential Traverse section of the Appalachian Trail, the High Sierra Camps Loop section of the Pacific Crest Trail, and the Ala Kahakai National Historic Trail.

There are well-developed national trails systems in many other countries too. England and Wales have designated sixteen national trails that total more than 2,500 miles. This book includes four of these trails: the Pembrokeshire Coast Path, the Pennine Way, the Thames Path, and part of the Hadrian's Wall Path. New Zealand has a national system of nine Great Walks that total 554 miles, and this book includes one of these trails, the Abel Tasman Coast Track. Mainland Europe has a vast system of international GR footpaths (GR is the acronym for the French *Grande Randonnee* and similar terms in other languages), mostly in France, Belgium, the Netherlands, Spain, Luxembourg, and Switzerland. These long-distance trails typically carry unromantic numbers instead of names. The Camino Portugués, in Portugal and Spain, which we include in this book, is a portion the GR 11.

Given the vast and intricate network of trails around the world, including regional and local trails, perhaps we should consider this an alternative and more authentic World Wide Web.

The Ala Kahakai National Historic Trail is part of the US national trail system.

The Presidential Traverse is one of the most striking sections of the Appalachian Trail.

Presidential Traverse

We'd done a substantial climb that day to reach Mizpah Spring Hut, one of eight huts managed by the Appalachian Mountain Club (AMC) in the dramatic White Mountains of New Hampshire. We'd just finished a family-style dinner at the hut when the "croo" (crew) reappeared in costume and launched into their funny, animated skit about the delicate arctic alpine vegetation left on the mountain summits after the glacial period 10,000 years ago and how hikers should avoid trampling these areas. This served as a great learning experience as well as the evening's entertainment. The AMC huts represent a rare opportunity in the United States, but one that's common in much of Europe and elsewhere—rustic accommodations sited a day's hiking distance apart along a network of trails. The AMC huts provide bunk space for hikers, common bathrooms (sorry, no showers), and communal meals prepared and served by crews of mostly college-age students. The huts make the White Mountains accessible to people who may not wish to, or be able to, backpack, but want to enjoy the mountains and the camaraderie of people who treasure the world-class hiking opportunities they present. Thanks to the AMC croos!

LOCATION
New Hampshire, United States

LENGTH
30 miles

ACCOMMODATIONS
Commercial: No
Huts/refuges: Yes
Backpacking/camping: Yes

BAGGAGE TRANSFER AVAILABLE
No

OPTION TO WALK SECTIONS
Yes

DEGREE OF CHALLENGE
Moderate–High

THE PRESIDENTIAL TRAVERSE is a hike of approximately 30 miles that climbs up and over seven dramatic White Mountain peaks in New Hampshire named for US presidents: Pierce, Eisenhower, Monroe, Washington, Jefferson, Adams, and Madison (from south to north). The hike is in the expansive White Mountain National Forest, encompassing about three-quarters of a million acres. All seven of the presidential peaks are over (some substantially over) 4,000 feet in elevation. Most of the peaks are reached by short side trails off the main route; hikers may choose not to stray off the route, but purists insist that hikers summit all seven peaks to qualify for having walked the "Presi Traverse."

Nearly all the route follows the iconic Appalachian Trail (AT), and the traverse is generally acknowledged as one of its most difficult sections. Usually hikers position themselves for the

Most of the Presidential Traverse follows ridgelines in the dramatic White Mountains.

Presidential Traverse by using the Appalachia Trailhead (on Route 2) or from Franconia Notch State Park (on Route US-3N). Though this is not an especially long walk, it requires a cumulative gain in elevation of 9,000 feet. Moreover, the trail is rough (very rough!) in places. And all this says nothing about the severity of the weather—more about that shortly.

As every schoolchild in New England knows, Mount Washington, at 6,288 feet, is the highest peak in the region and the most prominent mountain east of the Mississippi River. (Every schoolchild probably doesn't know that the mountain was called *Agiocochook*—Home of the Great Spirit—by some native tribes in the region.) Well above tree line and in the path of historic storm tracks, the mountain has the well-deserved reputation of having the worst weather in the world. The weather station at the summit recorded a wind gust of

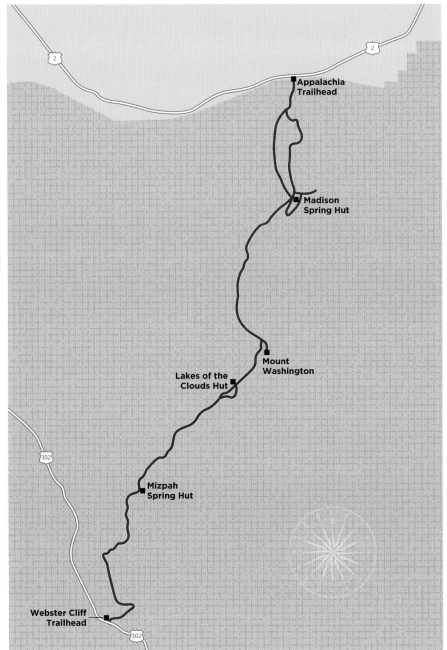

231 miles an hour in 1934 and, until recently, this was a world record (it's still the record in the United States). Because of its prominence above surrounding peaks, Mount Washington receives very large amounts of precipitation, averaging nearly 100 inches of moisture per year, much of it in the form of snow. A record 566 inches of snow fell on the mountain in 1968–69. Mount Washington and most of the neighboring peaks are cloaked in clouds much of the time, but when the weather allows, the views from the summit are staggering, extending to the Atlantic Ocean.

The geology of the White Mountains is complex. They're thought to be remnants of an earlier Appalachian Mountain chain that was once higher than the present-day Himalayas. However, inevitable erosion has taken place, the most prominent example being the last period of glaciation about 10,000 years ago. Evidence can be seen in the characteristic U-shaped valleys and passes, and in the massive glacial cirques—large portions of the upper slopes that were eroded off the southern sides of the mountains as the glaciers advanced. Tuckerman Ravine (which supports wilderness skiing sometimes lasting into June) on Mount Washington and King Ravine on Mount Adams are prime examples of these cirques. Because tree line is typically at 4,000 to 5,000 feet, the massive scale of this geologic history is readily apparent. A closer look will also reveal striations where rocks carried by the glaciers scraped across the bedrock. The ice age that caused this massive glaciation left plants on the summits that are now found almost exclusively in areas hundreds of miles to the north.

Much of the Presidential Traverse—from Crawford Notch to Mount Washington—follows the historic Crawford Path, the oldest continuously maintained trail in the United States. In 1819, Abel Crawford and his son, Ethan, cleared a path to tree line, and the trail was eventually extended to the summit of Mount Washington. In fact, many of the trails in the White Mountains were developed more than a hundred years before the designation of the Appalachian Trail. Because of the pride over this history, the trails generally carry their historic names in addition to being signed as the AT.

Mount Washington is justifiably called Monarch of the White Mountains because of its commanding presence, and it has received a great deal of attention since the mid-nineteenth century, most of it based on tourism and recreation. The Summit House hotel opened for business in 1852, and four heavy chains were used to anchor the roof; it burned in 1908. The competing Tip-Top

(ABOVE LEFT) A system of high-elevation huts run by the Appalachian Mountain Club provide accommodations and meals to hikers.

(ABOVE MIDDLE) Sleeping rooms are spare and shared with other hikers, but offer welcome comfort.

(ABOVE) Family-style meals are served at the Appalachian Mountain Club huts and offer great camaraderie.

(ABOVE) Lower-elevation portions of the trail are easy to follow, but can be rough.

(ABOVE RIGHT) Large cairns mark the trail at higher elevations on the Presidential Traverse and guide hikers when the weather is poor.

House was built in 1853 and is now a state historic site, recently renovated as a museum. A coach road was constructed in 1861 and is now the Mount Washington Auto Road, which allows motorized access to the summit. In addition, the Mount Washington Cog Railway—said to have the steepest grade of any railroad in the world (14 percent)—was built in 1869 and is still in operation. (Either of these could be used to break the Presidential Traverse in half.) Today, you'll find a visitor center, cafeteria, weather observatory, and radio antennas on the summit. But while much of the summit itself is heavily developed, most of the rest of the Presidential Traverse offers a great wilderness-like experience.

As with all walks, it's important to prepare for the Presidential Traverse. Weather is the most important consideration; as noted earlier, weather can be and often is severe, especially above tree line. Tragically, many people have died from exposure in the White Mountains; check the weather forecast closely before attempting the Presidential Traverse, and pack rain pants and coats and warm clothes no matter the forecast.

The AMC huts are a highlight of the trip. Three huts serve the Presidential Traverse: Mizpah Spring, Lakes of the Clouds, and Madison Spring, and they are located an easy day's hike apart. Be aware that the huts are popular, and reservations, especially for weekends, must be made well in advance. Because the huts are expensive to maintain (most supplies are toted up to the huts by the

croo), the cost to hikers is relatively high. Consider joining the AMC to get a discount at the huts and (more importantly) support the organization that has done so much for walkers for so long.

The trail can be rough in places, especially above tree line, so the going will be slow; we recommend hiking boots and poles. The AT portion of the trail is marked with white blazes, and much of the trail above tree line has large cairns for wayfinding when clouds have descended on the route. To make it easier for hikers as well as reduce the number of cars, the AMC operates a shuttle service between popular trailheads.

Walking the Presidential Traverse—a series of dramatic peaks above tree line that honors many American presidents—conjures up visions of an epic adventure, and the trail lives up to this expectation. It's clearly the "glamour" hike in the northeastern United States, and walking it will add substantially to your hiking credentials. The AMC huts add important elements of accessibility and enjoyment. We highly recommend this walk, but only when the weather allows.

(ABOVE LEFT) After completing the Presidential Traverse, consider treating yourself at the Mount Washington Hotel, as generations of hikers have done.

(ABOVE) The Presidential Traverse climbs steeply toward the summit of Mount Washington.

ALL OR NOTHING AT ALL?

We used to debate whether it's okay to walk just part of a long-distance trail if you can't (or don't care to) walk it all. Initially, we took a strictly "purist" position. The first long-distance trail we walked—Vermont's aptly named Long Trail—was America's first long-distance trail, wandering 270 miles along the ridgetops of the state's Green Mountains from the border with Massachusetts to Canada. We walked the trail in sections, using the roads that periodically bisect the trail to get on and off. We were so obsessed with our purist philosophy that we made a point of walking across the road between trail sections so we could say we'd walked every step of the trail. We laugh at this now.

Hikers on both the High Sierra Camps Loop Trail and the Pacific Crest Trail share the same path through serene Lyell Canyon.

There's no denying the deep sense of satisfaction you get from walking the full length of a long-distance trail. In addition to the walks in this book, we've walked dozens of long-distance trails in their entirety, including circling the Mont Blanc massif on the Tour du Mont Blanc, crossing the width of England on the Coast-to-Coast Trail, and backpacking the John Muir Trail in the Sierra Nevada. These and other trails are described in our book, *Walking Distance.*

But there are limitations to this purist approach. Some trails are simply too long to be walked in their entirety, at least by ordinary people, people who have some inherent limitations on their time and abilities. For example, most people can't—or won't—take the roughly five months needed to walk the 2,650-mile Pacific Crest Trail (PCT). But does that mean you shouldn't walk a portion of the trail? Can't that be satisfying as well? Is it really all or nothing at all? There are so many wonderful trails to walk—so many appealing cultural landscapes all around the world just waiting to be explored on foot. Isn't it better to walk a portion of these trails than not to walk them at all? Part of the High Sierra Camps Loop that we describe in this book is along the PCT, and we can attest to the joy of hiking that section, for example.

It's clear Bill Bryson struggled with this issue on his hike along the Appalachian Trail with his sidekick, Katz, described hilariously in his best-selling book *A Walk in the Woods.* They spent many weeks hiking the trail, but ultimately fell far short of completing it. Did that matter? He concludes:

I understand now, in a way I never did before, the colossal scale of the world. I found patience and fortitude that I didn't know I had. I discovered an America that millions of people scarcely know exists. I made a friend. I came home . . . We didn't walk 2,200 miles, it's true, but here's the thing: we tried. So Katz was right after all, and I don't care what anybody says. We hiked the Appalachian Trail.

It's probably obvious that we've changed our position on this issue. We still find great joy in walking the length of most of the trails we travel; we've walked the full length of nearly all the trails we describe in this book. But we've found it surprisingly liberating to moderate our initial purist views on this issue; walking only parts of some trails can give license to experiencing a greater diversity of the world's cultural landscapes.

For example, we just don't have the time or inclination to walk the full Appalachian Trail. But we've walked several sections of it, including the Presidential Traverse in the White Mountains of New Hampshire, a section that many AT hikers would agree is the most dramatic and strikingly beautiful, and we've included this portion of the trail in this book. We feel we're much better off having walked this and other sections of the AT than not having walked any of it for seemingly silly purist ideals. In addition, the six-month period it would have taken to walk the length of the AT was invested in walking a number of other, diverse trails, and we're happy with this decision. There's an old saying in the hiking community: walk your own walk. We recommend considering this pragmatic approach.

Hiking the Presidential Traverse, one of the most dramatic sections of the Appalachian Trail, was richly rewarding.

The air quality in the Marlborough Sounds is exceptional.

Queen Charlotte Track

It can be challenging to pack for a long-distance walk. What should you bring and how much? What will you do if you need something you don't have? We did pretty well for our four-day walk of New Zealand's Queen Charlotte Track. Nevertheless, we were pleased and amused on day three when we walked by a self-service "store" a local entrepreneur had constructed along the trail. An assortment of items that walkers might need—toothbrushes and toothpaste, Band-Aids, ponchos, warm hats, candy bars and other snacks—were housed in a small, homemade wooden cabinet. Relying on the trustworthiness of walkers, the items were priced and walkers were encouraged to leave the appropriate amount in the box at the bottom of the cabinet if they took something. We didn't need anything, but we've done other walks where we wished the Queen Charlotte Track entrepreneur had franchised the business!

ON THE NORTHWEST SHOULDER of New Zealand's South Island is a network of remarkable waterways that make up the Marlborough Sounds. Māori, the native people of New Zealand, believed that the Marlborough Sounds were created when Kupe, a legendary Polynesian explorer credited with discovering New Zealand, caught an octopus in nearby Cook Strait. The lashing tentacles of the octopus formed the sounds. Modern-day geologists tell us these fjord-like sounds are glacially carved valleys that have been filled, or "drowned," by waters of the Pacific Ocean over a period of thousands of years. The sounds include sheltered inlets, white sand beaches, and high headlands covered in tropical rain forests. Viewed from land, the water takes on a striking turquoise color. The Queen Charlotte Track winds its way through these headlands for 45 delightful miles, starting at historic Ship Cove, the site of Captain James Cook's favorite New Zealand anchorage, and ending in the quaint coastal village of Anakiwa. Most walkers take four to five days to complete the walk. There are a series of tiny villages and tourist accommodations for walkers along the way.

LOCATION
New Zealand

LENGTH
45 miles

ACCOMMODATIONS
Commercial: Yes
Huts/refuges: No
Backpacking/camping: Yes

BAGGAGE TRANSFER AVAILABLE
Yes

OPTION TO WALK SECTIONS
Yes

DEGREE OF CHALLENGE
Low–Moderate

(ABOVE) The Marlborough Sounds are not fjords; they're glacially carved valleys that have been "drowned" by the Pacific Ocean over thousands of years.

(BELOW) Most of the track is forested, but there are occasional plots where the land is used for small-scale agriculture.

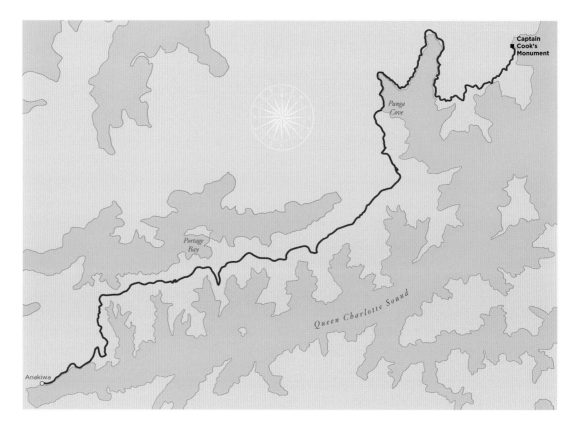

The sounds and surrounding headlands support an abundance of impressive native vegetation and animals. You'll encounter many weka, a flightless bird that New Zealanders call "cheeky"; they're curious, bold, and smart, so guard your food and other possessions carefully! All along the track we enjoyed seeing and (especially) hearing nectar-feeding bellbirds and tuis, with their fluted, musical calls. Dolphins often frolic offshore. Upper elevations support stately stands of virgin beech trees, some 600 to 700 years old, while lower elevations are cloaked in a rich rain forest, including many species of tree ferns. You'll see predator traps all along the way, a determined effort by the country's environmental agency to ward off exotic species; the traps contain poison and shouldn't be touched or tampered with.

The sounds have an interesting prehistory and history. Māori groups used the Marlborough Sounds (both the land and the sea), but population numbers were low. European settlement began when famous British explorer Captain Cook visited the sounds for the first time in 1770, finding his way to lovely Ship Cove, now the start of the Queen Charlotte Track. (Although Abel Tasman supposedly arrived in 1642, he did not get off the ship; whether due to cultural misunderstanding or aggression on one or both sides, the encounter was hostile.) Cook's interactions with the Māori were peaceful; he returned to this site on several occasions, naming Queen Charlotte Sound after the wife of King George III. The beach at Ship Cove has a large monument commemorating Cook's visits, and you can see where his sailors cleared away stones so they could beach their boats and make repairs.

Much of the track is along the ridgelines that separate the network of waterways comprising the Marlborough Sounds, which were named after an English general and statesman, and the route offers outstanding views of these stunningly beautiful waters; during the last half of the track, walkers can look into both Queen Charlotte Sound and Kenepuru Sound. The area's air quality is exceptional, and each view seems better than the last. Most of the track is forested, but there are occasional portions of agricultural lands and even aquaculture in the form of large fish farms.

The jumping-off point for the Queen Charlotte Track is the small tourist-friendly town of Picton (pronounced by the locals as PECK-ton), the northern terminus of the South Island's railroad (a delightful ride, one we highly recommend), highway networks, and port for one of the ferries that connects the South and North Islands. A passenger-only ferry ride is needed to access the beginning of the Queen Charlotte Track (a beautiful one-hour ride) and to return to Picton at the end of the walk (an equally beautiful half-hour ride). We especially enjoyed the seamanship of our boatman, who piloted and docked the boat without need of any crew. We were happy to see dolphins on both our ferry rides.

The track rises and falls along its route, but climbs to ridgelines and descents to isolated beaches are moderate. While views out over the sounds are numerous and lovely, some walkers might be disappointed at the relatively few beaches that are accessible. (Folks wanting more of a beach experience while walking in New Zealand should consider the Abel Tasman Coast Track, also described in this book.) Walking is not difficult as the track is well maintained and the surface is smooth; our trail running shoes were perfect. Wayfinding is easy on this well-marked route. Although camping is allowed, opportunities are limited and seemed to favor group outings; the campgrounds were full

The track rises and falls along its route, but climbs to ridgelines and descents to isolated beaches are moderate.

Viewed from above, the water takes on an appealing turquoise color.

of groups when we walked the track. Accommodations vary from traditional B&Bs and hotels to ecolodges, and there are a surprising number of choices tucked away off the track. As always, we suggest reservations.

New Zealand is justifiably proud of its locally produced foods, and the Marlborough Sounds region features seafood and wine, particularly its famous sauvignon blanc; the dinners were some of the best we've encountered when out walking, and we think you'll enjoy the terroir of this land, too. Many lodgings will prepare a tasty pack lunch if asked; these lunches are a winning choice over uninspired energy bars and trail mix.

A water taxi service will transfer luggage (and even tired walkers) if desired. The water taxis and occasional road crossings make it easy to walk the track in a series of day hikes. We encountered few other walkers when we were there in early December, New Zealand's summer season. However, on one of the weekend days, we encountered quite a few mountain bikers, a few of whom were inconsiderate. Some of the track crosses private lands and walkers must purchase a permit to access these

areas; these passes can be obtained at several locations in Picton and from a few businesses near the track.

The Queen Charlotte Track is a delightful walk offering strikingly beautiful views of Marlborough Sounds as well as occasional forays down to pristine beaches. This is a relatively easy walk, one that can be enjoyed by walkers of nearly all abilities. Though the water taxis can be used to walk parts of the trail, it would be a shame not to complete the full walk. The track provides a wonderful way to see the best of this unique part of New Zealand at a pace that allows a deep and rich appreciation for the area's beauty and natural and cultural history.

SLACKPACKING

What's "slackpacking?" you're thinking. Well, like walking itself, it's a relative term. At one end of the spectrum, there's strolling—a slow lap around the neighborhood after dinner; on the other end of the spectrum, there's backpacking—carrying all your gear on a trip that might last anywhere from a weekend to a few weeks or even months. And then there's slackpacking, which can include much of everything between. (There's also "glamping"—glamorous camping—in which a commercial outfitter transports your gear, sets up your tent, and cooks your dinners; this is also called "poshpacking.")

Slackpackers often hike relatively long (sometimes very long) distances. However, when the mood strikes, they abandon the trail at the end of the day, opting for the comfort of a warm shower and clean sheets instead of an icy dip in the river and a 20-degree rated sleeping bag. That's to say nothing of

Trails such as the Abel Tasman Coast Track have a series of modern, comfortable huts along the route.

the merits of a freshly cooked, locally sourced dinner (accompanied, perhaps, by an amusing wine) versus a pouch of freeze-dried lasagna washed down with yet another canteen of purified water.

A number of years ago, we decided to walk the Colorado Trail (described in our book, *Walking Distance*). This was a big undertaking for two reasons. First, the trail is challenging; it wanders 470 miles through the Rocky Mountains from Denver to Durango, much of it along the ridge of the Continental Divide. Like the mountains themselves the trail rises and falls, but much of the time is spent above 10,000 feet, sometimes well above. Second, most of the trail is pretty wild; it traverses eight ranges of the Rocky Mountains and five major river systems, crossing seven national forests and six wilderness areas. Sounds exciting, but maybe a little intimidating as well.

But a close inspection revealed that, as with most long-distance trails, there are a number of road crossings along the route (for better or worse). Moreover, a series of side trails feed into the main trail. And a Colorado map shows that the trail comes tantalizingly close to a string of colorful Colorado towns, including Breckenridge, Leadville, Buena Vista, Salida, Creede, Lake City, and Silverton. With some creative thinking, an epic slackpack began to come into focus.

We wound up walking the trail for a month, covering most of its miles. About half the nights we camped in this great wilderness, but the other half we stayed in local towns, sometimes in hostels and sometimes in B&Bs. In other words, we slackpacked the trail in the best sense of the term, one for which we are beginning to have greater appreciation. For several weeks, we thrilled in the breathtaking (in every sense of the word) beauty of the Colorado Rockies: the awe-inspiring geology, the lofty peaks, the lovely aspen groves, the stark

Many long-distance trails offer the opportunity to stay in local B&Bs. (Pennine Way)

and dramatic tundra, the lush wildflowers, the mule deer, elk, and bighorn sheep, the rushing streams, the blue skies, the wild weather. We think we now have a good sense of the landscape that is the Rocky Mountains.

But we have more than that. The Colorado Rockies, like most areas, are a *cultural* landscape, the product of a long-term and continuing dialogue between humans and nature. And both are worthy of attention and honor. The Colorado towns we visited are a reflection of the engaging history of the region, including its architecture, institutions, food, arts, and mythology. The people we met are as genuine and trust-worthy as they are colorful. They've shaped the landscape over the years, and the reciprocal is just as true.

The trails we recommend in this book span the spectrum of walking. For example, the Great Saunter is a walk (albeit a long one) in New York City. The Queen Charlotte Track is a hike that offers B&B-like accommodations along the way. The Four Pass Loop Trail in the Maroon Bells–Snowmass Wilderness is a backpacking trip. And Denali National Park and Preserve is a mostly trailless six-million-acre wilderness. Celebrate the whole spectrum of walking opportunities, choose the walks that meet your needs, and allow your needs to evolve with the course of time.

Much of the foreshore of Sydney Harbour has been preserved in public ownership and offers a wealth of walking opportunities.

Sydney

It was a beautiful Sunday morning, and we decided to take the ferry to Manly and walk out and around North Head, the dramatic peninsula that marks the northern flank of the entrance to Sydney Harbour. We got off the ferry and walked along the pedestrian mall to Manly Beach, where we were surprised to see so many people already on the sand and in the water. But what really caught our attention was the large number of kids—boys and girls maybe six to ten years old—organized into small groups, each led by several adults. Some of the groups were playing racing games on the sand, others were swimming through the surf, and some were trying hard to throw their adult leaders into the water. Watching for a while, we realized that these kids weren't just playing, they were being socialized into a vital part of living in Sydney, and probably Australia more generally. The out of doors seems important to so many people we saw in Sydney and surrounding communities, and being comfortable with the ocean is a fundamental part of that lifestyle. These kids were being prepared for life in a culture that values its environment. Of course, they didn't know anything about that—they were just having fun.

LOCATION
Australia

LENGTH
Variable

ACCOMMODATIONS
Commercial: Yes
Huts/refuges: No
Backpacking/camping: No

BAGGAGE TRANSFER AVAILABLE
No

OPTION TO WALK SECTIONS
Yes

DEGREE OF CHALLENGE
Low–Moderate

SYDNEY HARBOUR, first called Port Jackson, is the site of the first European presence in Australia. The harbor was "discovered" by Lieutenant (later Captain) James Cook in 1770 and named Port Jackson to honor the judge advocate of the British Fleet. Of course, the several native tribes living in the area at that time had little say in the matter. Eighteen years later, Governor Arthur Phillip sailed into the harbor and established a colony. In his first dispatch, he reported to the homeland that "we had the satisfaction of finding the finest harbor in the world."

Few people would disagree with him, even after more than two centuries. Geologically, Sydney Harbour is a drowned river valley that makes an especially large, deep, and well-protected harbor. It also showcases what may be Australia's greatest city, and certainly one of the most beautiful and vibrant cities in the world. The harbor features dramatic headlands, high sandstone cliffs, golden

The walk from Coogee Beach to Bondi Beach is just about everyone's favorite.

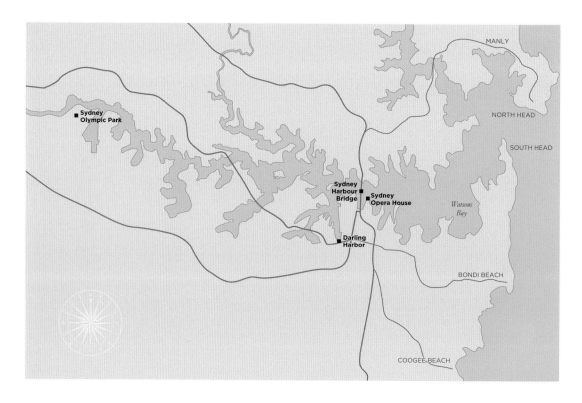

beaches, lush lagoons, rocky foreshores, turquoise waters, numerous bays, and patches of dense native bushland. The city itself is a mix of historic buildings and modern skyscrapers, with attractive suburban communities tucked into sheltered bays. And, of course, there's the Sydney Opera House and the Sydney Harbour Bridge, two iconic structures that are internationally known symbols of the city.

Most people know that Sydney was initially a British penal colony, and the contemporary people of Sydney seem to take a perverse pleasure in this origin and reputation. They are an outdoor-oriented, vital, and diverse society that takes great pleasure in their striking surroundings, flooding the harbor with their pleasure boats and the remarkable network of trails with what they call "bush-walkers," a term that strikes us as a bit of an overstatement. They've been remarkably foresighted (and a little lucky as well) to have reserved much of the coastline and its foreshore for public access and use. Many of these areas were originally reserved for military uses, but this purpose is now obsolete, and conservation and community groups have worked hard to save much of the land from development.

To the good fortune of residents and visitors, these areas support an extensive network of trails that offer a rich variety of walks that can easily be done as a series of day hikes. Sydney Harbour National Park is just one the harbor's many attractions. A wonderful system of ferries, supplemented by a network of trains and buses, provides convenient access. In fact, riding the ferries only adds to the pleasure of walking these trails.

The half-day walk that connects Coogee Beach to Bondi Beach—two of Sydney's most iconic beaches—is just about everyone's favorite. This path is hard along the coast, alternating between cliff tops and beaches, and in a few places the trail has been constructed out over the cliffs. Bondi Beach is big in both size and reputation—and with its lovely, powdery, white sand, it's a great place to hang out, swimming, surfing, and soaking up the Sydney lifestyle. At the south end of the beach is Bondi Icebergs Club, a swimming club where you can have an upscale lunch and try out the Bondi Baths, one of many large saltwater swimming pools along the coast. Here, waves from the sea break right into the pool. You'll pass several other beaches and saltwater pools along the walk, as well as the beautiful Waverley Cemetery and great spots to watch for whales between May and November. Coogee Beach has its own vibe, with lots of parkland just behind the sand. Buses provide the best public transportation.

(ABOVE LEFT) Many miles of trails around Sydney are perched on high oceanside cliffs.

(ABOVE) Popular Manly Beach on a Sunday morning shows how many Sydney residents value an outdoor lifestyle.

(ABOVE) Be sure to include the dramatic Sydney Harbour Bridge in your walking itinerary.

(BELOW) The extensive ferry system that serves the greater Sydney Harbour area provides easy access to many walks and is an attraction in itself.

You can continue this coastal walk north from Bondi Beach up and around South Head, and then into sheltered Watsons Bay for a full day's walk. On the long coastal portion of this walk, the trail stays mostly on the high cliff tops and is very dramatic. Intricate boardwalks navigate some of the steep areas, and a little road walking is necessary to skirt private property, including the Bondi Golf Course. You'll pass through several small parks and by the iconic Macquarie Lighthouse, a replica of the original structure that was designed by convict architect Francis Greenway. The lighthouse remains important for navigation, and its light can be seen more than 30 miles at sea. South Head is the peninsula that occupies the southern flank of Sydney Harbour, and also includes a candy-striped lighthouse. Part of this area is still a military post and is inaccessible to the public.

Rounding the head, there's a small nude beach and stunning views of the downtown section of Sydney. The community of Watsons Bay includes a wonderful park that flows right down to the water, as well as several restaurants—we recommend the fish and chips. Ferries provide a delightful ride between Watsons Bay and downtown Sydney.

North Head is the peninsula that makes up the northern flank of Sydney Harbour. Manly is this area's bustling town, and is served by a long and pleasant ferry ride. The town boasts that it is "only seven miles from Sydney and a million miles from care." Manly Beach is big, busy, and fun. The short walk around North Head offers a little more solitude, some areas of native bush, and several smaller, less heavily used beaches that have patches of rain forest and a tropical flare. We enjoyed seeing an enterprising young person selling ice cream treats from his boat at one of the beaches (and doing a good business); he'd ring a hand bell and swimmers and sunbathers would wade out to his little craft. Much of North Head was a military base; you'll see old gun emplacements, and a repurposed army building now serves as a visitor center.

Manly is at the western end of another delightful walk to Split Bridge (accessible by bus). This walk is right along the foreshore and passes through long stretches of native bushland and across a number of attractive beaches. It's best to do this walk at low tide to ensure beach access. At Grotto Point, the Aboriginal rock art sites are definitely worth seeking out.

Mosman Bay was one of our favorite walks, and took about a half day. A short ferry ride from downtown Sydney, the trail takes you around Cremorne Point, which features an attractive residential area of large homes with extensive landscaping and striking views of Sydney and the opera house. The area has remnants of native bush, including lots of tree ferns. It was a steep walk up and over Mosman Point, one of only a few places in our walks around Sydney that wouldn't be called "easy." We continued to the area that houses Taronga Zoo and took the ferry back from there.

Bicentennial Park, accessible by a ferry ride up the Paramatta River, offers a very different type of walk. This is one of the few areas that retains much of its original mangrove forest, and walkers use a system of boardwalks to make the wet area accessible. This area is adjacent to Olympic Park and has lots of facilities for family outings, including open fields, picnic areas, fountains, lakes, viewing platforms, and a restaurant.

There are several walks in the old, downtown portions of Sydney that shouldn't be neglected. Circular Quay is the heart of the ferry system and will quickly become familiar to you. This can be the starting and ending place for several walks. A half-day's loop walk from Circular Quay goes right by the Sydney Opera House (take time to walk around the building to appreciate it from several perspectives) and then through the city's impressive botanical garden (with its fruit bats). The plantings and grounds are impressive, but the area is heavily used for recreation as well—school groups, rugby players, runners, etc. We were there in November, and the jacaranda trees were in bloom throughout the city, one of the highlights for us.

Other walking destinations from Circular Quay include The Rocks (some of the very oldest parts of the city), Darling Harbour (a newer area of the city that includes tourist attractions such as the world's largest IMAX theater and an aquarium), and, more toward downtown Sydney, the historic Queen Victoria Building (an early shopping emporium that now houses shops and offers English tea service). By all means, walk across the mile-and-a-half Sydney Harbour Bridge to the charming neighborhood of Kirribilli. You can return to Circular Quay from the nearby ferry landing at Milsons Point/Luna Park, or walk through the neighborhood of Kirribilli and return from the Kirribilli ferry landing.

The logistics of walking in Sydney are pretty easy. The highly accessible ferry, train, and bus systems are user-friendly and multi-day passes are economical. Sydney can be hot at midday from December through March, so stay hydrated and use sun protection. Beaches and other attractions are noticeably busier on weekends. Residents of Sydney love fireworks and look for any excuse to mount a show over the harbor in the evenings; sometimes we didn't know what was being celebrated, but we always found the fireworks entertaining.

We spent ten days in Sydney, renting an apartment in the Kirribilli neighborhood. Each day we'd go out walking and enjoyed all our adventures. We left Sydney feeling fully entertained and with great admiration for the city, its environment, and people. There are lots of walks we didn't have time for and, of course, there are many we'd like to repeat, so we hope to get back again. Sydney is one of the world's great cities, and we think walking is the ideal way to appreciate it.

Many trails around Sydney lead down to neighborhoods, small harbors, and pocket beaches.

"EVERYTHING IS SOMEWHERE ELSE"

If walking is so great, why don't we walk more and drive less? An important part of the answer to this question is that we've designed our everyday world—the communities in which we live as well as the places we work—around the car rather than walking.

In her perceptive and wonderfully illustrated book, *Made for Walking: Density and Neighborhood Form*, Julie Campoli discusses some of the increasingly distressing aspects of the daily life of typical Americans across the country. For example, she describes the Hurst family, which lives in a single-family home in a low-density suburb—the ideal to which many Americans have traditionally aspired. But the rub is that Mr. Hurst must drive 22 miles to work in rush-hour traffic. Mrs. Hurst has it better, commuting just 5.5 miles. The two children go to schools that are 9 and 18 miles away. Most of the services they use—markets, shops, restaurants, etc.—are also well beyond reasonable walking distance. Consequently, the Hursts own several cars and use them nearly every day for multiple trips.

Even though there is a strong and growing impulse among many families to walk more in their everyday lives—for reasons of health, economy, and environment—the unfortunate reality is that this is simply not feasible, at least within the communities in which most of us live. Campoli titles the first chapter in her book *Everything Is Somewhere Else*, a metaphorical expression of the exasperation and frustration that a growing number of families mutter (maybe even scream) as they endure long commutes, traffic jams, the high cost of owning and operating a car, air pollution, lack of exercise, and not enough time left in the day for coveted leisure and genuine family time. As Campoli writes, "In most of the places we live and work, we can take a walk, but we can't walk to get somewhere because that somewhere is too far away." Campoli devotes most of her book to dissecting many American communities to learn why some are walkable and most are not.

But it's not like that everywhere. For example, Simon Armitage, British poet and reborn walker, says, "[Y]ou can really walk to places in Britain. It's not like walking from New York to Cleveland. You can actually set off and get to places here."

Frustration over the lack of "walkability" of communities is not new. Nineteenth-century Scottish geographer Patrick Geddes suggested that urban planning should begin with a walk. Writer and activist Jane Jacobs argued in her book, *The Death and Life of Great American Cities*, that "an unwalked city is a dead city; arguably it is no city at all." To advance walkability, contemporary community planners are now rallying around the "five Ds":

1. diversity (mixed land uses, including housing and commercial services)
2. density (both population and housing)
3. design (a pleasant streetscape)
4. distance to transit (public transit that is a short walk away)
5. destination accessibility (jobs and attractions)

Other elements of community design that can help encourage walking include limiting cheap and abundant parking, small blocks, narrow setbacks, multistory buildings, connected sidewalks, trees and other vegetation, variety in buildings, pedestrian street crossings, green spaces, buffers between roads and walkways, street furniture, good air quality, and shade. Research suggests that there is substantial latent demand for communities and neighborhoods that feature these characteristics. For example, a recent survey conducted for the National Association of Realtors found that a majority of respondents would chose a smaller house and yard to reduce their commute to twenty minutes or less, and nearly 90 percent would opt for a smaller home to live in a place with good schools, sidewalks, and services within walking distance.

These ideas are manifested in social movements such as "New Urbanism" and "New Pedestrianism," evolving sets of ideas designed to advance the walkability of communities. For example, "pedestrian villages" are designed to be compact neighborhoods with nonmotorized ways in the front of residences and businesses, and motorized vehicle access provided at the rear, underground, or on the periphery of the community. Venice, Italy, and Venice, California, are examples, as is the Disney town of Celebration, Florida, an Experimental Prototype Community of Tomorrow (EPCOT). Of course, there are an expanding number of pedestrian shopping malls and car-free town centers; central Copenhagen is one of the oldest and largest.

There are a number of pedestrian advocacy and support organizations, such as AmericaWalks and the European Local Transport Information Service. A number of walking audits—Walk Score, the Pedestrian Environment Review System (PERS), Walkonomics, RateMyStreet, and the Walk Space Score App—have been developed to help assess the walkability of communities. We encourage you to look up the score of your community; we hope you're pleased, but expect that you'll be disappointed. Conduct your own walkability audit and talk with your community planners about how to improve your score.

It's not uncommon now to see real estate listings that include a walkability score or assessment. The Leadership in Energy and Environmental Design (LEED) program has extended its work from buildings to neighborhood design

(LEED-ND), with a strong emphasis on walkability. National Geographic conducts a periodic "Greendex" study of seventeen nations that includes components on walking and transit use; the United States comes in a distant last on both criteria.

We should note that walkability is not all about aesthetics and quality of life (though these are enough to warrant concern)—it can also be a matter of life and death. For the most recent year of data, 4,735 pedestrians were killed by motor vehicles in the United States alone, and an estimated 66,000 were injured (a number that's thought to be substantially underestimated). The right to walk in one's community can also be seen as a social justice issue—walkability in low-income communities is often especially low. Writer Antonia Malchik says that we've even "criminalized" walking, fining people for "jaywalking."

Social movements such as "New Urbanism" and "New Pedestrianism" are advancing the walkability of the places where people live, work, and play. (Golden Gate Way)

The Thames Path brings walkers right past London's most iconic landmarks.

Thames Path

At first the river was little more than a creek, marshy in places. The peaceful, pastoral setting of the Thames Path didn't change much, but the river did. When we reached the village of Lechlade, the river was navigable for the first time. Here, a cluster of "narrow boats" had gathered, preparing to travel downstream, perhaps all the way to London. As the term narrow boat suggests, these have a distinctive configuration, designed to squeeze through the many locks on the river; boats can't exceed 7 feet in width and 72 feet in length or they won't fit through the narrowest and shortest locks in the system. Narrow boats played an important role in the Industrial Revolution, carrying cargo on the vast network of English rivers and canals. At first, horses on towpaths powered the boats, but later the internal combustion engine was popular. Now these boats have become very popular for recreation. One narrow boat stood out because of its colorful and attractive design; across the stern, we could see it was called *Sapphire*, in keeping with the rich blue paint. We waved as we passed, and the couple aboard gave us a wave back, the first of many such exchanges as it turned out. Narrow boats are not fast, but they're a little faster than a walker. So, after an hour or so, *Sapphire* passed us with another exchange of waves. But navigating the locks can take some time, especially if there are a number of boats waiting their turn. At the first lock, we strode on past *Sapphire*, offering another satisfying salute. This exchange of greetings carried on for much of our walk, and we looked forward to seeing *Sapphire* each day—it was an enjoyable routine. At one point we hadn't seen *Sapphire* for a few days and thought we'd lost her, but there she was in Windsor, nearly to London, where we enthusiastically exchanged greetings for what would turn out to be the last time.

LOCATION
England

LENGTH
184 miles

ACCOMMODATIONS
Commercial: Yes
Huts/refuges: No
Backpacking/camping: No

BAGGAGE TRANSFER AVAILABLE
Yes

OPTION TO WALK SECTIONS
Yes

DEGREE OF CHALLENGE
Low

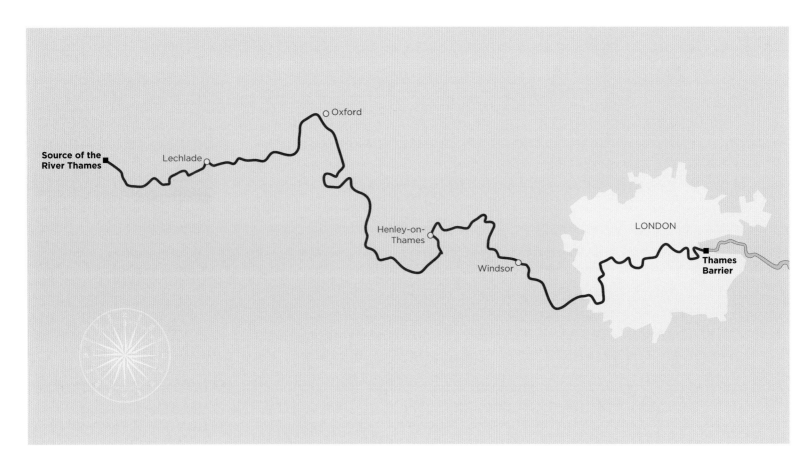

THE THAMES PATH is one of England's national trails, the only one to follow a river. It's only fitting that it follows the River Thames, England's greatest river, one that's also well known internationally. The trail follows the river's circuitous course from its source in the Cotswolds to where it meets the sea, a walk of 184 miles. It passes through "water meadows" (grasslands that are irrigated to enhance their productivity) and other agricultural lands, unspoiled rural villages, historic towns and cities, through London, and on to the Thames Barrier, an ingenious piece of engineering designed to prevent flooding in London and surrounding areas. The trail was initially proposed in the 1930s, but didn't become a reality until 1996. Much of the trail is on the original towpath that was created for the narrow boats that carried cargo up and down the river.

We started our walk with a short pilgrimage to the source of the river near Kemble. Here we found a large stone monument and a circle of small stones under an old ash tree marking the place where a spring usually gushes water, the very source of the river. However, the weather had been especially warm and dry that summer and we saw only some moist ground. At one time, there was also a statue of *Father Thames*, commissioned in 1854, but it was moved to a more secure location in the village of Lechlade. We saw the statue there, including the canoe paddle that someone had thoughtfully placed in Father Thames's hand.

From the marker stone we walked "downstream," and soon were in attractive marshy areas with interesting birds; then the marsh began to evolve into a creek with numerous ducks and swans. The land was primarily agricultural, and we walked along the margins of fields, sometimes having to shoo cows out of the way. At times we felt we were walking right through one of John Constable's nineteenth-century romantic landscapes, which glorified the classic English countryside. The first half of the Thames Path passes through four of England's Areas of Outstanding Natural Beauty; it's a stunning landscape in a very gentle way.

Lechlade, marking the beginning of the navigable portion of the river, is a beautiful village with a "wool church" (a characteristic Cotswold church built with the riches of the medieval wool trade); we encountered a flurry of boat activity. Here, the Ha'penny Bridge, named for the toll that was extracted to use it, crosses the Thames; it was the first of many historic and interesting bridges we enjoyed. Historically, narrow boats were loaded with Cotswold wool and stone bound for cities downstream, and many of the buildings in this region, even as far down the river as Oxford, were built with the attractive honey-colored stone, which seems to glow from within.

Travel on the river is made possible by a long system of locks that raise and lower the surface of the river to address changes in elevation as it descends to the sea. We found the locks fascinating, and they made good places to stop and take breaks. These locks are still vital to travel on the river, and it was great fun to watch them in operation. Boaters made their way into the locks and then closed the gates behind. Water then filled the lock (or drained from the lock, depending on whether the boat was traveling up- or downstream). Finally, the gate at the bow of the boat was opened and the boat was on its way. At many of the smaller locks, this was a self-service operation, up to the boat's crew to make this process happen. At the larger locks, paid staff operated the locks, and some were wonderfully efficient. Many still had the original lockkeepers cottages, which were very attractive, and some locks were beautifully landscaped and even had food concessions. Our favorite locks were Shepperton Lock and Mapledurham Lock, the first mechanized lock and one whose history dates back to at least 1086, when it's mentioned as a dam or weir in the Domesday Book. They sported lovingly tended flowerbeds and tea huts where we rewarded ourselves with sandwiches and drinks. We also enjoyed the gallery with local art at Mapledurham Lock.

Along some sections of the river we saw concrete bunkers that reminded us of the difficult times the English people faced in World War II. Of course, we were thrilled to walk through Oxford and

(ABOVE) Historically, narrow boats carried wool and stone from the Cotswold region to the cities downstream; nowadays many have been converted to pleasure craft, joining other boats cruising the River Thames.

(BELOW) There are forty-five locks on the River Thames, making it possible for boats to address the river's change in elevation as it descends to the sea.

tour through the attractive buildings that make up the historic college. This is a busy town, with students and others sculling on the river. Later, we walked through Henley-on-Thames, host of the famous Henley Regatta, established in 1839. The regatta is held over five days in July and attracts racing crews from all over the world. Farther along we dodged members of the rowing clubs at Putney; they were using the path as a staging area for putting their sculls into the river. Putney is the starting place for the Oxford and Cambridge boat races, credited (by some) as the oldest continuous sporting event. Sculling isn't the only recreational use of the River Thames. We enjoyed seeing many people walking, running, and biking along the riverbanks in many places, kids playing cricket, folks fishing, families picnicking, and recreational boats of many types. The River Thames remains an important part of everyday life for many Brits, and contributes enormously to the quality of life.

The Thames Path includes many attractions, big and small, that are important markers of British history and life. We walked by Iron Age forts and dikes that speak to the prehistory of the country and marveled at the authentic thatched-roof houses. We walked through lovely, lively towns such as Abingdon, a medieval market town with a beautiful seven-arch bridge approach. We walked through Runnymede, where the Magna Carta, recognizing basic human rights and a precursor to the American Constitution, was signed in 1215. Of course, sprawling Windsor Castle is a magnet for tourists who wander up and down picturesque Eton High Street. This is the oldest and largest occupied castle in the world and the Queen's official residence and favorite weekend home; it was established by William the Conqueror in the eleventh century. We peered through the gates at striking Hampton Court Palace and its extensive grounds. Yes, British royalty live in a much different world! Kew Gardens hosts the world's largest collection of living plants and enjoys recognition as a World Heritage Site; its 300-acre grounds are both educational and beautiful. We took a layover day here to walk the gardens and were glad we did, even though the gardens looked a little tired. We heard real Brits saying "crikey," "cheerio," and "brilliant."

Near the end of the path, of course, there's London. It's such a large city that it took us three days to walk through it, stopping to gawk at its world-famous buildings and institutions: the Houses of Parliament, the Tower of London, Big Ben, Tower Bridge, the giant Ferris wheel known as the London Eye. Not surprisingly, there are many options for exploring these iconic tourist destinations—a plethora of boat rides, tourist buses, etc.—but, as usual, we found walking gave us a satisfying introduction to the famous landscapes on the Thames, allowing us to choose what we'd visit later.

We marched on for another half day to reach the Thames Barrier, which shields London from large tidal surges that flow up the river from the sea. And here our two-week walk ended with a wave of ambivalence—glad to have successfully walked the Thames Path, but sorry that it was over. We

(ABOVE) Soon after leaving its source the River Thames becomes an attractive marshy area, but gives no hint of its eventual size and power.

(BELOW) Much of the Thames Path skirts agricultural land hard on the river shore.

Historic Windsor Castle is one of the landmark buildings walkers pass on the Thames Path; it was established in the eleventh century and is the Queen's official residence and favorite weekend home.

consoled ourselves with the reality that there were many more long-distance trails waiting to be walked.

The logistics of walking the Thames Path are pretty straightforward. It's a long but easy walk with little elevation change. It's well way-marked, and there are several good, detailed guidebooks. Reaching the beginning of the walk is probably the most difficult part, as it's quite rural. You can travel by train to Kemble and then take an infrequent bus to the starting point, or go to Cricklade, where there are more buses. Generally, the path is well served by public transportation, making it relatively easy to walk in sections. This is a popular choice for most Brits; we saw few folks who could be identified as thru-walkers (and, yes, there's a look.) A range of accommodations is available in the towns adjacent to the river, though fewer options are available in some of the small villages; we especially enjoyed staying in historic Thames-side lodgings. You can arrange to have your baggage sent by commercial service, if you like.

Walking the Thames Path is richly rewarding. Not only is it satisfying to walk the whole trail, but it's fulfilling to walk the full length of the river as well. When we finished the walk, we felt we had a much better sense of both the history and contemporary life of the English people and fully enjoyed the landscape that's been their home for so many generations. Crikey, the Thames Path is brilliant—cheerio!

TRAILS AS TRANSECTS

Transects are commonly used in the natural sciences to study plants and animals; a transect is a line that's used to inventory and monitor biological conditions. The large size of most natural areas makes it challenging to inventory all the plants and animals that might exist there, so a random sampling approach—a randomly drawn line or a transect—must be used. For example, a scientist might lay out such a line and count the number of each species of plants that touch the line; resulting data can be used to estimate the relative abundance of selected species. Transects can also be used to inventory cultural resources, such as Native American archeological sites. The underlying concept of transects is also being used to measure the rural-to-urban gradient in regional and city planning.

There is excitement about using the Appalachian Trail to help inventory and monitor environmental and cultural conditions across the fourteen states it traverses. (Presidential Traverse)

In an analogous way, trails can be thought of as a type of transect and might be used to study—either formally or informally—the natural and cultural conditions of the areas or regions they traverse. In fact, there is great excitement about using the Appalachian Trail in the eastern United States to help inventory and monitor environmental and cultural conditions across the fourteen states it traverses. This is not a new idea. The founder of the Appalachian Trail, Benton MacKaye, suggested in the 1930s that amateur naturalists could lead a grand investigation of trail ecology.

However, it wasn't until 1999 that this idea came to fruition in the form of the Appalachian Trail MEGA-Transect. This program includes agencies such as the National Park Service and US Forest Service, the nonprofit Appalachian Trail Conservancy, and citizen scientists. A number of "vital signs" are monitored along the trail, including rare plants, water quality, mountain birds, forest health, invasive plants, and ecological dynamics, such as the timing of bud break, flowering, animal migration, and amphibian breeding.

The Appalachian Trail MEGA-Transect has led to development of a multidisciplinary educational program called "A Trail to Every Classroom." Students can participate in the monitoring process, and resulting data helps transform classroom teaching into effective and exciting place-based education. This service-based learning can enhance and sustain local enthusiasm for volunteer-based management of the trail.

Megatransects are becoming more numerous, some of them very long and arduous. For example, Michael Fay conducted the MegaTransect across 2,000 miles of the Congo Basin in Africa. The journey took 455 days and surveyed the ecological condition of the area. Paul Salopek began his seven-year, thirty-million-step Out of Eden Walk in 2013,

Transects are lines on the landscape used to assess environmental conditions and how they change over time. (Pembrokeshire Coast Path)

following one of the routes taken by early humans to migrate out of Africa. The journey began in Ethiopia and will proceed through the Middle East and Asia, to Alaska by boat, then down the west coast of the Americas to the southern tip of South America. He writes, "I am going to swim upstream against the flow of information and try to slow people down to have them observe stories at a human pace—at about three miles per hour." His periodic dispatches are designed to "tell stories of humanity's ever unfolding journey." Support for both Fay and Salopek came from the National Geographic Society.

The concept of trails as transects doesn't have to be applied in a such a formal fashion. Just think of trails as a good way to "inventory" the natural and cultural features of the areas through which you walk. What are the important characteristics of the area? What makes this area distinctive? If you walk the trail periodically, how are these conditions changing over time and space? Using your own observations while walking will deepen your knowledge and enrich your experience.

The Val d'Orcia is a World Heritage Site, thought by some to be the "perfect" cultural landscape.

Val d'Orcia

We were excited to finally be walking the iconic landscapes of Italy's Tuscany region and were, of course, looking forward to the regional food. Our first day's walk brought us into the small walled city of Buonconvento, and we stopped at the tiny, modest restaurant that had been recommended. Tucked on one of the narrow, medieval streets, the restaurant (though reputedly a local favorite) was less than imposing, and the food was absolutely terrific. The fact that we could speak only a few words of Italian and our waiter could speak no English was no problem, and we ended up with a pasta dish that was the best we'd ever had. "Mama" was in the kitchen, directing all activity, and there was much back and forth between her, her small staff (probably family), and the locals who joined in the fun. We had room for *dolce* (dessert), and somehow conveyed to the waiter that he should choose; he responded by crossing the lane to an equally tiny bakery and presenting us with a Cabernet grape dessert that was obviously a local delicacy. What a fun dinner—delicious, authentic food combined with dinner theater—and we used that first meal as a standard for all others to follow.

LOCATION
Italy

LENGTH
59 miles

ACCOMMODATIONS
Commercial: Yes
Huts/refuges: No
Backpacking/camping: No

BAGGAGE TRANSFER AVAILABLE
Yes

OPTION TO WALK SECTIONS
Yes

DEGREE OF CHALLENGE
Low

Val d'Orcia means "Valley of the Orcia River," and this walk crosses a large, tranquil Tuscan valley, with walkers spending the night in a series of iconic hill towns. The valley is protected as an "artistic, natural, and cultural park," and its designation as a World Heritage Site proclaims the area "an exceptional reflection of the way the landscape was rewritten in Renaissance times to reflect the ideals of good governance and to create an aesthetically pleasing picture." The valley includes many important and defining features, including extensive vineyards, olive groves, fields of sunflowers and wheat, cypress-lined avenues, walled medieval hill towns, historic castles and abbeys, and isolated farmhouses. All these features fit gracefully within the foundational open structure of the landscape, defined by the rolling hills and valleys, long views, and the meandering Orcia River. Some observers have called this a utopian, "perfect landscape."

Afternoon sun enters the Abbey of Sant'Antimo, reputedly built by Emperor Charlemagne in AD 781.

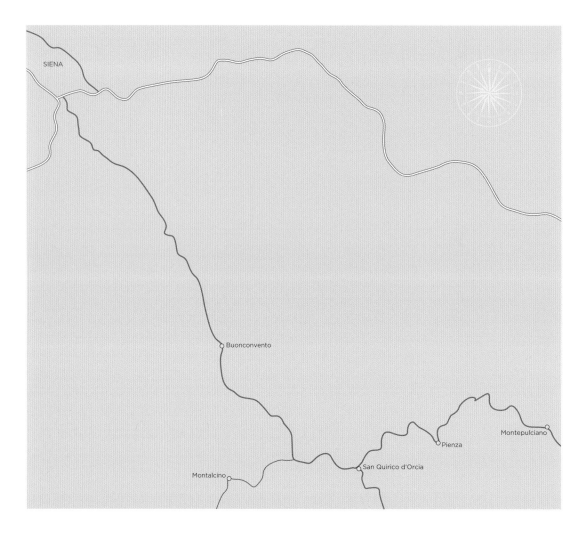

The area is celebrated by Renaissance painters as well as contemporary photographers, high-lighting the defining colors of the region, including the striking *terra di Sienna* hue and the yellow, red, and ochre-tinted shades of brown. If that weren't enough, the region offers an array of local foods, including wines (such as the internationally famous Brunello di Montalcino and Nobile di Montepulciano), olive oil, pecorino cheese (from sheep's milk), saffron, mushrooms, and chestnuts. These foods, and the visitors they attract, are designed to support the local economy, enhance the quality of life, and conserve the valley's history and distinctive sense of place.

When walking the Val d'Orcia, you have the option of spending each night in a different medieval hill town, each with unique charm.

The sense of history in the Val d'Orcia is palpable, and trying to keep all the players and places straight must be hard for Italian schoolchildren. The landscape itself is ancient, and everywhere you look there are significant buildings and sites of notable events. A cultural feature from early times is Bagno Vignoni, an area of thermal baths. Romans enjoyed these warm waters and they've been popular ever since; walkers can bathe here, too. Churches and fortifications date from the ninth century; our favorite was the Abbey of Sant'Antimo, reputedly build by Emperor Charlemagne in 781; rebuilt, it's considered one of the finest Romanesque churches in Italy.

Much of the area looks as it would have centuries ago. Our first night in Buonconvento is a good example. Buonconvento literally straddles the Via Francigena, the main pilgrim route from France to Rome. The town has an oval shape (somewhat unusual for a walled town) because it grew from a cluster of shops and services strung out along the road. Add in the mental image of Crusaders charging about, protecting humble pilgrims, and attacking forces from neighboring city-states (an ongoing process) and history becomes more real.

Another overnight stop was Rocca d'Orcia. A *rocca* (also called a *borgo*) is a defensive fortification or tower, sometimes attached to a castle (but in this case not). Rocca d'Orcia is reputed to be the oldest *borgo* in Italy, and we enjoyed visiting the inside of the tower, imagining defending

(ABOVE) The sunset provides dramatic light for viewing the surrounding countryside from Montepulciano, nicknamed "Florence on hills."

(ABOVE RIGHT) The tiny Vitaleta Chapel is reputed to be one of the most photographed churches in Tuscany; it's located between Pienza and San Quirico.

it against enemy forces. In spite of repeated attacks, it was held by the Sienese against Florentine assaults for a thousand years. We stayed a short walk away in a town with a public space and a stone plaza around the central well that has remained untouched since the twelfth century.

Pienza is another interesting hill town. It was the hometown of Pope Pius II; he wanted to promote Renaissance ideals and used what we call urban renewal to build a new central piazza featuring classically inspired designs. His architect was only able to complete three buildings (the Duomo, town hall, and a mansion for Pius's family) before the pope died, and these buildings employ tricks of geometry (nonrectangular walls, for example) to make the area appear larger and more open. Montepulciano has been called "Florence on hills" and the nickname is apt; here we stayed in a *palazzo* (palace) now run as a B&B; never have we stayed in such a large and grand room.

History is everywhere! The buildings themselves sometimes employ stones from centuries past and it's fun to note the idiosyncrasies. The artwork inside was done by the masters you studied in art history. Even the use of land has historical precedence, and we were pleased to note many large farm estates now operating as ecotourism centers (*agriturismos*).

Perhaps you already sense that food was a highlight on this walk, but let's not forget the wine. In restaurants it was common for the waiter to bring a bottle to the table. When ready to leave, the waiter would "eyeball" the wine remaining in the bottle and charge an appropriate amount. (You have to request the bill in Italy because Italians believe in leisurely meals and will leave you in peace until you indicate you're ready to depart.)

The wine estates we passed are significant players in the local economy, and while the landscapes and structures are historic, agriculture has become industrialized in this part of Tuscany. While the route sometimes takes walkers along agricultural roads, entering any of the fields is forbidden. (We don't know if the prohibition is due to concerns about crop damage or about espionage by competitors.) We will admit to tasting a few grapes that dropped off an overloaded truck that crossed in front of us; they probably made delightful wine, but they were not for eating raw. One afternoon we enjoyed watching a mechanical device harvest grapes by running between the rows and shaking the vines so that the ripe grapes fell into a hopper—no peasants will be tucking up their skirts and stomping those grapes as viticulture is high tech now.

Occasionally you may spot a falcon or eagle soaring over the landscape (roughly 140 bird species have been observed in Tuscany), and it wasn't unusual to surprise a pheasant. Both deer and porcupine (introduced as food by the Romans) are numerous, and we were pleased to see a beaver. The cypress trees of Tuscany are world-famous symbols of the region, depicted in art for centuries; tall and spindly, they often march up the gentle slopes or highlight a building. Nonnative, these trees were brought to Europe by the Etruscans and Phoenicians, and were popular in ornamenting Roman villas.

The doors of the old homes in the medieval hill towns offer graceful vignettes of history.

This is an easy walk—generally covering short distances each day and with little elevation change (with the exception of walks up to those hilltop towns). Much of the route is along gravel roads with little or no automobile traffic. While many walking routes are possible in this area, our route was designed by a local walking tour company to help ensure that we didn't trespass on private property and that we enjoyed some of the very best of this area. This walk can be done nearly year-round, but the winters are likely to be pretty cool. We walked the route in September—the weather was delightful and the region not at all crowded. Dinners can be challenging for walkers wanting to get to bed early as they are typically late and long, including at a minimum, *antipasto* (appetizer), *primo* (first), *secondo* (second), and *dolce* (dessert) courses. We like to eat early after a day of walking, so we would often just get the first course (e.g., pizza or pasta) and hopefully have room for dessert. While this confounded our waiters, who were used to more thorough diners, it worked well for us. Breakfasts are just the opposite—very minimal. The joke is that the classic Italian breakfast is a cigarette and a cappuccino. We suggest you pack some nutritious snacks for a midmorning pick-me-up. Trains took us to and from the walk, and the first one was quaint—only two cars (including the engine).

Val d'Orcia offers a gentle, beautiful walk through one of the most striking cultural landscapes in the world. We talk often about doing this walk again, perhaps in another season or perhaps on a slightly different route to other towns. (Tuscany and Siena offer a wealth of options.) The only negative we can think of is that you may gain (not lose) weight in spite of active days.

CULTURAL LANDSCAPES

Some walkers are drawn to natural areas or even to wilderness, while others appreciate more developed areas, even cities. The reality is that all the places we walk can be thought of as "cultural landscapes," places that reflect both nature and culture; it's mostly a matter of degree.

Wilderness areas reflect nature and natural processes, but have also been shaped—for better or for worse—by humans. Examples include the very trails we walk on, the prehistoric activities of native peoples, and the contemporary effects of issues such as air pollution and global climate change. Cities are primarily artifacts of civilization, but they also include elements of nature such as parks and other open spaces, they continue to be affected by natural processes such as weather and climate, and they include the efforts of many people to live more sustainably by recycling and use of public transit. The idea of cultural landscapes offers us a rich set of opportunities

The Kumano Kodo presents a rich blend of nature and culture.

to appreciate both nature and culture, especially the places that blend the two in distinctive, harmonious, and sustainable ways.

Geographer Peirce Lewis defines cultural landscapes as "our unwitting autobiography, reflecting our tastes, our values, our aspirations, and even our fears, in tangible, visible form." Conservationist Nora Mitchell describes cultural landscapes (which she also calls "storied landscapes") as places "that have been shaped over time by people adapting to their natural environment, sometimes over many generations," adding that "the character of a cultural landscape is the result of this relationship between people and place, reflecting traditions, memories, beliefs, sense of beauty, and use of natural resources." She also suggests that, with practice and sensitivity, we can "read" these cultural landscapes and more deeply appreciate their history and significance. We might best think about these places as manifestations of how people have shaped the land and vice versa. More than a thousand cultural landscapes around the world have been designated World Heritage Sites, a program derived from a 1992 international treaty known as the World Heritage Convention.

The harmony of nature and culture is a subtle but often overlooked refrain in environmental literature. Our greatest nature writers have made strong statements admonishing us to save the environment from human encroachment. Thoreau, for example, wished to "say a word for nature" and concluded that "in Wildness is the preservation of the world." But a closer reading suggests that balance and moderation were his ultimate goals. The "half cultivated" bean field at his Walden Pond retreat was a useful metaphor for the need to incorporate elements from both nature and culture. "I would not," he wrote, "have every part of a man cultivated, any more than I would

Cultural landscapes offer rich opportunities to appreciate both nature and culture, especially in places like the Amalfi Coast, which blend the two in distinctive, harmonious, and sustainable ways.

have every acre of earth." He went on to write: "The natural remedy [to the inherent tension between civilization and wilderness] is to be found in the proportion which the night bears to the day, the winter to the summer, thought to experience." Contemporary environmental philosophers continue to warn about the false and potentially dangerous dichotomy between humans and nature.

Like Thoreau's bean fields, trails can be metaphors as well. They are literal and figurative pathways into nature and human nature, into history and natural history. The landscape is natural (at least, for the most part), but the trails themselves are human artifacts, often with important historical meaning, and many with good intentions. They are gifts from one generation to the next, and they reflect the societies that create and nurture them (we call it trail-building and maintenance in our mundane and understated everyday language). We are well served to take the time to stop and more fully appreciate our trails and the cultural landscapes through which they pass. Just as we botanize when we hike, stopping to identify and appreciate the beauty and complexity of the natural world, we should engage with the cultural diversity of our outdoor spaces and places, recognizing and honoring the people who live, work, and play there, and the cultures that are reflected in the trails they have given us.

The walks we describe in this book reflect a full range of cultural landscapes. For example, Alaska's Denali National Park and Preserve is obviously on the wilderness end of the spectrum, while portions of the Golden Gate Way through San Francisco are clearly on the urban end. But in reality, both of these walks—indeed all the walks we describe—pass through cultural landscapes, and we encourage you to see, honor, and appreciate the ways in which both nature and culture have contributed to their integrity and aesthetics.

Springs, seeps, and small tributaries create pockets of lush vegetation deep in the Virgin River Narrows.

Virgin River Narrows

We like this hike so much we've done it several times. At the end of the experience, we emerge from the mouth of the canyon—the distinctive "narrows" section of Zion Canyon that's been incised by the North Fork of the Virgin River—inspired and invigorated, but also tired, wet, and sometimes cold. The last mile is an easy walk along a paved path that leads to the end of the 6-mile road through the wider, more open portion of beautiful Zion Canyon. Here we board one of the park's frequent shuttle buses, which takes us to the campground or on to the tourist-friendly gateway town of Springdale. The bus is always a welcome sight, a chance to let someone else do the driving while we stare out the window at the staggering scenery. Zion's shuttle bus system is the poster child for the growing movement toward public transit in the national parks. In the 1990s, there were as many 5,000 cars a day on the dead-end road into Zion Canyon, all competing for the area's 450 parking spaces. The road was congested and noisy, visitors were frustrated, there were collisions with wildlife, and cars spewed pollution and wasted energy. In 2000, the park instituted a mandatory shuttle bus system in Zion Canyon. Visitors are still welcome in the canyon, but they must leave their cars at the visitor center or in Springdale. Some people initially opposed the shuttle bus system, but it's been a remarkable success. Buses are powered by propane, seat sixty-six people (the equivalent of about twenty-five cars), and drivers often provide commentary and point out park features. Zion Canyon is calmer, quieter, and cleaner. A growing number of national parks have instituted shuttle bus systems and more are planned, as they're a great way to manage the parks in a more sustainable way.

LOCATION
Utah, United States

LENGTH
16 miles

ACCOMMODATIONS
Commercial: Some (nearby)
Huts/refuges: No
Backpacking/camping: Yes

BAGGAGE TRANSFER AVAILABLE
No

OPTION TO WALK SECTIONS
No

DEGREE OF CHALLENGE
High

———————— ≈ ————————

ZION NATIONAL PARK sits in the southwest corner of Utah. It's not an especially big park by national park standards (just under 150,000 acres), but it's a glorious one, packed with views and attractions throughout. This is an arid landscape of great and colorful slickrock canyons, towering cliffs, and magical spires and arches. Some of the canyons are "slot" canyons, narrow, sinuous, steep-walled, formed by rivers that cut deeply into the park's comparatively soft sandstone. Zion includes many slot canyons, but the Virgin River Narrows is the granddaddy of them all. It's a 16-mile route through a canyon that narrows to 20 to 30 feet across, with near vertical walls that rise over a thousand feet. The North Fork of the Virgin River runs through the canyon—sometimes from wall to wall—and staying dry isn't an option.

The walk through the canyon can be done in three ways. The first and best option (because it allows you to really appreciate all that you're seeing) is a two-day hike from the top of the narrows section of the canyon. There are several campsites tucked into a few of the wider spaces in the canyon, and this overnight hike is what we describe in the following several paragraphs. The walk can also be done as a long day hike from the top of the Narrows, or as an out-and-back day hike starting from the mouth of the canyon; we'll describe these options as well.

The first walk begins with a beautiful hour-and-a-half drive from the gateway town of Springdale, following the park road out through the east entrance, and then heading north on a paved and then dirt road to Chamberlain Ranch, where there's a small parking area. Portions of this road are not passable in a standard (non-four-wheel-drive) car when conditions are wet, and the route may be closed in winter. Most hikers arrange to be dropped off here rather than leave their cars

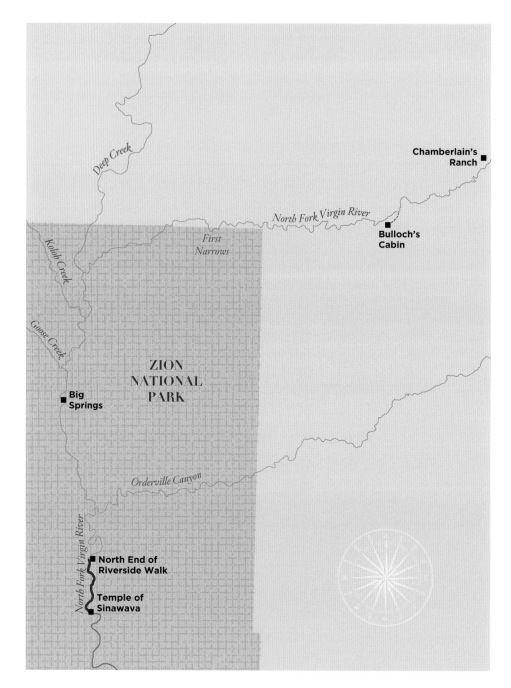

HIkers explore the downstream entrance to the Virgin River Narrows.

(which, of course, would have to be retrieved later). If you can't find anyone to give you a ride, there are dependable shuttle services based in Springdale. Chamberlain Ranch is private property, so please be respectful of the owner's willingness to allow access, including leaving all gates as you find them.

From the parking area, ford the river, assuming water levels are not too high—not above your knees. Indeed, if the water is high, you shouldn't enter the canyon. Follow the dirt road to just beyond Bulloch's Cabin, constructed from hand-hewn local timber. The road ends shortly after the cabin, at which point you should follow the river as it enters the narrows.

Frequent river crossings are necessary as the river moves from one side of the canyon to the other. The characteristic steep walls of the Narrows are intermittent at first, allowing for tall conifers and shrubby maples. Soon, the canyon walls become nearly continuous, and a number of small nameless tributaries—and a few larger ones—flow into the canyon. At one point, the river flows over a 12-foot waterfall, which can be avoided by a using a trail that goes off to the left. Soon after,

In some places the Virgin River Narrows is so confined that the sunlight penetrates only briefly each day.

several deep pools must be waded or even swum in high water. At the confluence with Deep Creek, more water flows into the canyon, substantially raising the level of the river. Most of the designated campsites are found a mile or two beyond Deep Creek; hikers learn their assigned site when they pick up their hiking permit (see below).

Downstream from tiny Goose Creek, there are a series of pools that can be deep and tricky due to the faster current of the river, which has picked up volume from the upstream side canyons. Big Spring appears on river right, and is often used to collect drinking water; treat it before consuming. Big Spring marks the upper end of an especially dramatic 3-mile section of the Narrows, where the nearly sheer canyon walls rise a thousand feet above the river and only a sliver of sky can be seen; this area is colloquially known as "Wall Street." Orderville Canyon joins the river from the left and is worth exploring upstream as far as you like.

About a mile below Orderville Canyon is Mystery Canyon, also on the left, where the tributary flows over the curved canyon wall and spills into the river. The Narrows section of the canyon widens quickly after this point, bringing you to a paved walkway on the left of the river that leads to the Temple of Sinawava trailhead and the associated shuttle bus stop.

Highlights of the walk include the fluted, nearly sheer, terra-cotta-colored walls of the canyon, the occasional sandstone grottos, the lush hanging gardens of maidenhair fern and monkeyflower growing around the frequent seeps and springs in the canyon walls, and water ouzels, small birds that "fly" underwater in their search for aquatic insects. And walking in the river is all part of this great adventure.

We mentioned that the Narrows can be done as a day hike following the same route as described above. However, this is a long and challenging hike of twelve or more hours, leaving little time to enjoy and appreciate the canyon. A very early start is required, especially considering the hour-and-a-half drive to the head of the canyon.

Many Zion visitors do a shorter day hike *up* the Virgin River Narrows. From the shuttle bus stop at the Temple of Sinawava trailhead, follow the paved Riverside Walk for a mile and then enter the river as it flows out of the narrows. Walk upstream, mostly in the water, for as far as you like. It's about fifteen minutes to reach Mystery Canyon, and another mile or so to Orderville Canyon, a popular destination/turn-around point. You can walk on to Big Springs, about 4 miles from where you entered the water, but day hikers are not allowed beyond this point. It's about a seven-hour round-trip to Big Springs, and it is slower going upstream than down.

There are a number of logistical concerns with this walk. The first and most important is the danger of flash floods, which are not uncommon. You should check at the park visitor center about weather conditions and water levels, and never enter the canyon if there is the threat of rain anywhere in the river's large watershed. In much of the Narrows portion of this walk, there is nowhere to find shelter against the power of a flash flood and accompanying debris.

Another concern is hypothermia; the water in the North Fork of the Virgin River is usually cold. Moreover, the Narrows portion of Zion Canyon receives relatively little direct sunlight, which can make it difficult to get warm after long exposure to the river water. Be sure to carry warm clothes in a waterproof bag (put *everything* in waterproof bags!), eat high-energy food before you get chilled, and don't wear cotton clothing.

Take a headlamp even if you don't expect to be in the canyon after dark. There is no maintained trail in the Narrows portion of the canyon, the route includes many river crossings and often involves traveling in the water, or even swimming short sections. The footing can be very rough and challenging as the river bottom is often comprised of large, algae-covered stones—sort of like slippery bowling balls. Sturdy footwear is essential. Outfitters in Springdale rent specially designed footwear and other equipment, though we've always done the hike using our own gear. Hiking poles are especially useful. Drinking water is available in only a few places (water in the river is often heavily silt-laden) and must be treated. It's best to carry the water you'll need—a gallon per day per person is recommended, especially in the summer. If you're doing the hike from the head of the canyon, as an overnight backpacking trip or as a day hike, you'll need a permit; check the park's website for details. A day hike moving upstream to Big Springs from the lower end of the canyon does not require a permit. The best time to hike the canyon is in summer or fall, though thunderstorms are more frequent in the summer. When water levels are too high or when the National Weather Service issues flash flood warnings, the National Park Service temporarily closes the canyon.

The Virgin River Narrows is one of the most iconic walks in the national parks. It asks a lot of hikers, but it returns even more. Prepare for this walk by carefully planning when and how you're going to do it and what equipment you'll need to do it safely. Check the official Zion National Park website for details about permits and local conditions, and check in with rangers at the Zion visitor center. Then enjoy this trek, which is on many hikers' top ten lists.

Frequent river crossings are necessary as the stream meanders from one side of the canyon to the other; occasional pools require walkers to wade or even swim through short sections.

"STEP AWAY FROM THE VEHICLE . . ."

There's an encouraging movement toward public transit in parks and at other walking attractions to minimize the potential impacts of cars. The US national parks are a good example. The national park system now accommodates more than 300 million annual visits, and many of these visits are in the form of "driving for pleasure" through the parks to see their iconic attractions. But all these cars can be troublesome—they pollute the air, endanger wildlife, cause traffic congestion, and require large areas to be converted into parking lots. Some cynics are suggesting that the name should be changed from "national parks" to "national parking lots."

Buses on the Denali Park Road will stop anywhere to let off and pick up hikers.

The Yosemite shuttle picks up and drops off hikers on the Tioga Road in Yosemite National Park; this service works well for hikers on the High Sierra Camps Loop.

This has led to efforts to minimize automobile use in the national parks and related areas by coaxing people out of their cars and into various forms of what is called "alternative transportation"—even "intelligent transportation"—such as public transit, bikes, and, of course, walking.

Several of the walks we recommend in this book are served by innovative and effective means of public transit.

For example, Acadia National Park's Island Explorer bus system serves most of the park's major attractions, including its wonderful system of carriage roads. Using the Island Explorer relieves traffic congestion on park roads, reduces air pollution and greenhouse gas emissions, frees drivers from worrying about finding a parking place, and facilitates one-way walks along the carriage roads (i.e., let the bus drop you off at one trailhead and pick you up at another). And using the Island Explorer is free!

Zion National Park has gone a step further, requiring use of a shuttle bus system in Zion Canyon, and the result has been remarkable: there's no traffic congestion, parking isn't an issue, wildlife is protected, the air is cleaner, and the canyon is much more quiet and peaceful. The transit system enhances enjoyment of both of the walks in this park we recommend in this book: the Virgin River Narrows and Zion Rim-to-Rim.

Of course, no one needs to tell walkers about the benefits of "alternative transportation"—we live it by definition. Walking is our own form of "intelligent transportation." When it comes to the environment, walkers are naturally inclined to "walk the talk." As we all know, walking is the preferred way to really see and experience parks and the other great cultural landscapes of the world.

Zion Rim-to-Rim is a grand traverse of
Zion National Park.

Zion Rim-to-Rim

We admit it—we're a bit spooked by "exposure"—steep drop-offs that could be dangerous if not taken seriously. Many years ago, we signed up for a week-long climbing course with the Yosemite Mountaineering School but washed out on the second day; we're just a little afraid of heights, and this is one of the reasons we tend to stick to the trails. But there's a route in Zion National Park—Angels Landing, one of the most famous in the national parks—that requires a white-knuckle scramble along a knife-edge for about a half-mile to the top of the formation. The margins of the trail drop off 1,500 feet in both directions. The National Park Service has installed metal chains along strategic portions of the route, much like we've encountered on *via ferrata* sections of trails in the Dolomites and other areas in the Alps. We gritted our teeth and carefully inched our way out to the top of Angels Landing, where we were rewarded with sweeping views up and down dramatic Zion Canyon, much like it's seen from the perspective of an eagle. We paused just long enough to acknowledge the view and take a few pictures before carefully inching our way back to the psychological security of the West Rim Trail. Was it worth it? Yes! Do we want to do it again? No!

LOCATION
Utah, United States

LENGTH
28 miles

ACCOMMODATIONS
Commercial: Some (nearby)
Huts/refuges: No
Backpacking/camping: Yes

BAGGAGE TRANSFER AVAILABLE
No

OPTION TO WALK SECTIONS
Yes

DEGREE OF CHALLENGE
Moderate–High

Zion National Park, in the southwest corner of Utah, is one of the early national parks in the United States; it didn't take long for the public to recognize its remarkable and dramatic beauty. It was established as Mukuntuweap National Monument in 1909, the name meaning "straight canyon" in the language of the Paiute Indians. However, the name was later changed to Zion to recognize Mormon settlement of the area. In religious teachings, Zion means place of peace and refuge, and to many people the area retains this character, though in a more secular way. This is an arid landscape of great and colorful slickrock canyons, towering cliffs, and magical spires and arches.

Combining two of the park's longest and most significant trails offers walkers the unusual opportunity to trace a broad cross section of the park—an approximately 30-mile trek that connects the East and West Rims of the park. The West Rim Trail begins in the highest elevations in the park—nearly 8,000 feet—and descends about 5,000 feet over approximately 16 miles to the floor of Zion Canyon. A short hike over the Virgin River and across Zion Canyon brings you to the Weeping Rock Trailhead, and then you climb steeply to the East Rim Trail, gaining nearly 2,500 feet (and losing about 1,000 feet) over approximately 11 miles. This leads to the east entrance to the park. Of course, the hike can be done in either direction, but the West Rim is higher than the East Rim, and going west to east means a little less uphill hiking.

The West Rim Trail offers a special richness of features and views and is probably the most popular backpacking trail in the park. It begins at the Lava Point Trailhead and rambles across the large Horse Pasture Plateau and through associated forests. The trail wanders up and down, offering stunning views into a variety of colorful canyons that include some the park's iconic geologic formations, including North and South Guardian Angels and a number of distinctive domes and beehives. Several springs support grassy meadows and provide opportunities to collect drinking water (though you should check with rangers about the status of these springs and always treat water before drinking it). You'll also encounter tall ponderosa pines, Gambel oaks, bigtooth maples, spruce, and Douglas fir.

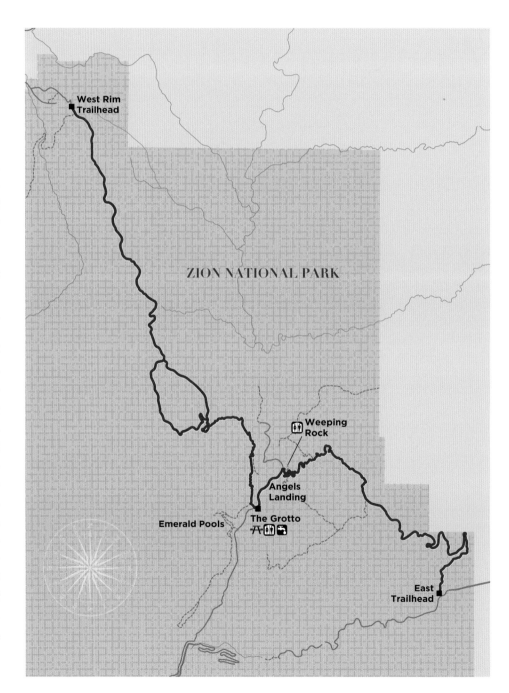

As the trail approaches the steep descent into Zion Canyon, the action really begins. An expanse of slickrock leads to the base of Angels Landing at Scout Lookout, and the exposed side trail that leads out to Angels Landing starts here. If you choose to follow this route, with its iron rungs and fixed chains, stop at Scout Lookout and refresh yourself with food and water. The out-and-back trail to Angels Landing takes an hour or more, depending on how many people have the same idea. Since Angels Landing is pretty accessible from Zion Canyon, it can be quite crowded.

Back on the West Rim Trail, head down Walter's Wiggles, a series of twenty-one tight switch-backs descending a 60-degree slope; this trail section is named for the first superintendent of the park. Stop to admire this triumph of trail-making, one of the most artistic "crafted" trails in the national park system.

After descending gently through refreshing Refrigerator Canyon, the trail then drops sharply on a paved path that leads to the floor of Zion Canyon, the most popular region of the park. A bridge leads over the Virgin River to the Grotto Trailhead, from which you can walk (or take the free shuttle bus) north to the trailhead at Weeping Rock. We suggest that before you cross the river, you take a short walk to the Emerald Pools, one of the park's major attractions and worth the detour.

Before launching yourself up the Observation Point Trail, a steep route that climbs the east wall of Zion Canyon, we also suggest you consider another short detour, this time to Weeping Rock, a favorite of many Zion visitors. Then begin the climb (continuing on the Observation Point Trail) that will lead you through Echo Canyon and up to the East Rim Trail. There are two attractive add-on options as you climb. The first is a relatively short side trip into magical Hidden Canyon, where you can scramble as far as you like. Second, where the East Rim Trail branches off the Observation Point Trail, you can continue up to Observation Point, where there are sweeping views—some of the best in the park—of Zion Canyon.

From the junction with the Observation Point Trail, the East Rim Trail is an undulating and varied hike leading east to the park entrance. There's a more challenging section through a generally open area of slickrock where the trail is marked with cairns; pay attention to wayfinding here. The upper elevations of the trail pass through ponderosa pine, dwarf pinyon pine, and Utah juniper forests, along with manzanita. A short side trail leads to Stave Spring, the only reliable source of water. The trail passes an impressive pour-off in generally dry Jolley Gulch, where we saw evidence of a large, recent flash flood.

As you approach the end of the trail, there are dramatic views of classic Zion "checkerboard" mesas, sandstone formations where (over time) geologic forces, weather, and temperature changes have fashioned distinctive crosshatched grooves in the rock. Although it's mostly uphill from the Weeping Rock trailhead to Jolley Gulch, it's mostly downhill from there to the trailhead near the

Hikers walk through a narrow gap near the intersection of the Observation Point Trail and the East Rim Trail.

(ABOVE) The descent along the Observation Point Trail opens to sweeping views of stunning Zion Canyon.

(ABOVE RIGHT) The lower portion of the West Rim Trail includes a series of dramatic views into Zion Canyon.

east entrance. Despite being a truly spectacular route over varied terrain, we saw only a few other hikers on the East Rim Trail section of the route.

The natural history of Zion National Park is dominated by its geologic heritage, a millennia-long sequence of sediment deposition, uplift, and erosion. The park is part of the huge geographical region known as the Grand Staircase, a reference to the alternate layers of limestone (remains of marine organisms collected at the bottom of freshwater and saltwater seas) and sandstone (formed by vast sand dunes) that are exposed throughout the region. More recently, the expansive Colorado Plateau has been uplifted thousands of feet by tectonic forces, and rivers have carved it into a series of canyons, some broad like the lower reaches of Zion Canyon and some narrow "slot canyons," like the Virgin River Narrows at the head of Zion Canyon (also described in this book). The Navajo sandstone layer, up to 2,000 feet thick, dominates much of Zion National Park. Its naturally occurring iron oxide has dissolved and washed away from its upper layers, where the walls of Zion Canyon are bone white, but the lower layers often appear a reddish or rusty color.

The natural variation of the park—a wide range of elevations and occasional access to water—results in four major life zones: desert, riparian, woodland, and coniferous forest, and these zones support a great variety of plant and animal life. Highlights include mule deer, ringtails, foxes, mountain lions, and a great variety of birds, including eagles. Exotic plants include night-blooming (and poisonous) sacred datura and lush hanging gardens of ferns and monkeyflowers where water seeps from canyon walls.

Archeologists estimate that human presence in the park goes back to the Basket Maker culture; these pre-Ancestral Puebloans grew maize, squash, and beans on the floodplains, but little physical evidence remains of them or of subsequent Native American tribes. The area was explored by Spanish missionaries in the eighteenth century, and settled by Mormons in the nineteenth century. Remnants of a brief ranching period can still be seen in the park and the surrounding area.

There are some important logistical considerations in walking rim to rim through Zion. The Lava Point and East Park Entrance trailheads are far apart by road; the most practical approach is to arrange a ride with one of the outfitters/guides in the gateway town of Springdale. The ideal way to conduct this walk is as a multi-day backpacking trip, spending two days on the West Rim Trail and two days on the Observation Point/East Rim Trail. Most of these trails are in the wilderness portion of the park, and you'll need a permit to camp in the wilderness. You could give yourself a break when you reach the floor of Zion Canyon by taking the free shuttle bus to the Zion Lodge or into Springdale and spending the night. Another approach would be to day-hike the West Rim Trail to the floor of Zion Canyon, spend the night, and then arrange for a ride to the east entrance of the park and day-hike the East Rim Trail/Observation Point Trail to the floor of Zion Canyon. However, these are strenuous day hikes and leave little or no time to explore the many side trails. Check in at the visitor center to get the latest information on trail conditions, including availability of water.

The West Rim's higher elevation and deeper snow cover usually mean that the hiking season doesn't start until late spring and lasts only until early fall; the East Rim has a slightly longer open season. In both cases, summer days can be very hot; we recommend hiking in the spring or fall. You'll need to take the usual sun precautions for high desert hiking (protective clothing and lots of sunscreen). You'll need to drink a lot of water, so you should plan on carrying water even if the streams are flowing.

Zion National Park is a true standout in the US national park system, a remarkably varied and beautiful place, and one of our favoritess. Walking the Zion Rim-to-Rim offers hikers an unusual opportunity to fully experience (and appreciate) the diversity of this wonderful area. Hike Zion Rim-to-Rim, and make this one of your favorite parks, too.

Popular Angels Landing offers sweeping views of Zion Canyon, but is a white-knuckle scramble along a dramatic knife-edge; the National Park Service has installed iron rungs and fixed chains to help walkers over the most exposed areas.

WALKING THE TALK

History can be read as a millennia-long struggle to free ourselves from the need to walk. Freedom from walking has always been highly coveted, coming first to the rich and powerful: slaves carried masters, knights rode horses, the rich owned carriages, and the upper and now middle classes in much of the world drive cars. Today, only the less fortunate are forced to walk.

Walking has suffered an especially steep decline over the last hundred years in response to the revolution in transportation. As Ralph Waldo Emerson observed, "Civilized man has built a coach, but has lost the use of his feet."

While all forms of mechanized transport have allowed increasing numbers of people to ride rather than walk—a

In an especially appropriate turn of contemporary phrase, we must "walk the talk." By choosing to walk, we make a lifestyle choice, fulfill a commitment to ourselves, and make a statement about what we think is important for us and the world. (Kumano Kodo)

choice most people have exercised when presented the option—it's the car that has relegated walking to the back seat. Most people drive back and forth to work, to the store, running errands; most children take the bus or are driven to school, socializing them to mechanized transportation. In the process, we've transformed much of the world to accommodate the driver—at a cost to the walker. City streets are straightened and widened for more and faster traffic, making walking difficult, unpleasant, and often dangerous. And vast suburbs have been developed on a scale that accommodates the car, rather than on a human scale. American historian Lewis Mumford wrote that the car is responsible for "the end of the pedestrian," and that "[i]n America we have pushed the elimination of the pedestrian to its ultimate conclusion—the drive-in market, the drive-in movie theater, and the drive-in bank."

The decline of walking has caused considerable angst among people who choose to walk (or who would like to have that choice). In *Wanderlust,* Rebecca Solnit suggests taking an ecological approach by considering walking an "indicator species for various kinds of freedoms and pleasures: free time, free and alluring space, and unhindered bodies." In this context, walking might be considered "endangered." She argues that modern transportation and technology lead us to transcend space and time, alienating us from the material world and leaving us "disembodied." "It is the unaugmented body that is rare now," she writes, "and that body has begun to atrophy as both a muscular and a sensory organ."

Joseph Amato, author of *On Foot: A History of Walking*, suggests that the car has altered our relationship with the world, making the walker "feel like a trespasser on the earth," and that in the process it has "transformed . . . human senses of space, time, and freedom." Social critic Marshall McLuhan warned against allowing technology to rule our lives, observing that cars have transformed cities into places where traditional walking patterns now constitute illegal "jaywalking." Sociologist Jean Baudrillard observed, "As soon as you start walking in Los Angeles you are a threat to public order, like a dog wandering in the road."

But things are changing, as some people are now *choosing* to walk instead of ride. The choice to walk is in response to an apparent yearning to be more active and healthy, to do things in a more sustainable way, and to be more directly in touch with the world around us. The deliberate pace of walking allows us to more fully sense the world, to see its richness of detail, to touch, hear, smell, and even taste it. The choice to walk is based on principles such as appreciation of natural and cultural diversity, direct and authentic contact with people and the places they live, a need to slow our hectic lives, protection of the distinctive places that make our world so interesting, and investment in these places through direct economic benefits.

Walking the great natural and cultural landscapes of the world is an ideal way to pursue all these objectives. Walking's deliberate, human-scale pace encourages a deep understanding and appreciation of nature and culture, and this ultimately leads to preservation of special places. Walking contributes to personal health and fitness, and can have relatively little environmental or social impact. The small scale of walking makes use of facilities and services provided by local people, and resulting economic benefits flow directly to these communities. And walking is one of the most democratic and accessible recreation activities, demanding no extraordinary athletic ability, requiring relatively little cost, and it is appropriate for nearly all ages.

At the beginning of the twenty-first century, most countries have established extensive systems of public parks, forests, and trails, and these demand exploration and the close inspection that is only possible on foot. Government agencies and nonprofit citizen groups continue their good work toward expansion of these places and the opportunities they present to walkers. All parts of the world have great cultural landscapes where people and the environment are intertwined in distinctive, harmonious, enduring, and sustainable ways, and many of these regions can be walked on safe, well-marked and well-managed trails, served by public transportation and local facilities and services. Many cities are working hard and successfully to accommodate the needs of walkers through pedestrian malls, better sidewalks and lighting, and greenways to connect home, work, and recreation.

Walking is simple. As Geoff Nicholson writes in *The Lost Art of Walking*, walking is analog in a digital world. In *A Philosophy of Walking*, Frédéric Gros writes that "[p]utting one foot in front of the other is child's play," and that "[t]o walk, you need to start with two legs. The rest is optional." But walking can also be profound. We walk because it's a celebration of our evolutionary heritage, it stimulates our thinking, it's a form of political expression, it contributes to conservation and sustainability, it deepens our understanding and appreciation of the world, it can be a means to explore spirituality, and it makes us healthier and happier in the process.

In today's world, walking is a choice we must consciously make; it's more conventional to sit and ride. In an especially appropriate turn of contemporary phrase, we must "walk the talk." By choosing to walk, we make a lifestyle choice, fulfill a commitment to ourselves, and make a statement about what we think is important for us and the world. As Rebecca Solnit writes, "To walk in a sitting and riding society is always, at least potentially, the beginning of a Renaissance."

Trail Finder

Trail	Location	Length (miles)	Type of trail	Accommodations			Baggage transfer	Option to walk sections	Seasons	Permits/fees	Degree of challenge
				Commercial (e.g., inns, B&Bs)	Huts/ refuges	Backpacking/ camping					
Abel Tasman Coast Track	New Zealand	32	Point-to-point	Yes	Yes	Yes	Yes	Yes	Year-round	Fee for huts and campsites	Low–Moderate
Acadia Carriage Roads	Maine, United States	50	Variable	Yes (nearby)	No	Yes (nearby)	No	Yes	Spring through fall	Fee for park entrance	Low
Ala Kahakai National Historic Trail	Hawaii, United States	Up to 175	Point-to-point	Yes (nearby)	No	Yes	No	Yes	Year-round	Fee for park entrance	Low–Moderate
Amalfi Coast	Italy	Variable (a few days to a week)	Variable	Yes	No	No	Yes	Yes	Year-round	No	Moderate
Aravaipa Canyon Wilderness	Arizona, United States	22 (Round-trip)	Point-to-point or out-and-back	No	No	Yes	No	No	Year-round	Yes	Moderate
Backbone Trail	California, United States	65	Point-to-point	Yes (nearby)	No	Some	No	Yes	Year-round	Fee for park entrance	Moderate
Camino Portugués	Portugal and Spain	150	Point-to-point	Yes	Yes	No	Yes	Yes	Spring through fall	No	Low–Moderate
Cumberland Island National Seashore	Georgia, United States	Variable (a few days or more)	Variable	Yes	No	Yes	No	Yes	Year-round	Fee for park entrance and ferry	Low
Denali National Park and Preserve	Alaska, United States	Variable (a few days to a few weeks)	Variable	Some (nearby)	No	Yes	No	Yes	Summer through fall	Fee for park entrance and shuttle bus; backpacking permit required	Moderate–High

Trail	Location	Length (miles)	Type of trail	Commercial (e.g., inns, B&Bs)	Huts/ refuges	Backpacking/ camping	Baggage transfer	Option to walk sections	Seasons	Permits/fees	Degree of challenge
Golden Gate Way	California, United States	Variable (up to a week)	Point-to-point	Yes	Yes	Yes	No	Yes	Year-round	No	Low–Moderate
Grand Canyon Rim Trail	Arizona, United States	14	Point-to-point	Yes	No	Yes	No	Yes	Year-round	Fee for park entrance	Low
Great Glen Way	Scotland	80	Point-to-point	Yes	No	Yes	Yes	Yes	Spring through fall	No	Low–Moderate
Great Saunter	New York City, United States	32	Loop	Yes	No	No	No	Yes	Year-round	No	Low
Great Wall of China	China	Variable (up to a week)	Point-to-point	Yes (nearby)	No	No	Yes	Yes	Spring through fall	Guide service required	Moderate–High
Havasu Canyon	Arizona, United States	22+	Out-and-back	Yes	No	Yes	Yes	No	Spring through fall	Yes	Moderate
High Sierra Camps Loop	California, United States	50+	Loop	No	Yes	Yes	No	Some	Summer through early fall	Fee for park entrance and camping permit	Moderate
Kumano Kodo	Japan	Variable (up to two weeks)	Point-to-point	Yes	No	No	Yes	Yes	Spring through fall	No	Moderate
Maroon Bells–Snowmass Wilderness	Colorado, United States	27+	Loop	No	No	Yes	No	Some	Summer through early fall	No	High
Needles	Utah, United States	Variable (up to a week)	Variable	No	No	Yes	No	Yes	Spring through fall	Fee for park entrance and camping permit	Moderate
Paris	France	Variable	Variable	Yes	No	No	No	Yes	Year-round	No	Low
Pembrokeshire Coast Path	Wales	186	Point-to-point	Yes	No	Some	Yes	Yes	Spring through fall	No	Moderate

Trail Finder / 243

Trail	Location	Length (miles)	Type of trail	Accommodations Commercial (e.g., inns, B&Bs)	Huts/ refuges	Backpacking/ camping	Baggage transfer	Option to walk sections	Seasons	Permits/fees	Degree of challenge
Pennine Way	England and Scotland	270	Point-to-point	Yes	No	Some	Yes	Yes	Spring through fall	No	Moderate–High
Popo Agie Wilderness	Wyoming, United States	Variable (a few days to a few weeks)	Variable	No	No	Yes	No	Yes	Summer through early fall	Permit required; fee for driving through Wind River Indian Reservation	Moderate–High
Presidential Traverse	New Hampshire, United States	30	Point-to-point	No	Yes	Yes	No	Yes	Summer through early fall	Fee for huts	Moderate–High
Queen Charlotte Track	New Zealand	45	Point-to-point	Yes	No	Yes	Yes	Yes	Year-round	Fee for walking across private lands	Low–Moderate
Sydney	Australia	Variable	Variable	Yes	No	No	No	Yes	Year-round	No	Low–Moderate
Thames Path	England	184	Point-to-point	Yes	No	No	Yes	Yes	Spring through fall	No	Low
Val d'Orcia	Italy	59	Point-to-point	Yes	No	No	Yes	Yes	Spring through fall	No	Low
Virgin River Narrows	Utah, United States	16	Point-to-point	Some (nearby)	No	Yes	No	No	Spring through fall	Fee for park entrance and permit	High
Zion Rim-to-Rim	Utah, United States	28	Point-to-point	Some (nearby)	No	Yes	No	Yes	Spring through fall	Fee for park entrance and camping permit	Moderate–High

References

Algeo, Mathew. *Pedestrianism: When Watching People Walk Was America's Favorite Spectator Sport*. Chicago: Chicago Review Press, 2014.

Amato, Joseph. *On Foot: A History of Walking*. New York: New York University Press, 2004.

Armitage, Simon. *Walking Home*. New York: Liveright, 2014.

Brame, Rich, and David Cole. *Soft Paths: Enjoying the Wilderness Without Harming It*. Mechanicsburg, PA: Stackpole Books, 2011.

Bryson, Bill. *A Walk in the Woods: Rediscovering America on the Appalachian Trail*. New York: Broadway Books, 1998.

Campoli, Julie. *Made for Walking: Density and Neighborhood Form*. Cambridge, MA: Lincoln Institute of Land Policy, 2012.

Feller, Bruce. *Walking the Bible: A Journey by Land Through the Five Books of Moses*. New York: HarperCollins Publishers, 2001.

Gros, Frédéric. *A Philosophy of Walking*. New York: Verso, 2014.

Harmon, Will. *Leave No Trace: Minimum Impact Outdoor Recreation*. Nashville, TN: Falcon, 1977.

Huffington, Arianna. 2013. "Hemingway, Thoreau, Jefferson, and the Virtues of a Good Long Walk," *Huffington Post*, August 29, 2013.

Jacobs, Jane. *The Death and Life of Great American Cities*. New York: Vintage Press, 1992.

Leakey, Mary. "Footprints in the Ashes of Time," *National Geographic*. April 1979.

Lieberman, Daniel. *The Story of the Human Body: Evolution, Health, and Disease*. New York: Vintage, 2014.

Macfarlane, Robert. *The Old Ways: A Journey on Foot*. New York: Viking Penguin, 2012.

Manning, Robert, and Martha Manning. *Walking Distance: Extraordinary Hikes for Ordinary People*. Corvallis, OR: Oregon State University Press, 2013.

Nicholson, Geoff. *The Lost Art of Walking*. New York: Riverhead Books, 2009.

Solnit, Rebecca. *Wanderlust: A History of Walking*. New York: Penguin Books, 2001.

Strayed, Cheryl. *Wild: From Lost to Found on the Pacific Crest Trail*. New York: Vintage Books, 2013.

Thoreau, Henry David. "Walking," *Atlantic Monthly*. June 1862.

Tilden, Freeman. *Interpreting Our Heritage*. Chapel Hill, NC: University of North Carolina Press, 2008.

Waterman, Laura, and Guy Waterman. *Backwoods Ethics: A Guide to Low-Impact Hiking and Camping*. Woodstock, VT: Countryman Press, 2003.

White, Edmund. *The Flaneur: A Stroll through the Paradoxes of Paris*. New York: Bloomsburg Publishing, 2008.

Williams, David. *Cairns: Messengers in Stone*. Seattle, WA: The Mountaineers Books, 2012.

About the Authors

Robert Manning is Steven Rubenstein Professor of Environment and Natural Resources and Director of the Park Studies Laboratory at the University of Vermont. He teaches and conducts research on the history, philosophy, and management of parks, wilderness, and related areas. He has won the university's highest awards in both teaching and research. **Martha Manning** is an artist working in fiber and printmaking. Her work has been published in national magazines and shown in nationally juried shows.

Kumano Kodo